LIVEWIRE

FUGITIVE

VITA AYALA | RAÚL ALLÉN | PATRICIA MARTÍN | SAIDA TEMOFONTE

CONTENTS

Collection Cover Art: Adam Pollina
with Ulises Arreola

Associate Editor: David Menchel
Editors: Joseph Illidge and Heather Antos (#2-4)

Dan Mintz
Chairman

Fred Pierce
Publisher

Walter Black
VP Operations

Matthew Klein
VP Sales & Marketing

Robert Meyers
Senior Editorial Director

Mel Caylo
Director of Marketing

Travis Escarfullery
Director of Design & Production

Peter Stern
Director of International Publishing & Merchandising

Karl Bollers
Senior Editor

Lysa Hawkins
Heather Antos
Editors

David Menchel
Associate Editor

Drew Baumgartner
Assistant Editor

Jeff Walker
Production & Design Manager

Julia Walchuk
Sales & Live Events Manager

Emily Hecht
Sales & Social Media Manager

Connor Hill
Sales Operations Coordinator

Danielle Ward
Sales Manager

Gregg Katzman
Marketing Coordinator

Ivan Cohen
Collection Editor

Steve Blackwell
Collection Designer

Russ Brown
President, Consumer Products,
Promotions & Ad Sales

Oliver Taylor
International Licensing Coordinator

Zane Warman
Domestic Licensing Coordinator

Livewire™: Fugitive. Published by Valiant Entertainment LLC. Office of
Publication: 350 Seventh Avenue, New York, NY 10001. Compilation copyright ©
2019 Valiant Entertainment LLC. All rights reserved. Contains materials originally
published in single magazine form as Livewire #1-4. Copyright © 2018 and 2019
Valiant Entertainment LLC. All rights reserved. All characters, their distinctive
likeness and related indicia featured in this publication are trademarks of
Valiant Entertainment LLC. The stories, characters, and incidents featured in this
publication are entirely fictional. Valiant Entertainment does not read or accept
unsolicited submissions of ideas, stories, or artwork. Printed in the U.S.A.
First Printing. ISBN: 9781682153017.

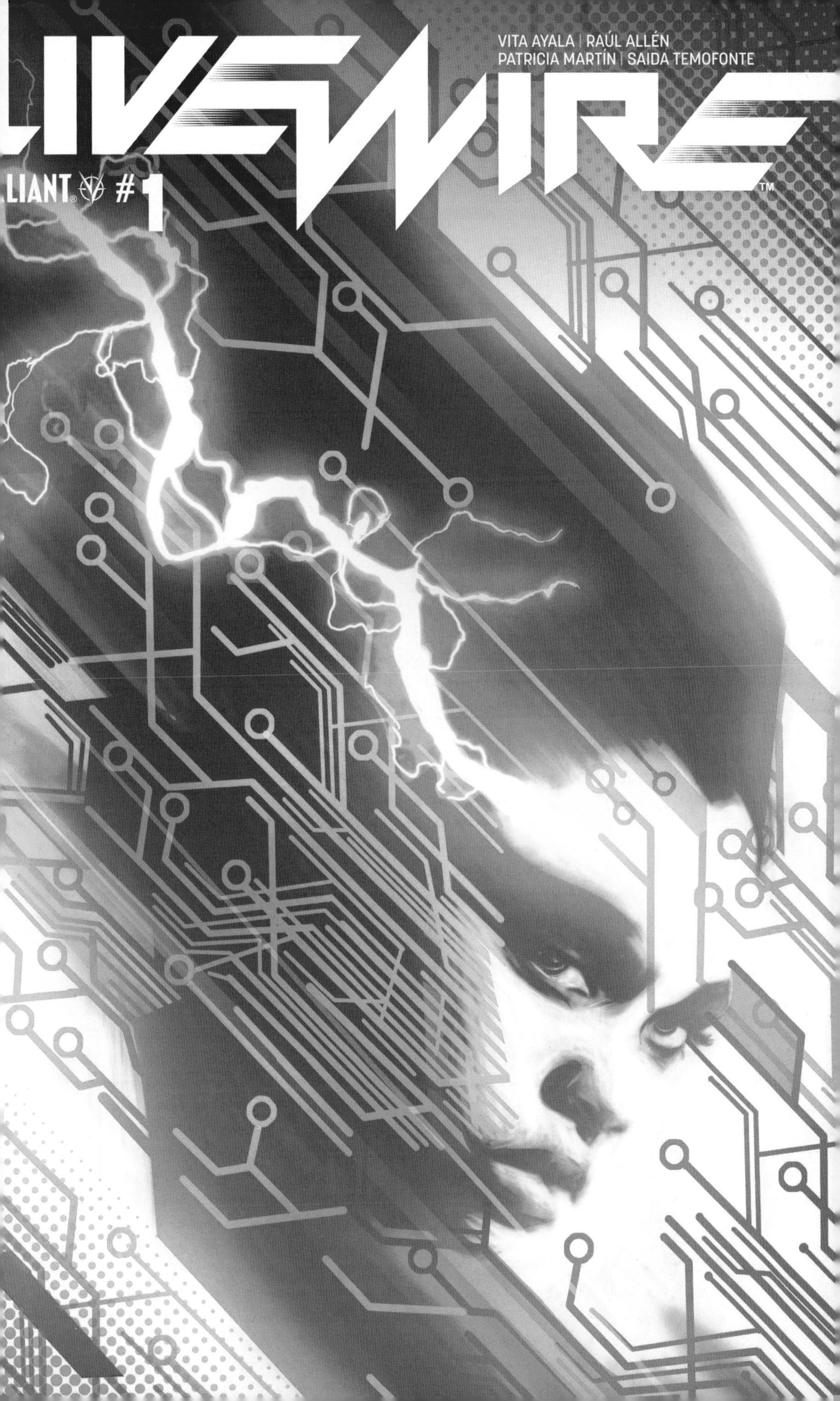
VITA AYALA | RAÚL ALLÉN
PATRICIA MARTÍN | SAIDA TEMOFONTE
LIVEWIRE™
LIANT
#1

Guardian. Warrior. Fugitive.

Meet Amanda McKee, the
superpowered psiot known as
Livewire. With her incredible
teletechnopathic abilities, Amanda
has unrestricted access to the
digital world that keeps our own
afloat, able to control anything
from a social media account to the
satellites in the atmosphere. But
Amanda was never interested in
control, only helping those in need
– a hero, until the United States
Government betrayed her and her
fellow psiots, forcing her to take
extreme actions to ensure her
own survival.

Now, Amanda is picking up
the pieces, one digital
fractal at a time...

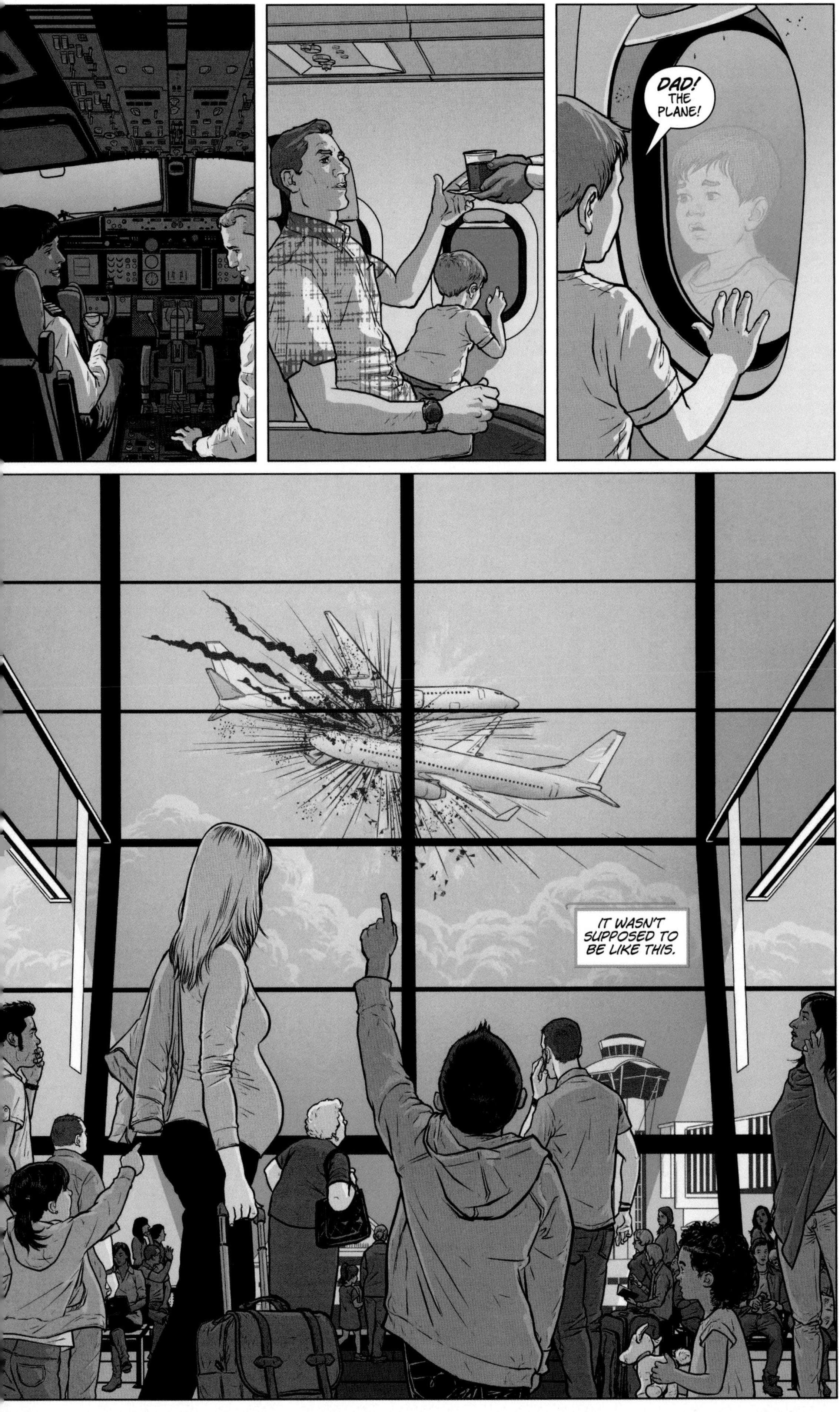
DAD! THE PLANE!
IT WASN'T SUPPOSED TO BE LIKE THIS.

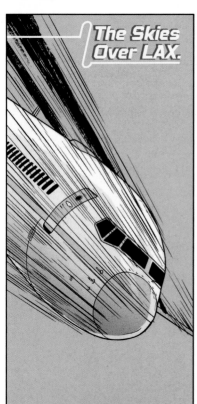

I HAVE PLAYED MANY ROLES IN MY LIFE.

AAIEE!

DADDY HELP ME!

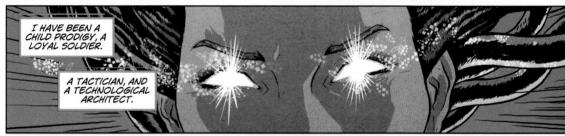

I HAVE BEEN A CHILD PRODIGY, A LOYAL SOLDIER.

A TACTICIAN, AND A TECHNOLOGICAL ARCHITECT.

YOU'RE ALRIGHT, I HAVE YOU.

ENTIRE UNIVERSES OF DATA HAVE COME FROM MY FINGERTIPS.

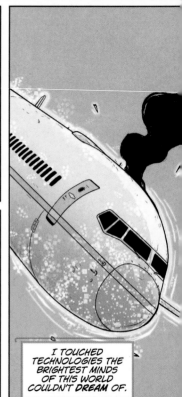

I TOUCHED TECHNOLOGIES THE BRIGHTEST MINDS OF THIS WORLD COULDN'T DREAM OF.

T-THANK YOU!

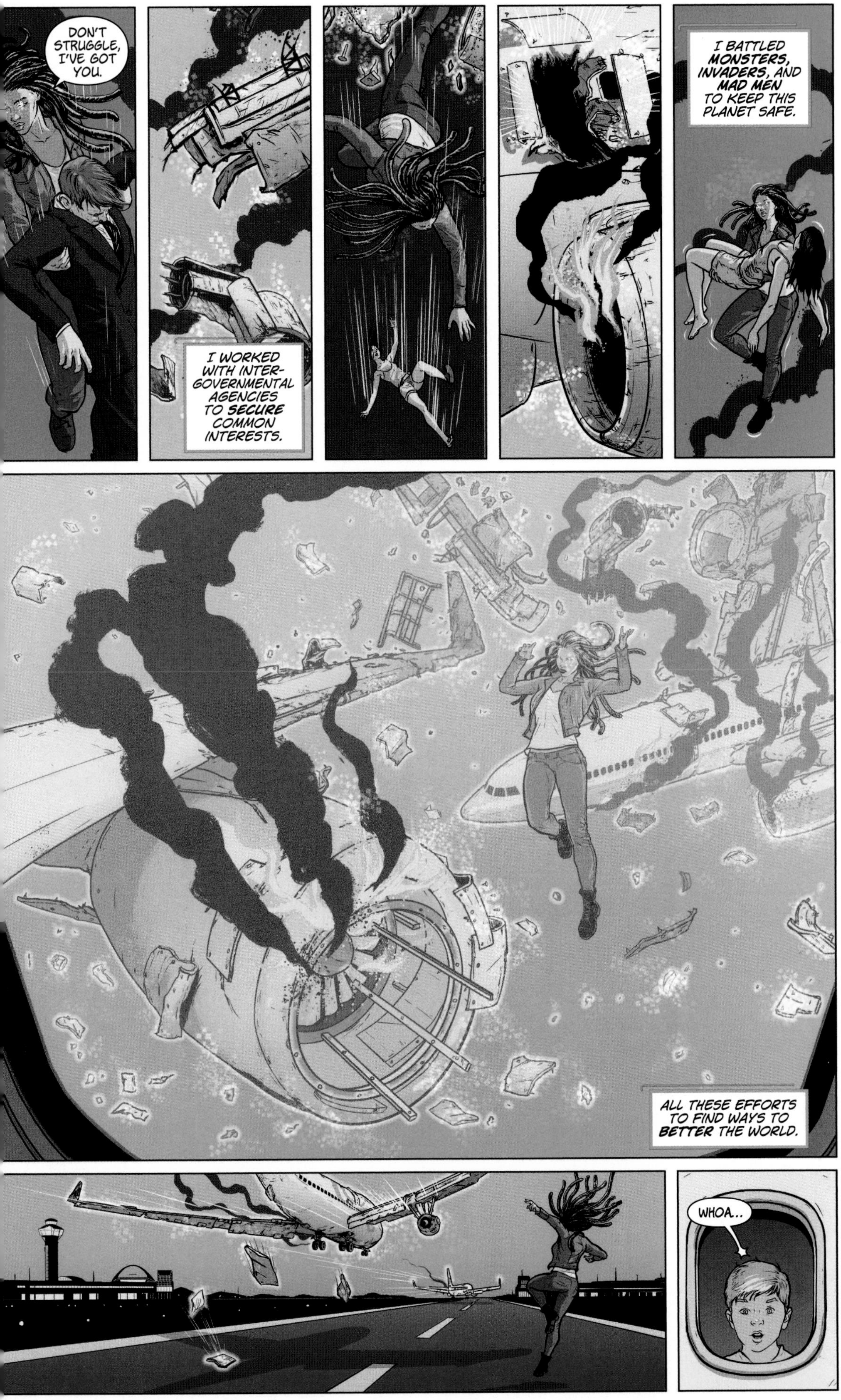
DON'T STRUGGLE, I'VE GOT YOU.
I WORKED WITH INTER-GOVERNMENTAL AGENCIES TO SECURE COMMON INTERESTS.
I BATTLED MONSTERS, INVADERS, AND MAD MEN TO KEEP THIS PLANET SAFE.
ALL THESE EFFORTS TO FIND WAYS TO BETTER THE WORLD.
WHOA..

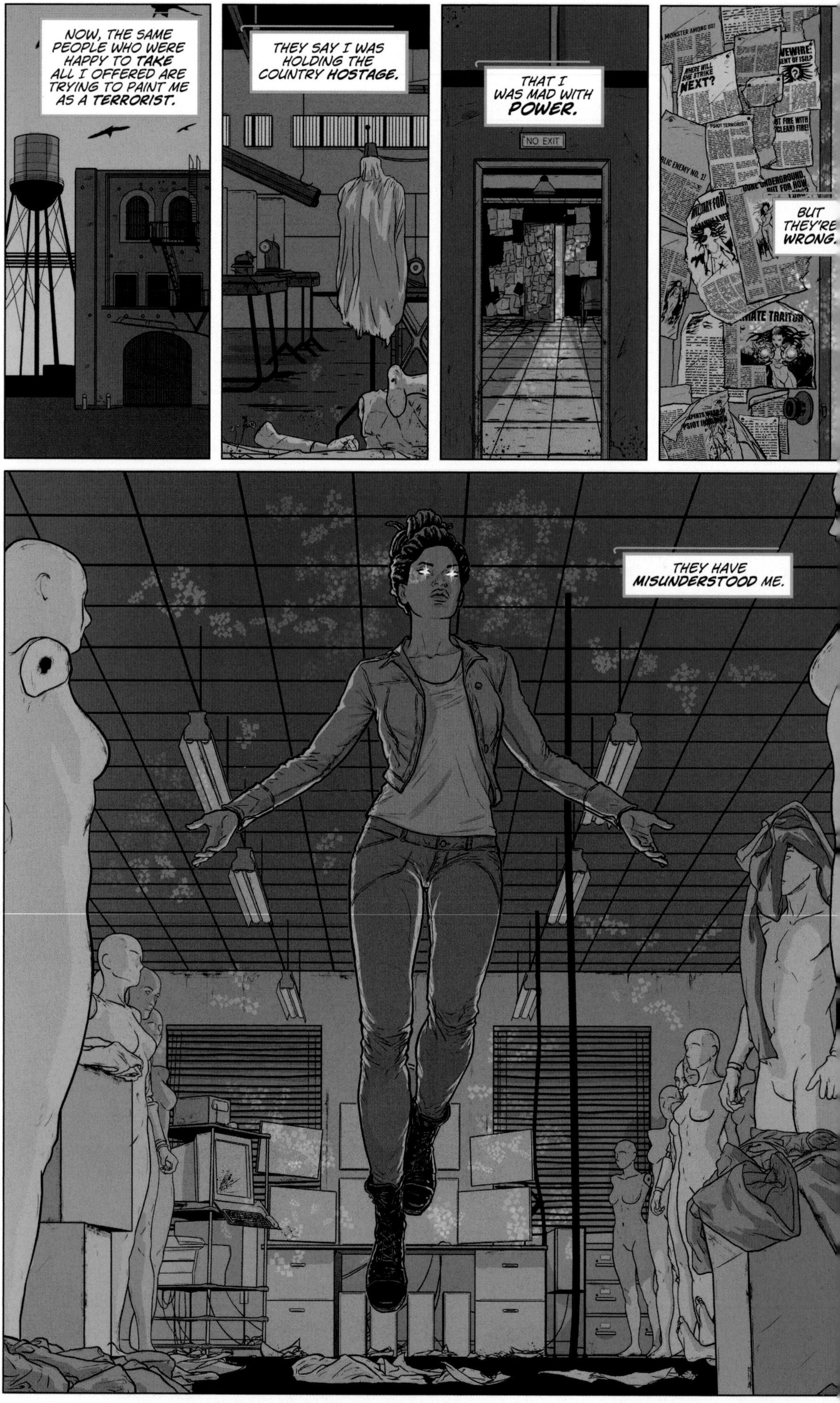
NOW, THE SAME PEOPLE WHO WERE HAPPY TO TAKE ALL I OFFERED ARE TRYING TO PAINT ME AS A TERRORIST.
THEY SAY I WAS HOLDING THE COUNTRY HOSTAGE.
THAT I WAS MAD WITH POWER.
NO EXIT
MONSTER AMONG US!
WHERE WILL SHE STRIKE NEXT?
PSIOT TERRORIST!
BUT THEY'RE WRONG.
THEY HAVE MISUNDERSTOOD ME.

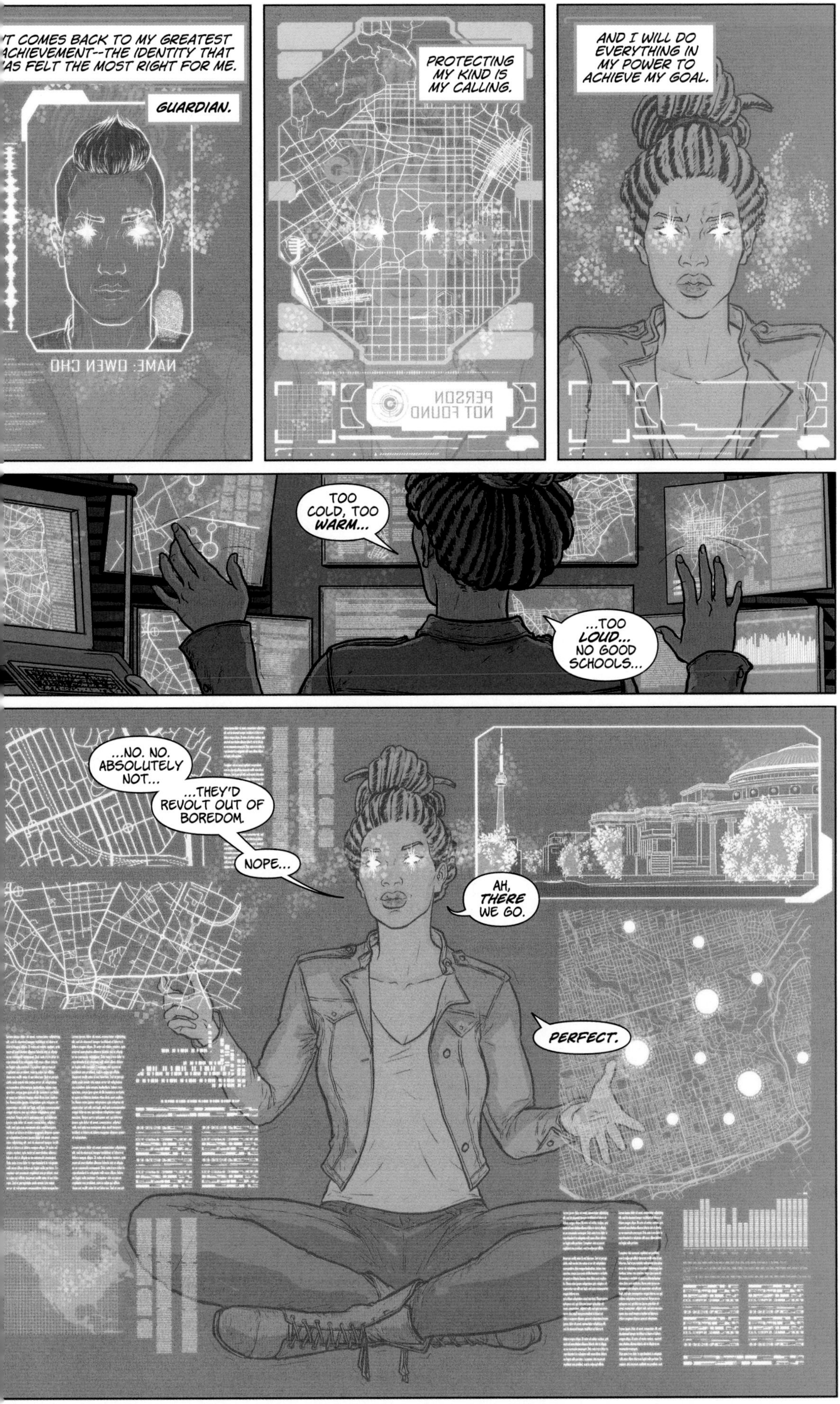

'T COMES BACK TO MY GREATEST ACHIEVEMENT--THE IDENTITY THAT 'AS FELT THE MOST RIGHT FOR ME.
GUARDIAN.
NAME: OWEN CHO
PROTECTING MY KIND IS MY CALLING.
PERSON NOT FOUND
AND I WILL DO EVERYTHING IN MY POWER TO ACHIEVE MY GOAL.
TOO COLD, TOO WARM...
...TOO LOUD... NO GOOD SCHOOLS...
...NO. NO. ABSOLUTELY NOT...
...THEY'D REVOLT OUT OF BOREDOM.
NOPE...
AH, THERE WE GO.
PERFECT.

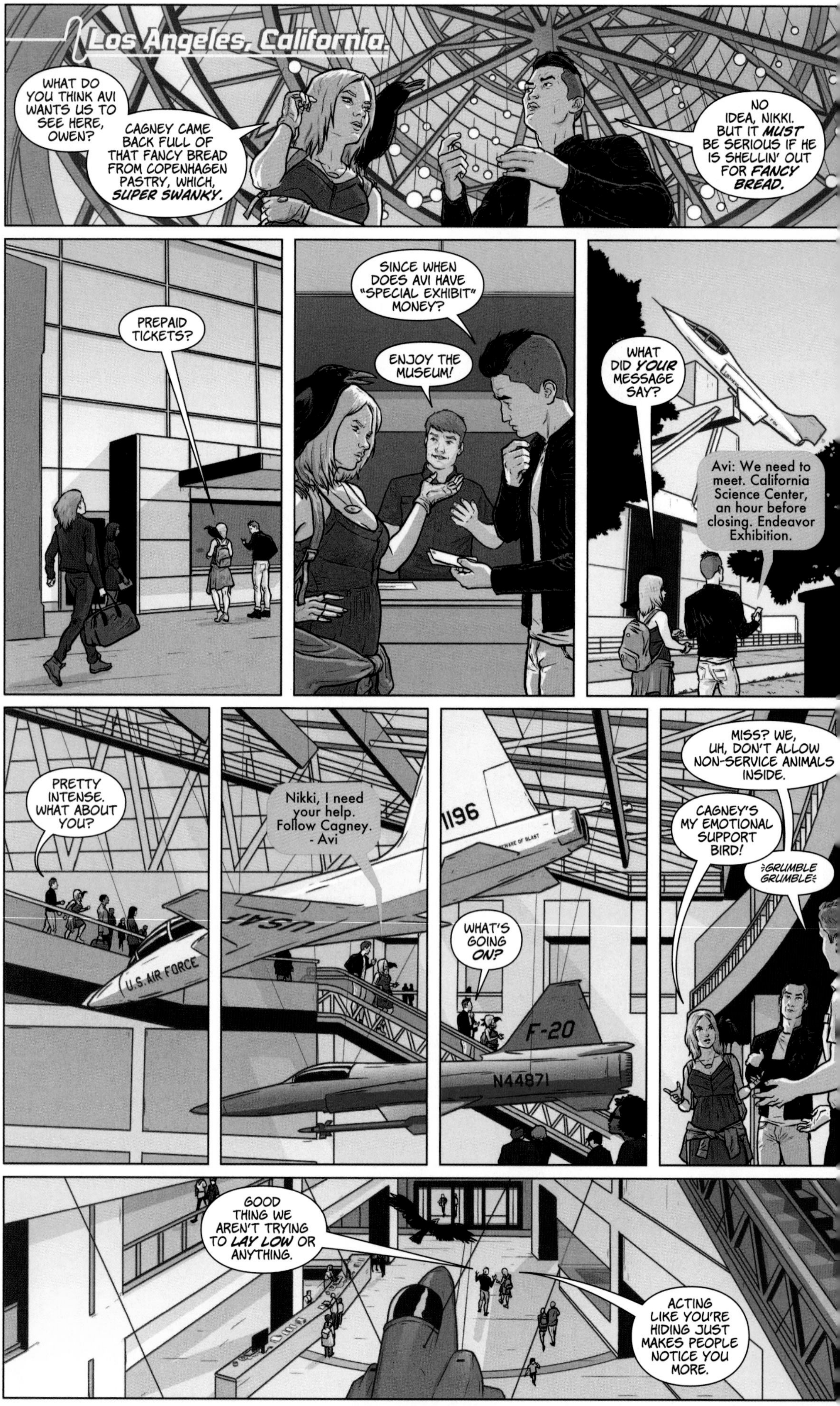
Los Angeles, California.
WHAT DO YOU THINK AVI WANTS US TO SEE HERE, OWEN?
CAGNEY CAME BACK FULL OF THAT FANCY BREAD FROM COPENHAGEN PASTRY, WHICH, SUPER SWANKY.
NO IDEA, NIKKI. BUT IT MUST BE SERIOUS IF HE IS SHELLIN' OUT FOR FANCY BREAD.
PREPAID TICKETS?
SINCE WHEN DOES AVI HAVE "SPECIAL EXHIBIT" MONEY?
ENJOY THE MUSEUM!
WHAT DID YOUR MESSAGE SAY?
Avi: We need to meet. California Science Center, an hour before closing. Endeavor Exhibition.
PRETTY INTENSE. WHAT ABOUT YOU?
U.S. AIR FORCE
Nikki, I need your help. Follow Cagney. - Avi
USAF
1196
WHAT'S GOING ON?
F-20
N44871
MISS? WE, UH, DON'T ALLOW NON-SERVICE ANIMALS INSIDE.
CAGNEY'S MY EMOTIONAL SUPPORT BIRD!
GRUMBLE GRUMBLE
GOOD THING WE AREN'T TRYING TO LAY LOW OR ANYTHING.
ACTING LIKE YOU'RE HIDING JUST MAKES PEOPLE NOTICE YOU MORE.

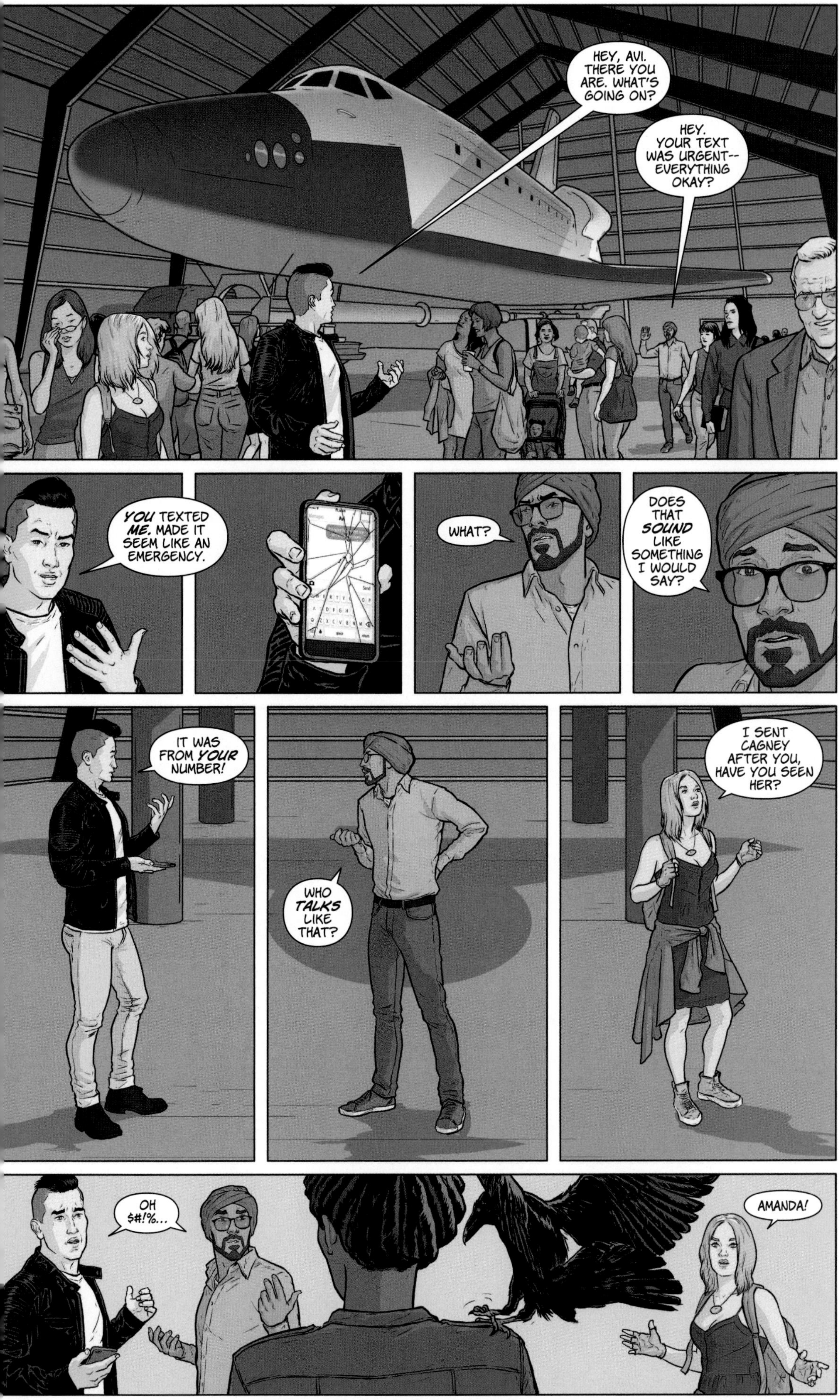
HEY, AVI. THERE YOU ARE. WHAT'S GOING ON?
HEY. YOUR TEXT WAS URGENT-- EVERYTHING OKAY?
YOU TEXTED ME. MADE IT SEEM LIKE AN EMERGENCY.
WHAT?
DOES THAT SOUND LIKE SOMETHING I WOULD SAY?
IT WAS FROM YOUR NUMBER!
WHO TALKS LIKE THAT?
I SENT CAGNEY AFTER YOU, HAVE YOU SEEN HER?
OH $#!%...
AMANDA!

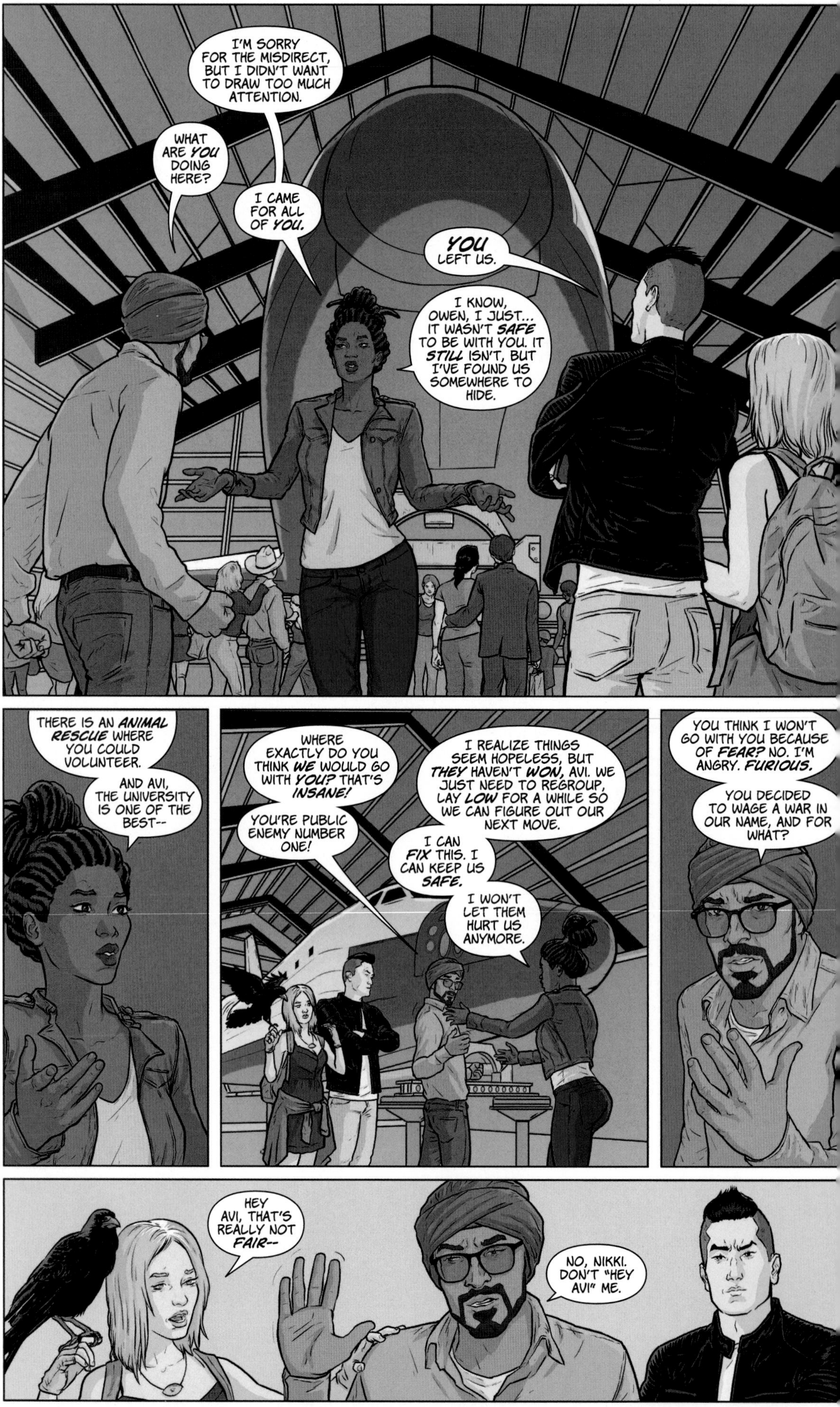

I'M SORRY FOR THE MISDIRECT, BUT I DIDN'T WANT TO DRAW TOO MUCH ATTENTION.
WHAT ARE *YOU* DOING HERE?
I CAME FOR ALL OF *YOU.*
YOU LEFT US.
I KNOW, OWEN, I JUST... IT WASN'T *SAFE* TO BE WITH YOU. IT *STILL* ISN'T, BUT I'VE FOUND US SOMEWHERE TO HIDE.
THERE IS AN *ANIMAL RESCUE* WHERE YOU COULD VOLUNTEER.
AND AVI, THE UNIVERSITY IS ONE OF THE BEST--
WHERE EXACTLY DO YOU THINK *WE* WOULD GO WITH *YOU?* THAT'S *INSANE!*
YOU'RE PUBLIC ENEMY NUMBER ONE!
I REALIZE THINGS SEEM HOPELESS, BUT *THEY* HAVEN'T *WON,* AVI. WE JUST NEED TO REGROUP, LAY *LOW* FOR A WHILE SO WE CAN FIGURE OUT OUR NEXT MOVE.
I CAN *FIX* THIS. I CAN KEEP US *SAFE.*
I WON'T LET THEM HURT US ANYMORE.
YOU THINK I WON'T GO WITH YOU BECAUSE OF *FEAR?* NO. I'M ANGRY. *FURIOUS.*
YOU DECIDED TO WAGE A WAR IN OUR NAME, AND FOR WHAT?
HEY AVI, THAT'S REALLY NOT *FAIR*--
NO, NIKKI. DON'T "HEY AVI" ME.

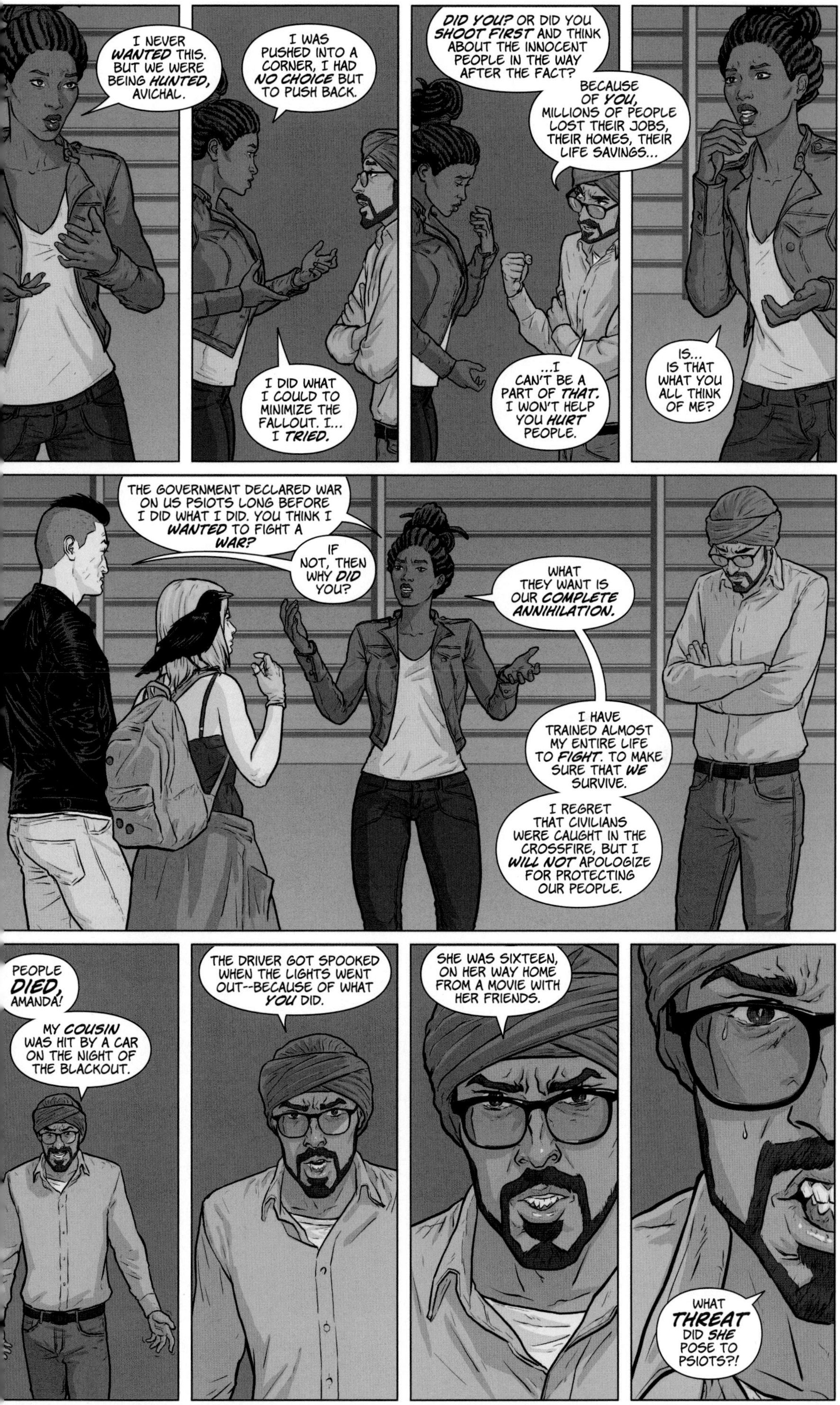
I NEVER WANTED THIS. BUT WE WERE BEING HUNTED, AVICHAL.
I WAS PUSHED INTO A CORNER, I HAD NO CHOICE BUT TO PUSH BACK.
I DID WHAT I COULD TO MINIMIZE THE FALLOUT. I... I TRIED.
DID YOU? OR DID YOU SHOOT FIRST AND THINK ABOUT THE INNOCENT PEOPLE IN THE WAY AFTER THE FACT?
BECAUSE OF YOU, MILLIONS OF PEOPLE LOST THEIR JOBS, THEIR HOMES, THEIR LIFE SAVINGS...
...I CAN'T BE A PART OF THAT. I WON'T HELP YOU HURT PEOPLE.
IS... IS THAT WHAT YOU ALL THINK OF ME?
THE GOVERNMENT DECLARED WAR ON US PSIOTS LONG BEFORE I DID WHAT I DID. YOU THINK I WANTED TO FIGHT A WAR?
IF NOT, THEN WHY DID YOU?
WHAT THEY WANT IS OUR COMPLETE ANNIHILATION.
I HAVE TRAINED ALMOST MY ENTIRE LIFE TO FIGHT. TO MAKE SURE THAT WE SURVIVE.
I REGRET THAT CIVILIANS WERE CAUGHT IN THE CROSSFIRE, BUT I WILL NOT APOLOGIZE FOR PROTECTING OUR PEOPLE.
PEOPLE DIED, AMANDA!
MY COUSIN WAS HIT BY A CAR ON THE NIGHT OF THE BLACKOUT.
THE DRIVER GOT SPOOKED WHEN THE LIGHTS WENT OUT--BECAUSE OF WHAT YOU DID.
SHE WAS SIXTEEN, ON HER WAY HOME FROM A MOVIE WITH HER FRIENDS.
WHAT THREAT DID SHE POSE TO PSIOTS?!

YOU MAY NOT HAVE *MEANT* TO HURT THEM.

BUT THAT DOESN'T CHANGE WHAT HAPPENED.

AVI...

WOULD YOU DO IT AGAIN, RIGHT NOW, IF YOU HAD THE CHANCE TO GO BACK? HUH?

I...AVI, YOU *HAVE* TO UNDERSTAND--

WE DON'T *HAVE* TO DO ANYTHING.

UNLESS YOU'RE GONNA *FORCE* US TO? YOU GONNA DO THAT?

I WOULD *NEVER* FORCE YOU TO DO ANYTHING AGAINST YOUR WILL. YOU *KNOW* THAT, OWEN.

SOLID. THEN YOU'LL HAVE NO PROBLEM WITH US *GOING.*

I--I'M SORRY, WE JUST...

YOU HAVE NO *IDEA* WHAT YOU DID WRONG, DO YOU?

YOU CAN'T ASK ME TO REGRET FIGHTING TO KEEP YOU *ALIVE*, AVI.

"BY ANY MEANS NECESSARY," RIGHT?

WERE YOU TRYING TO PROTECT PSIOTS, OR WERE YOU TRYING TO *CONTROL* THE GOVERNMENT?

I HAVE NO INTEREST IN *RULING* ANYTHING. IF I DID, THERE ARE *SMARTER* WAYS TO DO IT THAN *THIS.*

I CARE ABOUT YOU--YOU ARE MY *FAMILY.* I AM TRYING TO *SAVE* US!

SEEM LIKE SOMETH I'VE HE *BEFO*

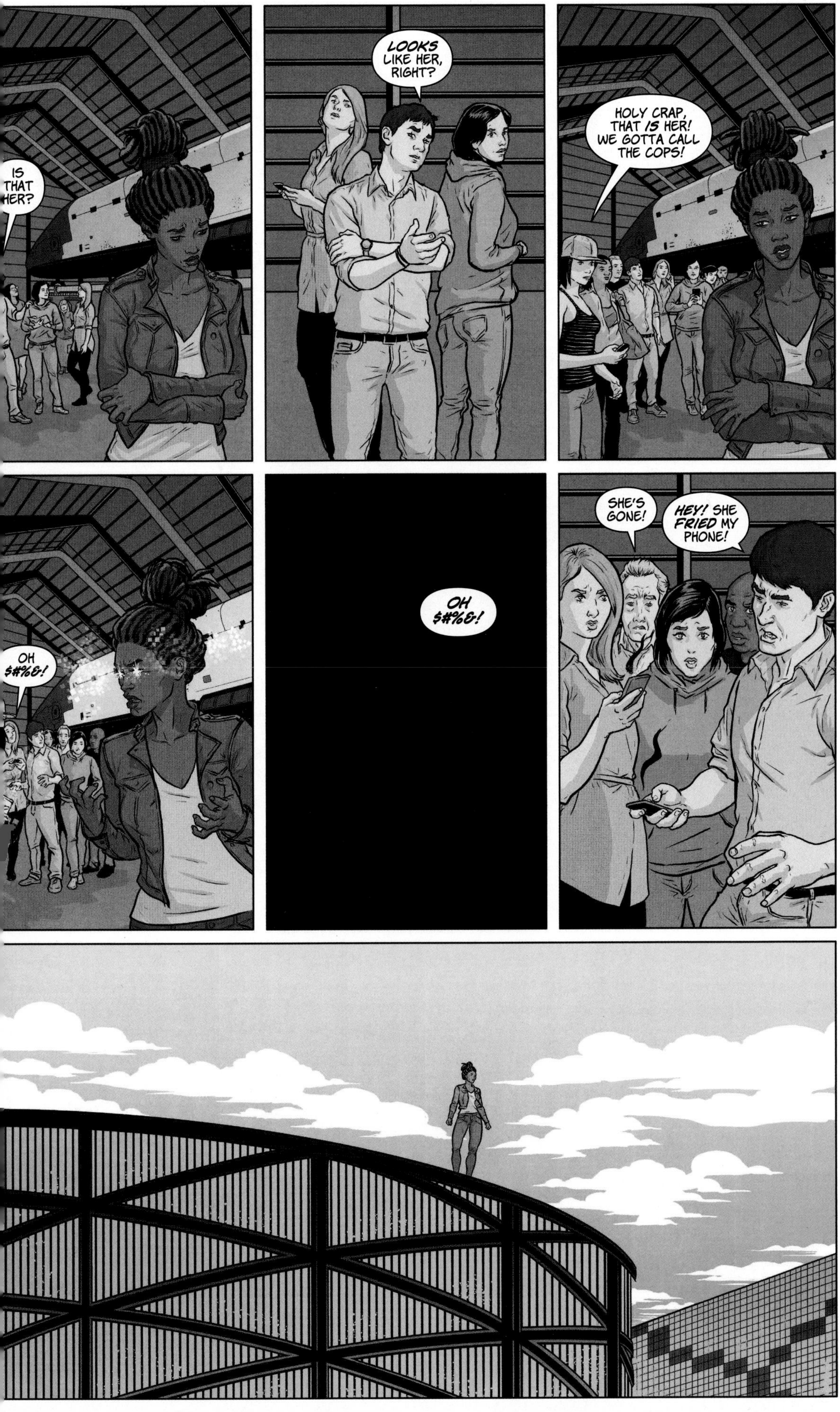
IS THAT HER?
LOOKS LIKE HER, RIGHT?
HOLY CRAP, THAT IS HER! WE GOTTA CALL THE COPS!
OH $#%&!
OH $#%&!
SHE'S GONE!
HEY! SHE FRIED MY PHONE!

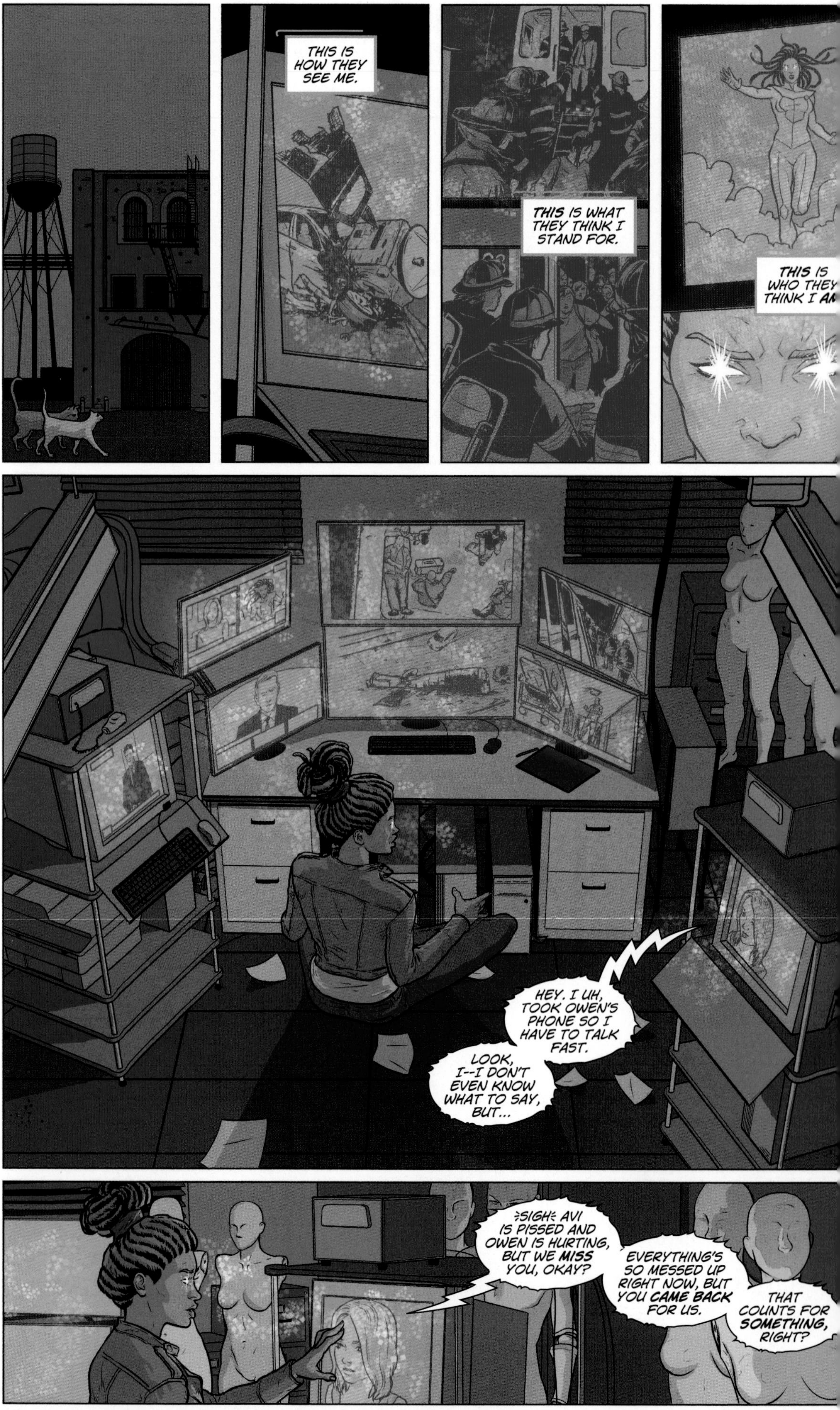
THIS IS HOW THEY SEE ME.
THIS IS WHAT THEY THINK I STAND FOR.
THIS IS WHO THEY THINK I AM
HEY. I UH, TOOK OWEN'S PHONE SO I HAVE TO TALK FAST.
LOOK, I--I DON'T EVEN KNOW WHAT TO SAY, BUT...
SIGH AVI IS PISSED AND OWEN IS HURTING, BUT WE MISS YOU, OKAY?
EVERYTHING'S SO MESSED UP RIGHT NOW, BUT YOU CAME BACK FOR US.
THAT COUNTS FOR SOMETHING, RIGHT?

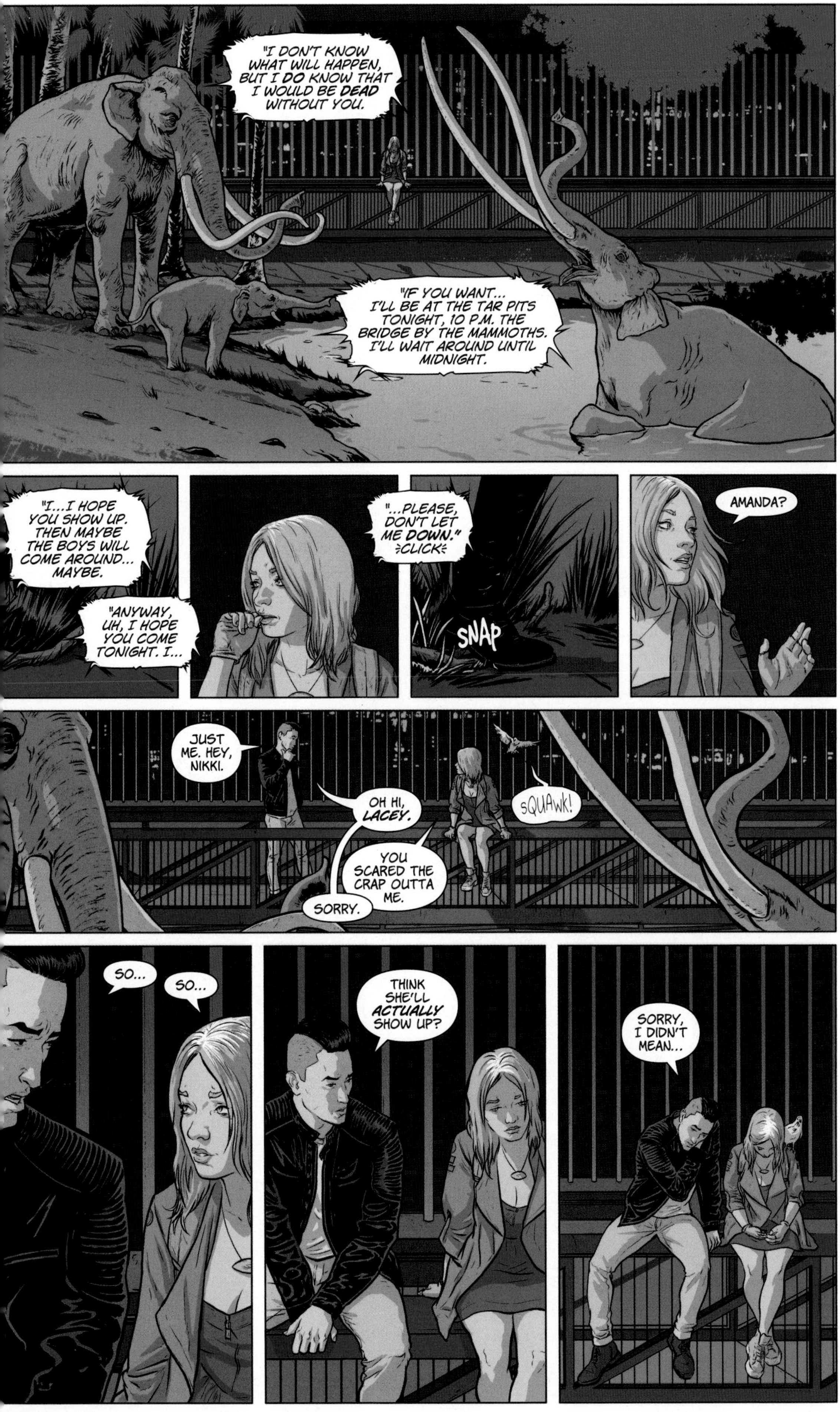
"I DON'T KNOW WHAT WILL HAPPEN, BUT I DO KNOW THAT I WOULD BE DEAD WITHOUT YOU.
"IF YOU WANT... I'LL BE AT THE TAR PITS TONIGHT, 10 P.M. THE BRIDGE BY THE MAMMOTHS. I'LL WAIT AROUND UNTIL MIDNIGHT.
"I...I HOPE YOU SHOW UP. THEN MAYBE THE BOYS WILL COME AROUND... MAYBE.
"ANYWAY, UH, I HOPE YOU COME TONIGHT. I...
"...PLEASE, DON'T LET ME DOWN."
CLICK
SNAP
AMANDA?
JUST ME. HEY, NIKKI.
OH HI, LACEY.
SORRY.
YOU SCARED THE CRAP OUTTA ME.
SQUAWK!
SO...
SO...
THINK SHE'LL ACTUALLY SHOW UP?
SORRY, I DIDN'T MEAN...

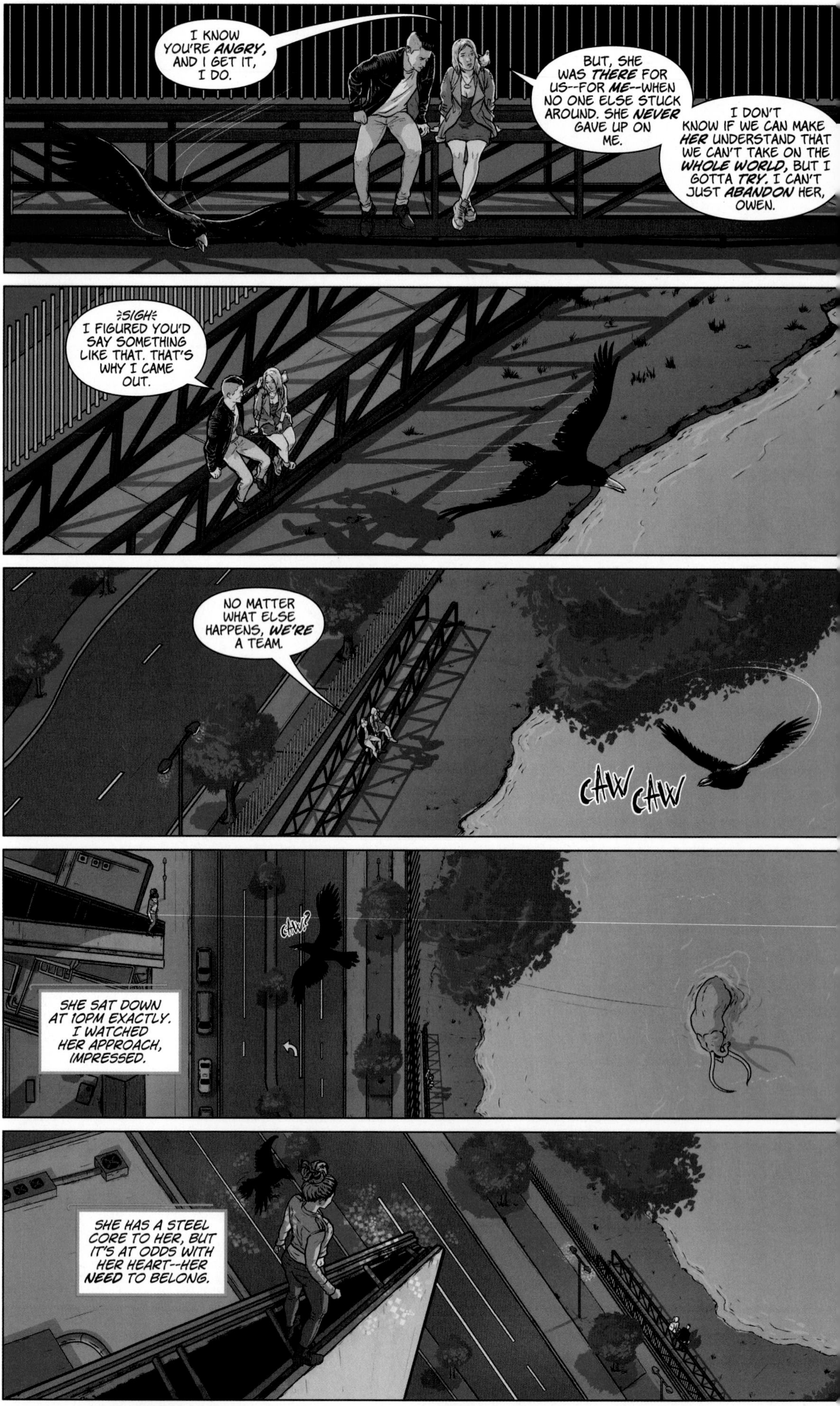

I KNOW YOU'RE ANGRY, AND I GET IT, I DO.
BUT, SHE WAS THERE FOR US--FOR ME--WHEN NO ONE ELSE STUCK AROUND. SHE NEVER GAVE UP ON ME.
I DON'T KNOW IF WE CAN MAKE HER UNDERSTAND THAT WE CAN'T TAKE ON THE WHOLE WORLD, BUT I GOTTA TRY. I CAN'T JUST ABANDON HER, OWEN.
SIGH I FIGURED YOU'D SAY SOMETHING LIKE THAT. THAT'S WHY I CAME OUT.
NO MATTER WHAT ELSE HAPPENS, WE'RE A TEAM.
CAW CAW
CAW?
SHE SAT DOWN AT 10PM EXACTLY. I WATCHED HER APPROACH, IMPRESSED.
SHE HAS A STEEL CORE TO HER, BUT IT'S AT ODDS WITH HER HEART--HER NEED TO BELONG.

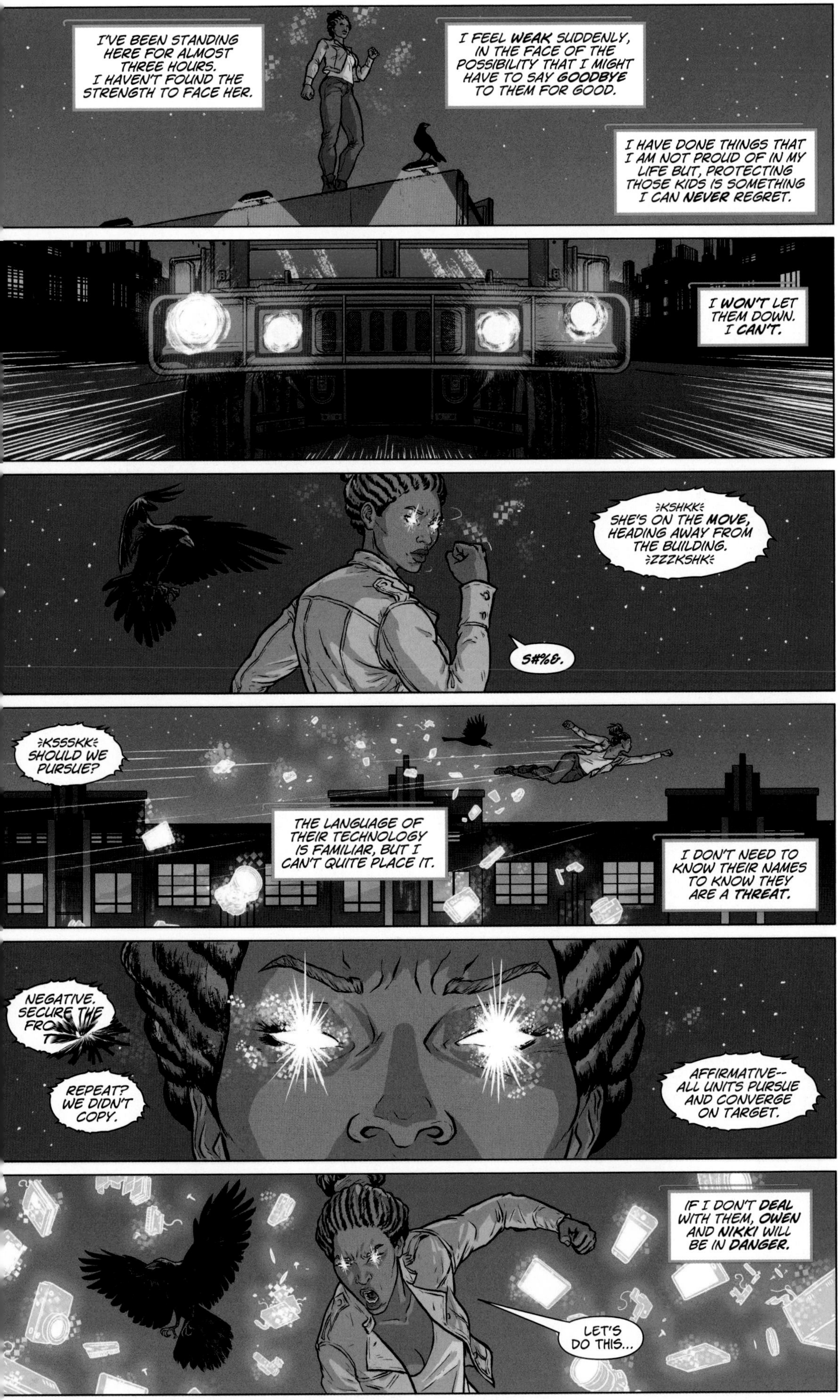
I'VE BEEN STANDING HERE FOR ALMOST THREE HOURS. I HAVEN'T FOUND THE STRENGTH TO FACE HER.
I FEEL **WEAK** SUDDENLY, IN THE FACE OF THE POSSIBILITY THAT I MIGHT HAVE TO SAY **GOODBYE** TO THEM FOR GOOD.
I HAVE DONE THINGS THAT I AM NOT PROUD OF IN MY LIFE BUT, PROTECTING THOSE KIDS IS SOMETHING I CAN **NEVER** REGRET.
I **WON'T** LET THEM DOWN. I **CAN'T.**
KSHKK SHE'S ON THE **MOVE,** HEADING AWAY FROM THE BUILDING. ZZZKSHK
S#%&.
KSSSKK SHOULD WE PURSUE?
THE LANGUAGE OF THEIR TECHNOLOGY IS FAMILIAR, BUT I CAN'T QUITE PLACE IT.
I DON'T NEED TO KNOW THEIR NAMES TO KNOW THEY ARE A **THREAT.**
NEGATIVE. SECURE THE FRO
REPEAT? WE DIDN'T COPY.
AFFIRMATIVE-- ALL UNITS PURSUE AND CONVERGE ON TARGET.
IF I DON'T **DEAL** WITH THEM, **OWEN** AND **NIKKI** WILL BE IN **DANGER.**
LET'S DO THIS...

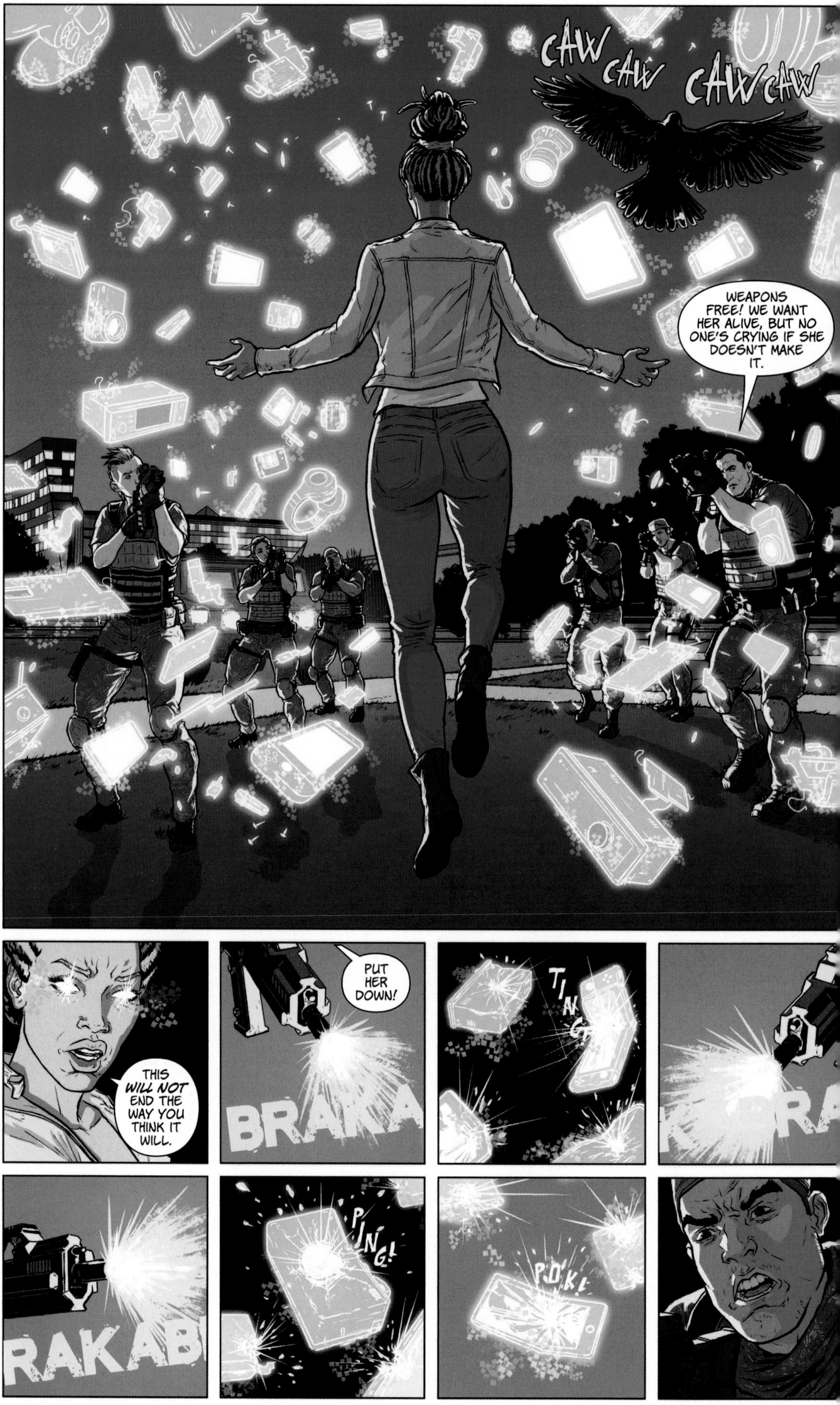
CAW CAW CAW CAW
WEAPONS FREE! WE WANT HER ALIVE, BUT NO ONE'S CRYING IF SHE DOESN'T MAKE IT.
THIS *WILL NOT* END THE WAY YOU THINK IT WILL.
PUT HER DOWN!
BRAKA
RAKAB
PING!
POK!

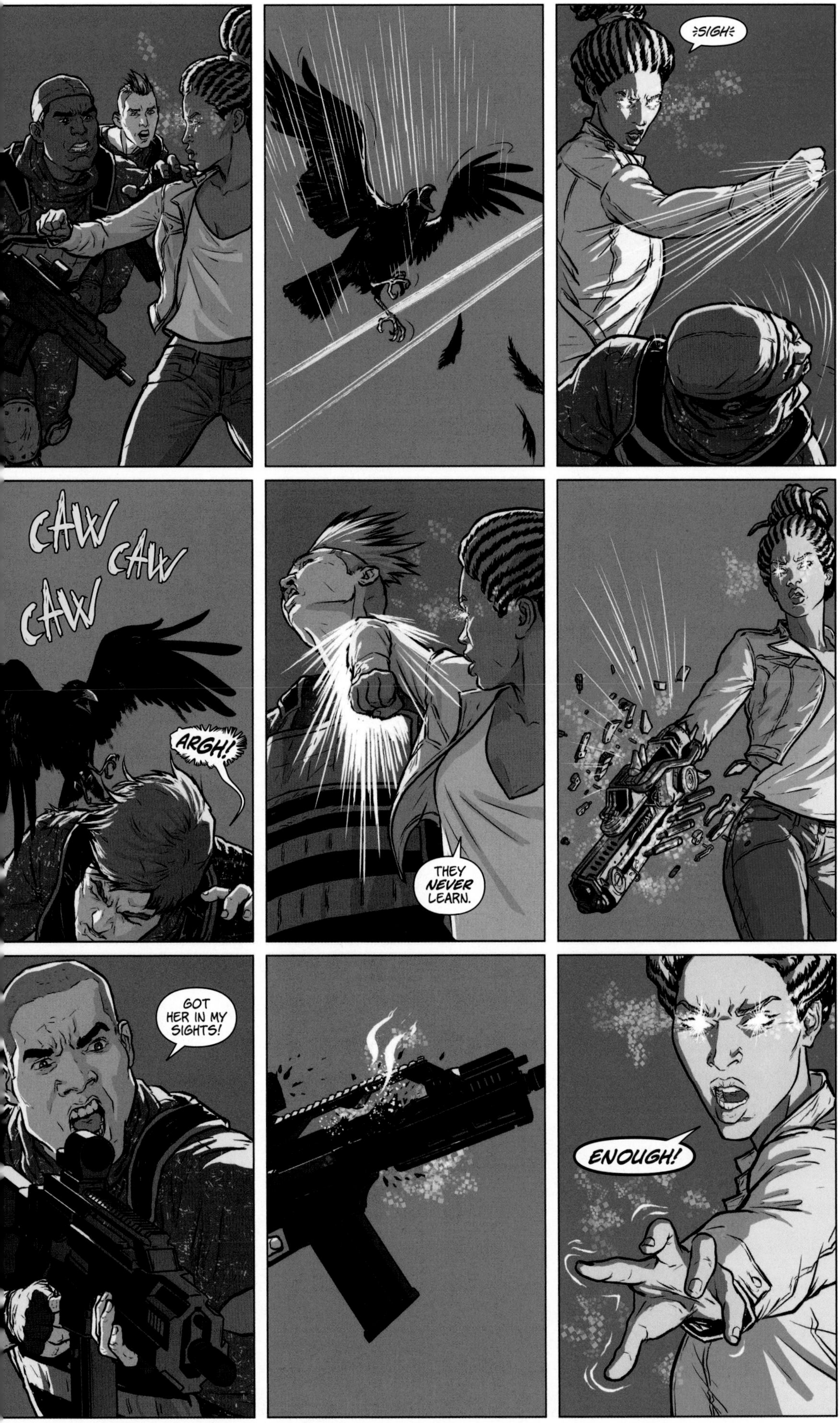

SIGH
CAW CAW CAW
ARGH!
THEY NEVER LEARN.
GOT HER IN MY SIGHTS!
ENOUGH!

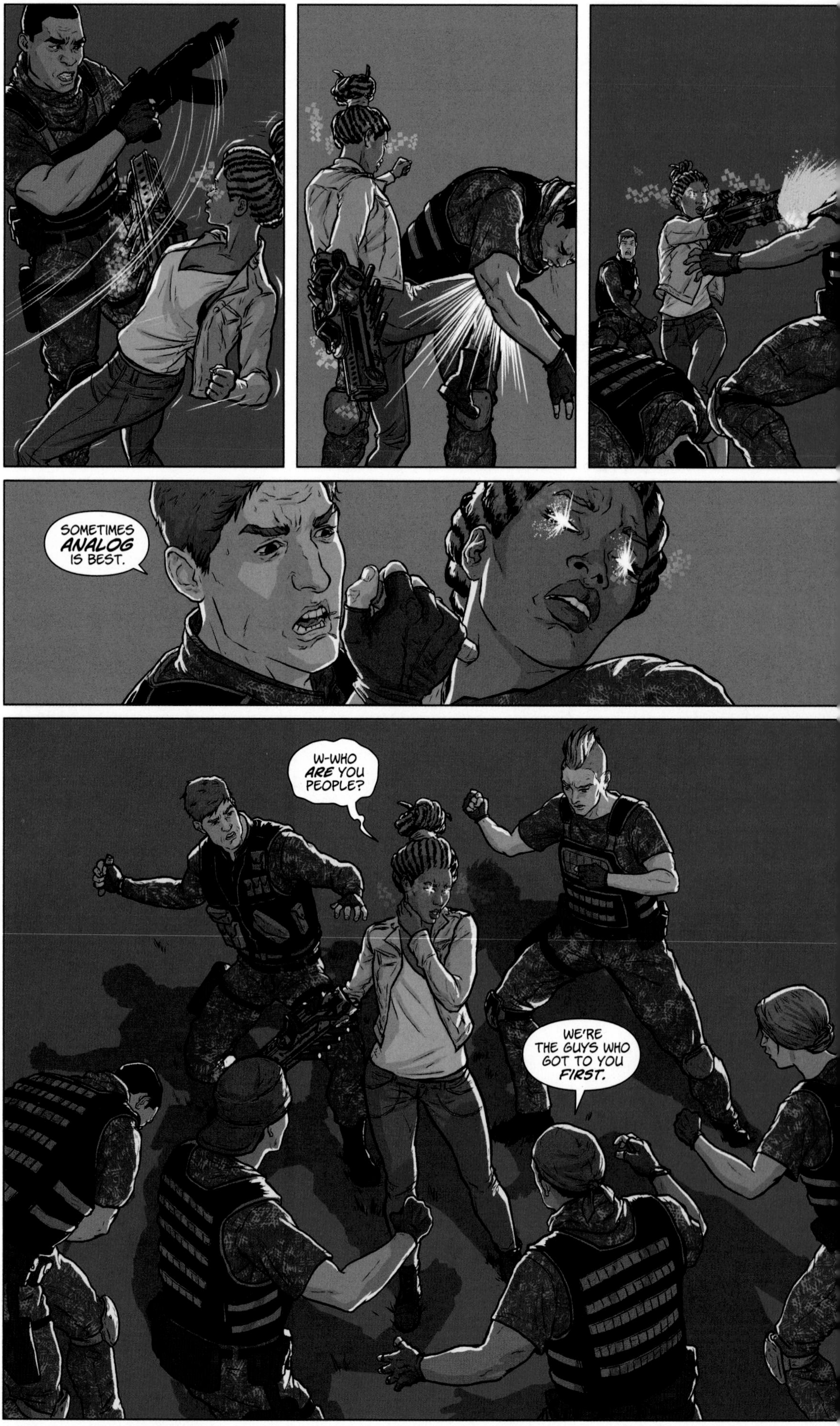
SOMETIMES ANALOG IS BEST.
W-WHO ARE YOU PEOPLE?
WE'RE THE GUYS WHO GOT TO YOU FIRST.

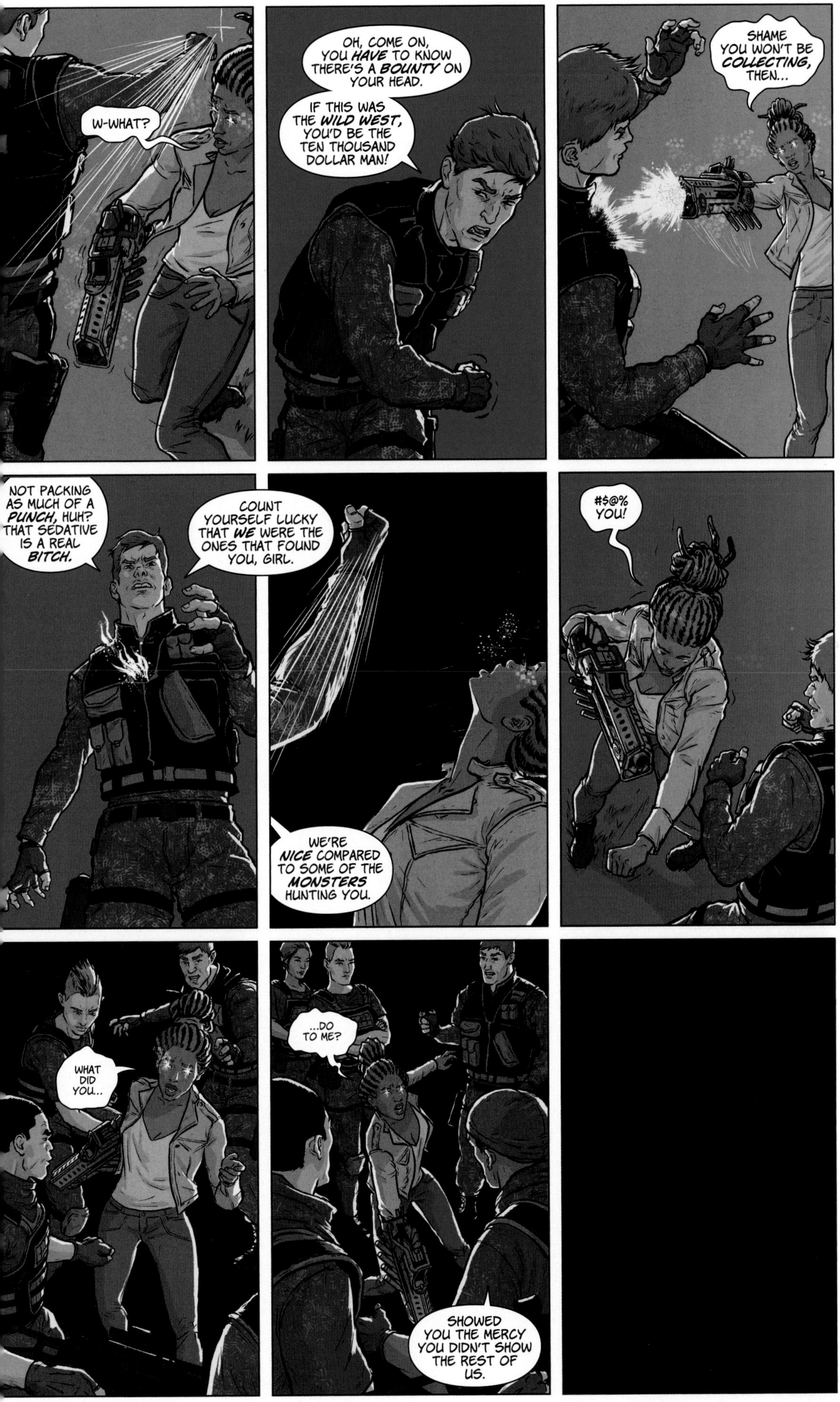
W-WHAT?
OH, COME ON, YOU HAVE TO KNOW THERE'S A BOUNTY ON YOUR HEAD.
IF THIS WAS THE WILD WEST, YOU'D BE THE TEN THOUSAND DOLLAR MAN!
SHAME YOU WON'T BE COLLECTING, THEN...
NOT PACKING AS MUCH OF A PUNCH, HUH? THAT SEDATIVE IS A REAL BITCH.
COUNT YOURSELF LUCKY THAT WE WERE THE ONES THAT FOUND YOU, GIRL.
WE'RE NICE COMPARED TO SOME OF THE MONSTERS HUNTING YOU.
#$@% YOU!
WHAT DID YOU...
...DO TO ME?
SHOWED YOU THE MERCY YOU DIDN'T SHOW THE REST OF US.

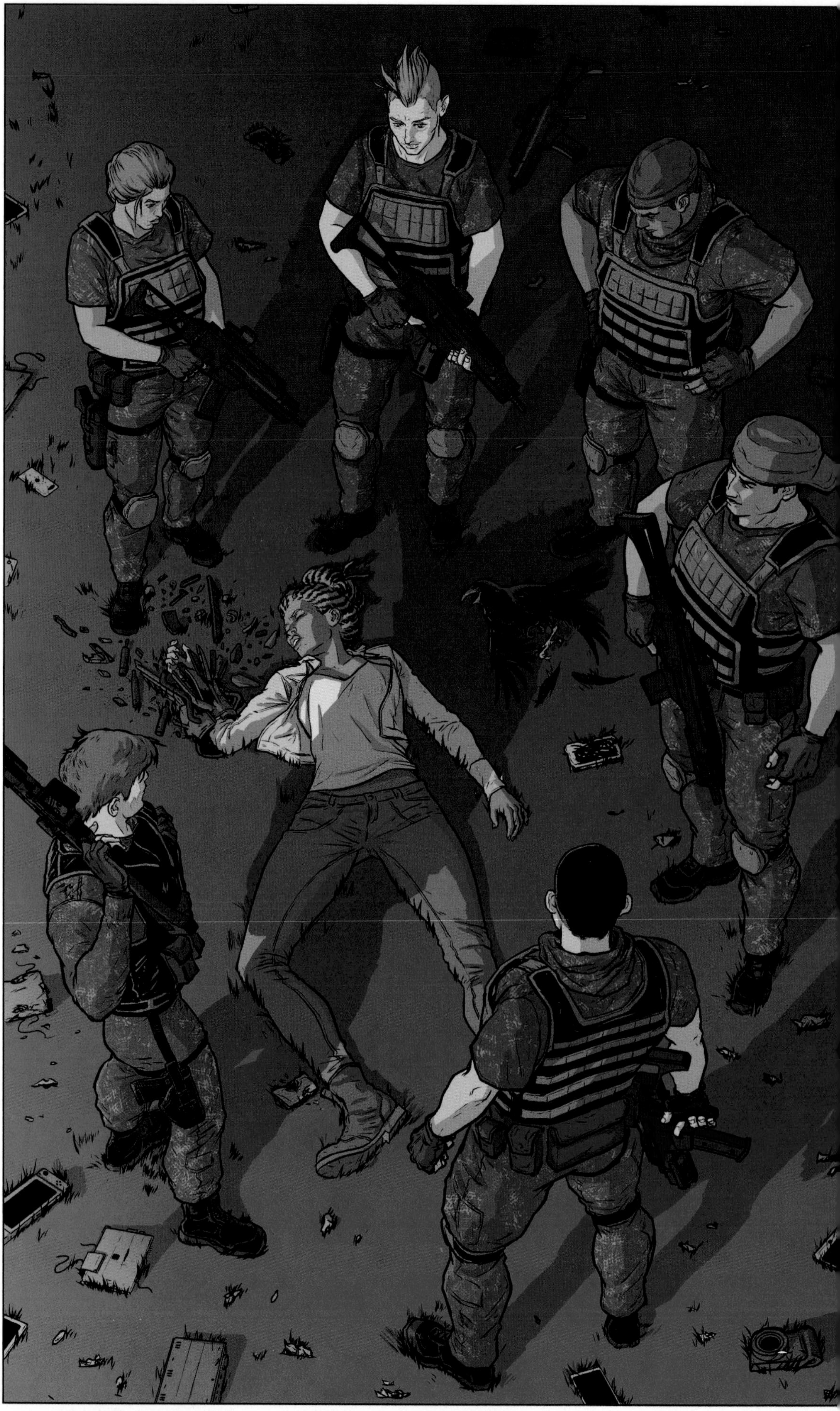

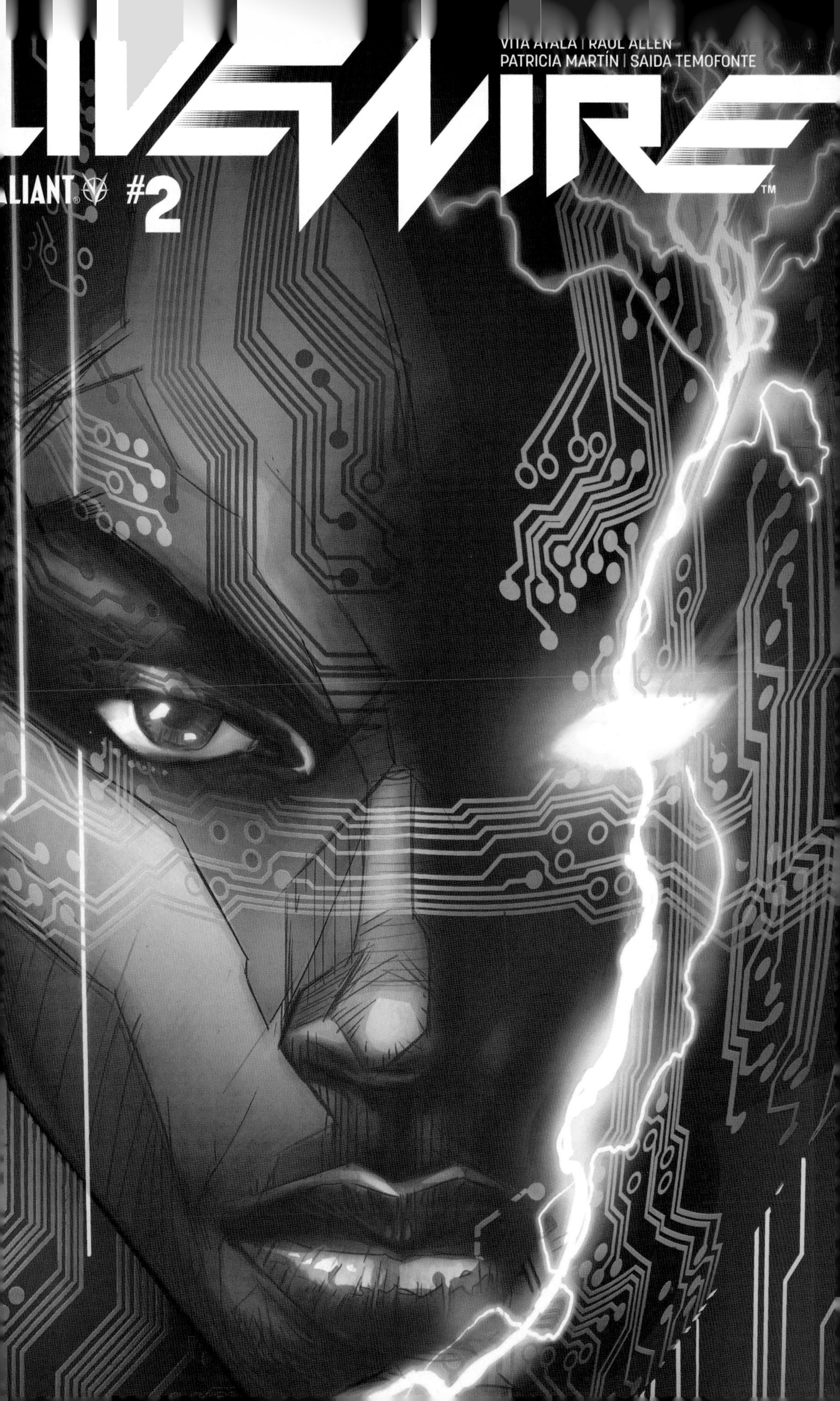
VITA AYALA | RAÚL ALLEN
PATRICIA MARTÍN | SAIDA TEMOFONTE
LIVEWIRE™
VALIANT
#2

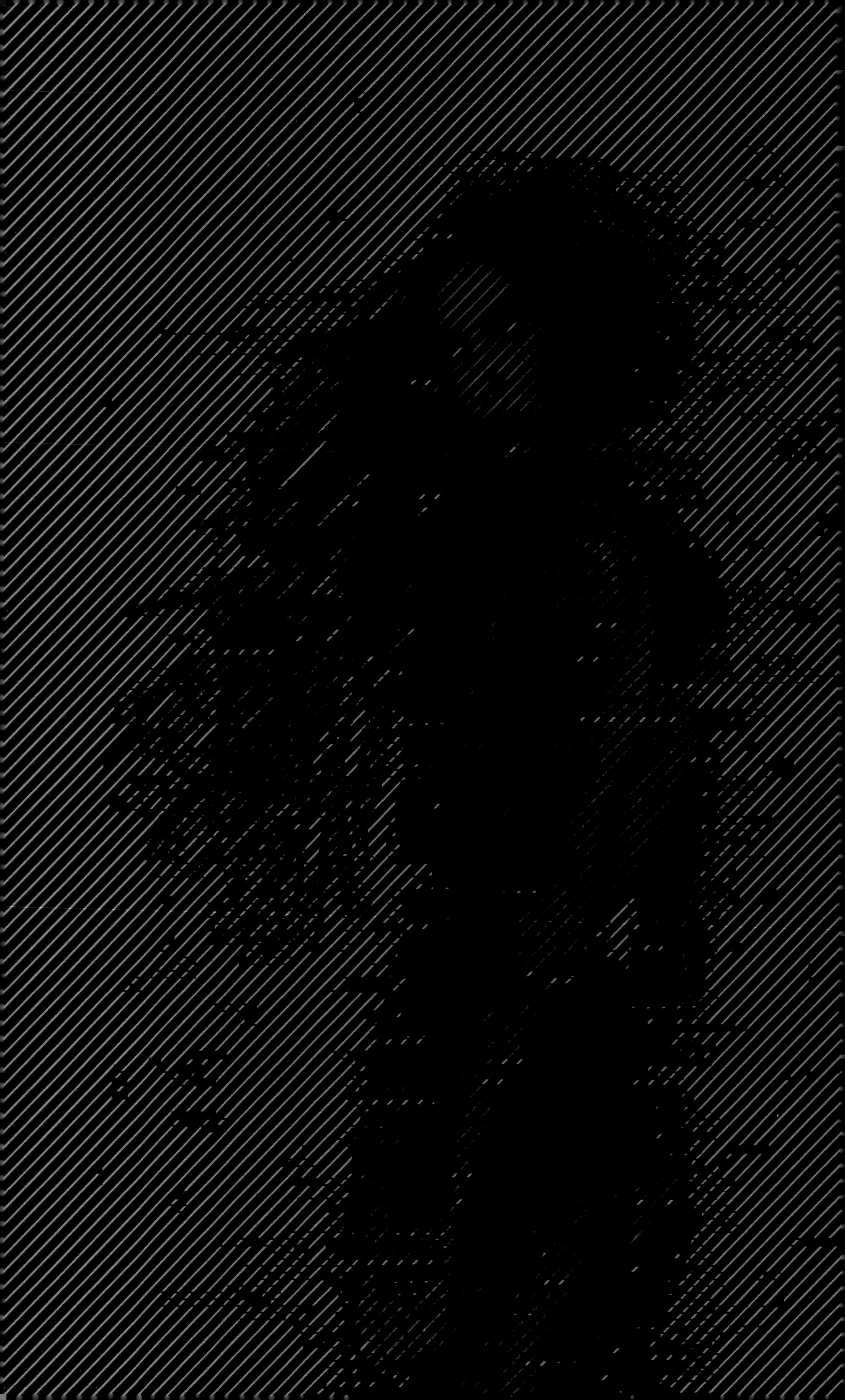

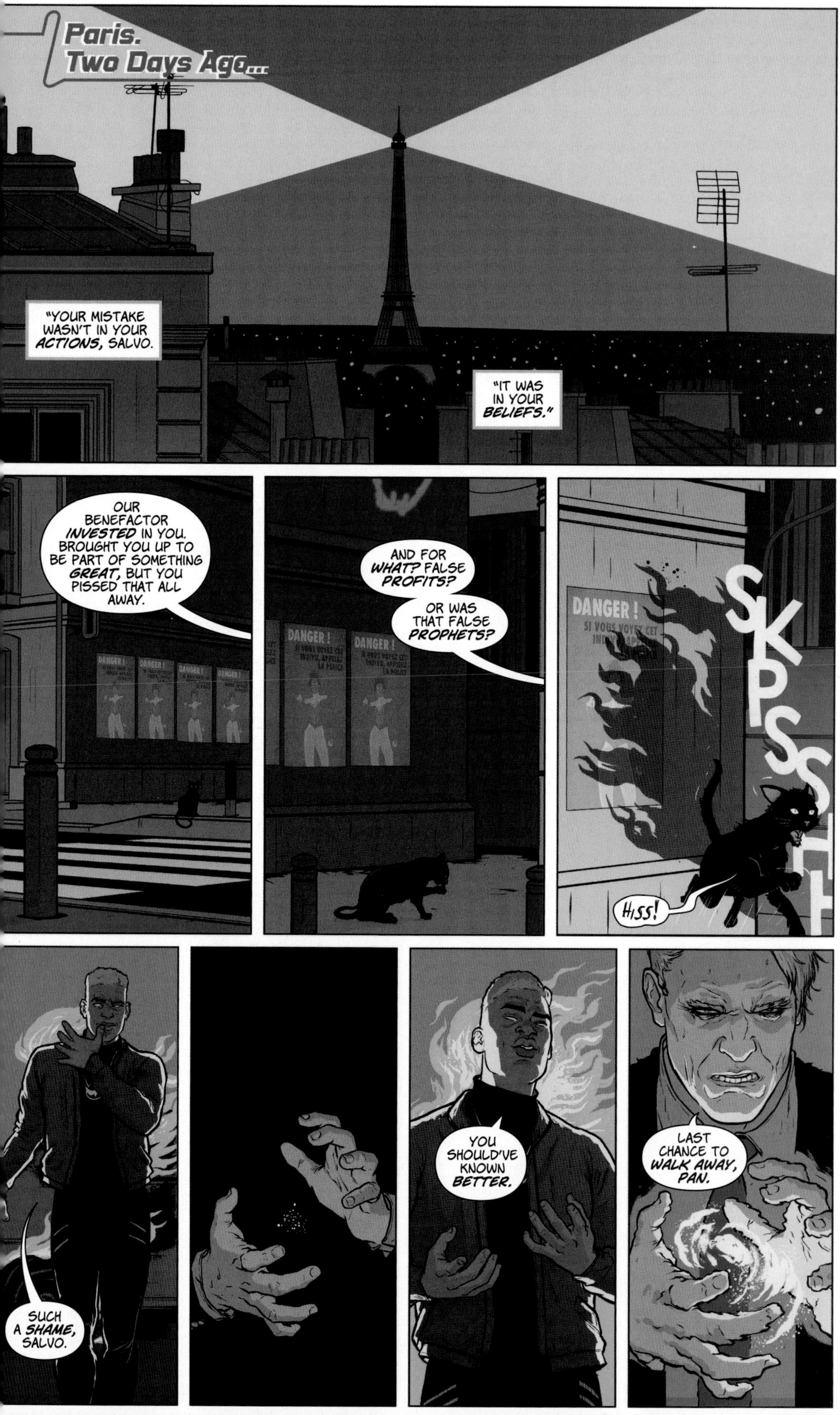

Paris.
Two Days Ago...
"YOUR MISTAKE WASN'T IN YOUR ACTIONS, SALVO.
"IT WAS IN YOUR BELIEFS."
OUR BENEFACTOR INVESTED IN YOU. BROUGHT YOU UP TO BE PART OF SOMETHING GREAT, BUT YOU PISSED THAT ALL AWAY.
AND FOR WHAT? FALSE PROFITS?
OR WAS THAT FALSE PROPHETS?
DANGER !
SKPSSH
HISS!
SUCH A SHAME, SALVO.
YOU SHOULD'VE KNOWN BETTER.
LAST CHANCE TO WALK AWAY, PAN.

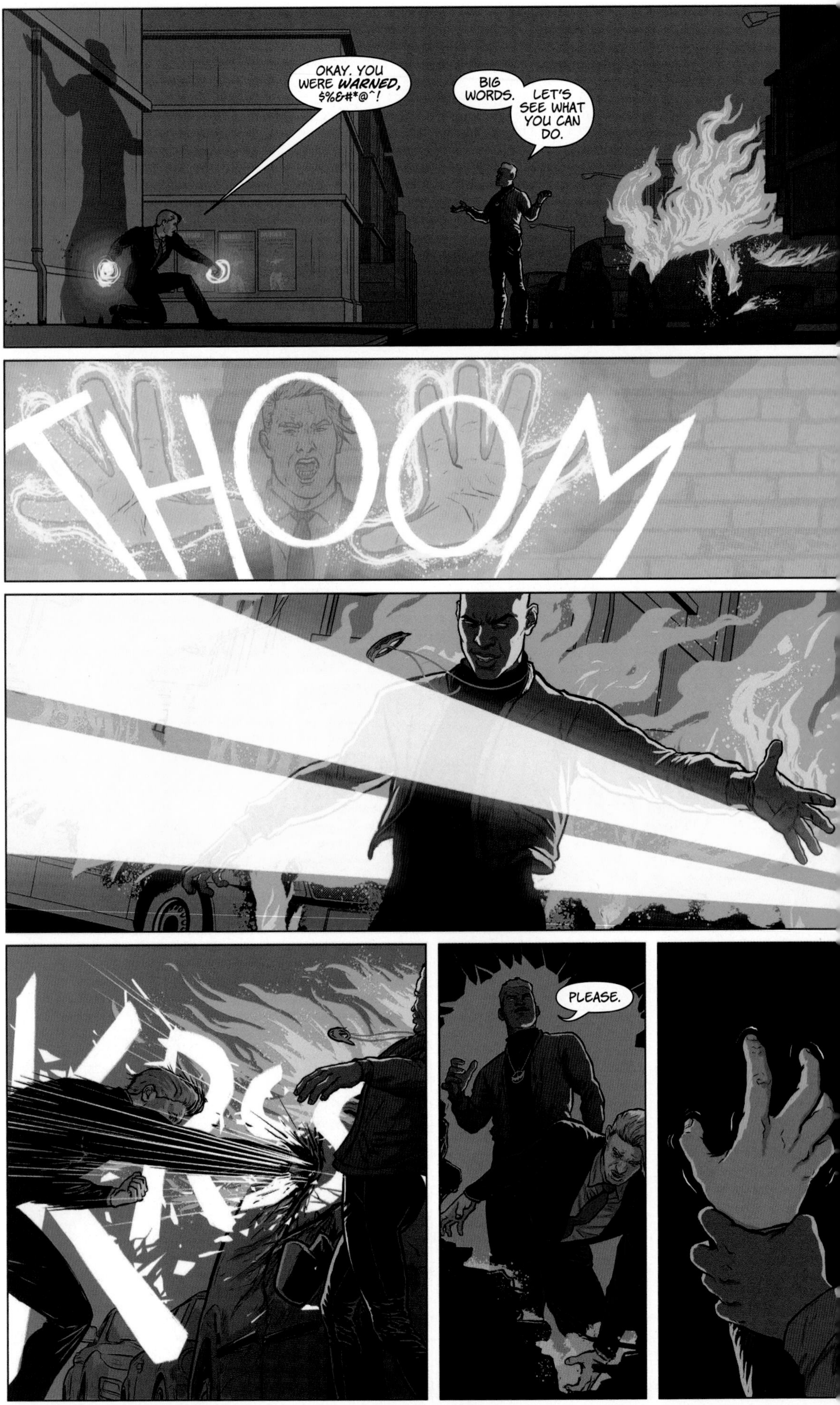
OKAY. YOU WERE WARNED, $%&#*@^!
BIG WORDS.
LET'S SEE WHAT YOU CAN DO.
THOOM
PLEASE.

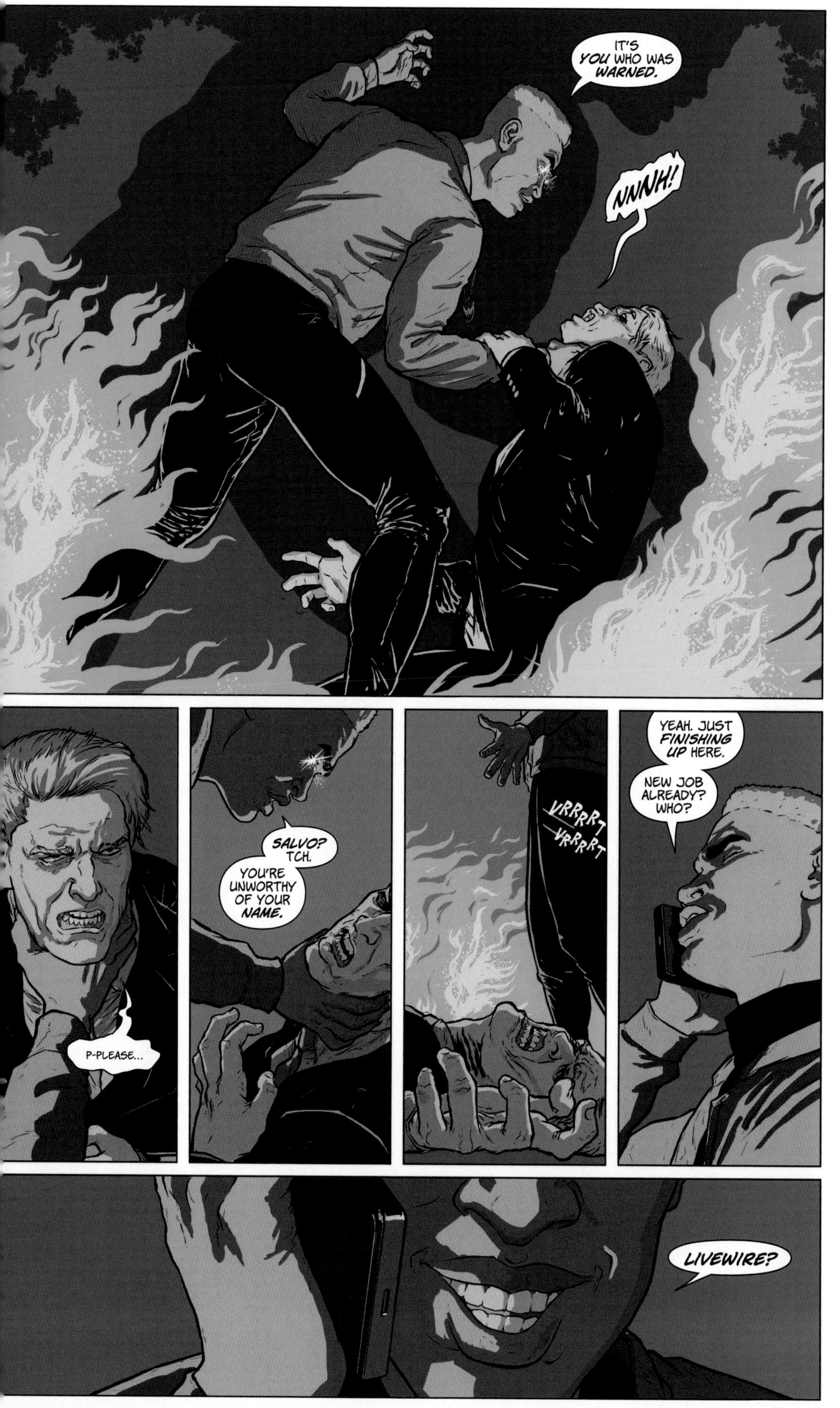
IT'S YOU WHO WAS WARNED.
NNNH!
P-PLEASE...
SALVO? TCH.
YOU'RE UNWORTHY OF YOUR NAME.
VRRRRT VRRRRT
YEAH. JUST FINISHING UP HERE.
NEW JOB ALREADY? WHO?
LIVEWIRE?

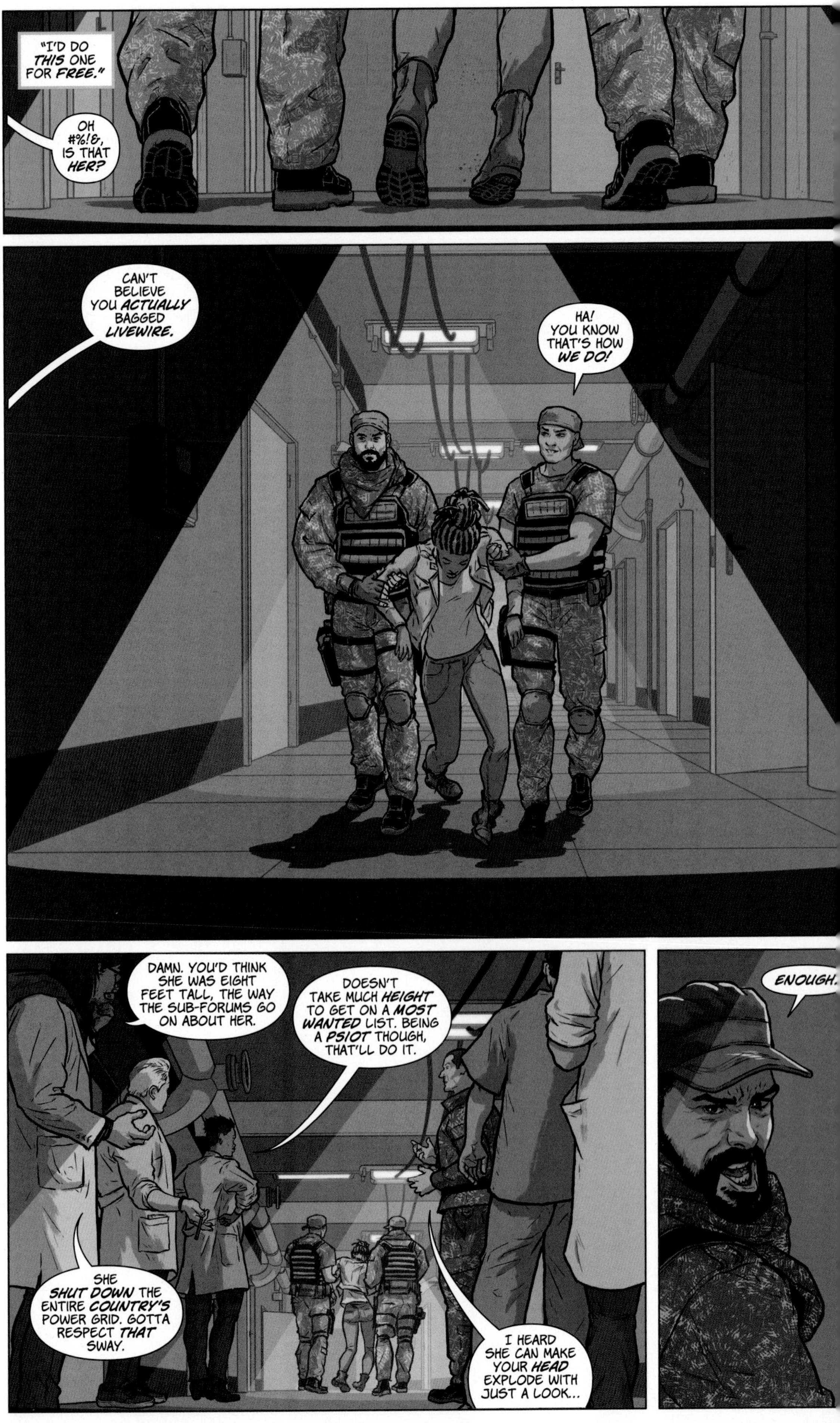
"I'D DO THIS ONE FOR FREE."
OH #%!&, IS THAT HER?
CAN'T BELIEVE YOU ACTUALLY BAGGED LIVEWIRE.
HA! YOU KNOW THAT'S HOW WE DO!
DAMN. YOU'D THINK SHE WAS EIGHT FEET TALL, THE WAY THE SUB-FORUMS GO ON ABOUT HER.
DOESN'T TAKE MUCH HEIGHT TO GET ON A MOST WANTED LIST. BEING A PSIOT THOUGH, THAT'LL DO IT.
SHE SHUT DOWN THE ENTIRE COUNTRY'S POWER GRID. GOTTA RESPECT THAT SWAY.
I HEARD SHE CAN MAKE YOUR HEAD EXPLODE WITH JUST A LOOK...
ENOUGH.

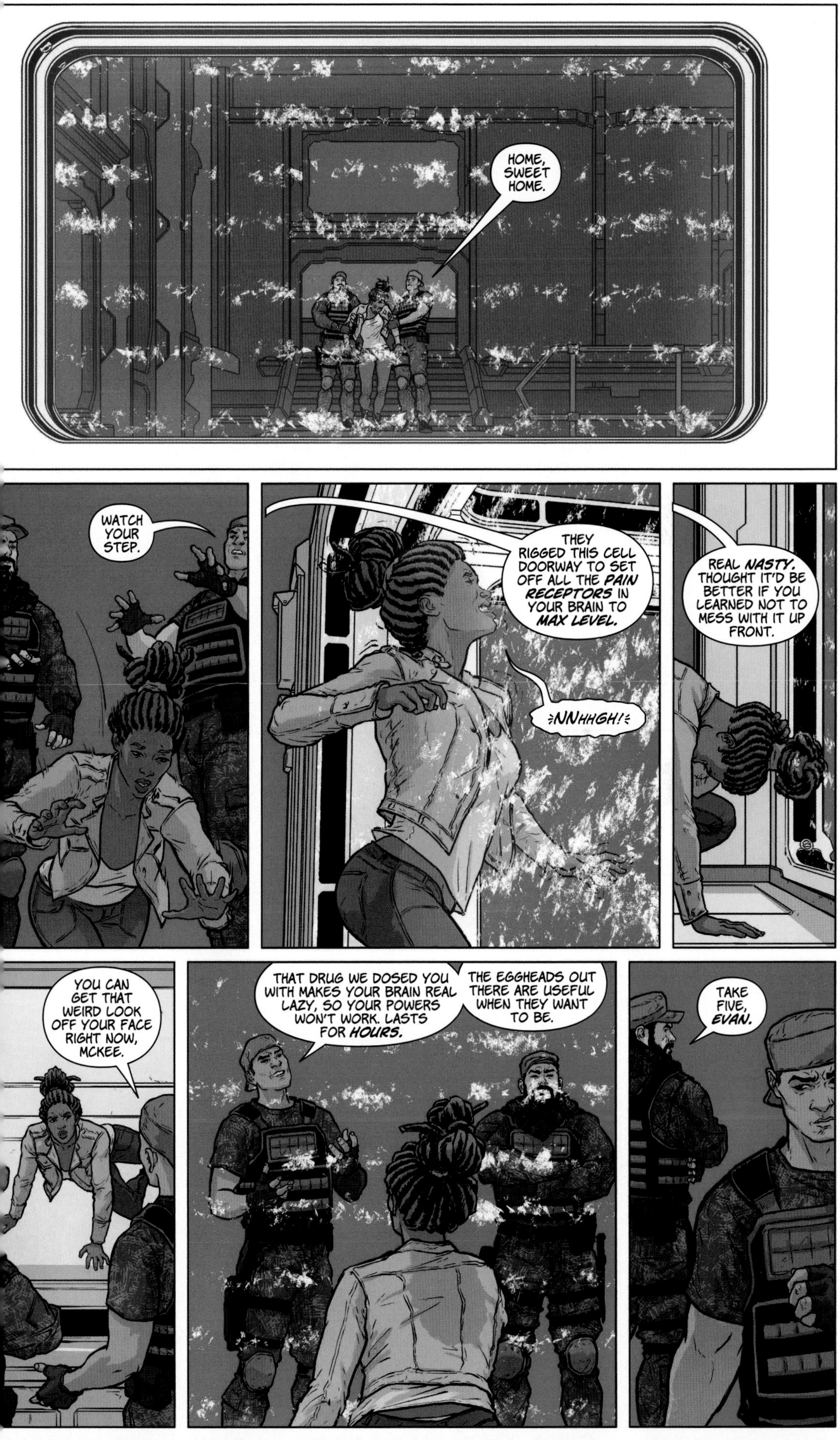
HOME, SWEET HOME.
WATCH YOUR STEP.
THEY RIGGED THIS CELL DOORWAY TO SET OFF ALL THE PAIN RECEPTORS IN YOUR BRAIN TO MAX LEVEL.
NNHHGH!
REAL NASTY. THOUGHT IT'D BE BETTER IF YOU LEARNED NOT TO MESS WITH IT UP FRONT.
YOU CAN GET THAT WEIRD LOOK OFF YOUR FACE RIGHT NOW, MCKEE.
THAT DRUG WE DOSED YOU WITH MAKES YOUR BRAIN REAL LAZY, SO YOUR POWERS WON'T WORK. LASTS FOR HOURS.
THE EGGHEADS OUT THERE ARE USEFUL WHEN THEY WANT TO BE.
TAKE FIVE, EVAN.

THAT'S BETTER. WE HAVE SOME *BUSINESS* TO TALK ABOUT.

I DOUBT THAT.

YOU THINK YOU'RE CLEVER, DON'TCHA?

YOU THINK BECAUSE YOU PEOPLE HAVE POWERS, YOU'RE ABOVE IT ALL?

HOW ORIGINAL. LET ME GUESS, THIS IS WHERE THE PETTY INTIMIDATION AND BRUTALITY STARTS?

YOU'RE NOTHING BUT A COWARD. A *TERRORIST.*

LISTEN UP, YOU *FREAK.* GOOD PEOPLE *DIED* WHEN YOU DECIDED TO TURN OFF THE POWER TO THE COUNTRY.

PEOPLE WORTH A *HUNDRED* OF YOU PSIOTS.

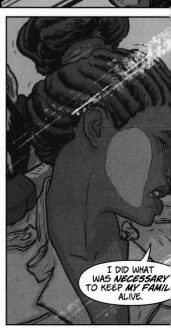

I DID WHAT WAS *NECESSARY* TO KEEP *MY FAMILY* ALIVE.

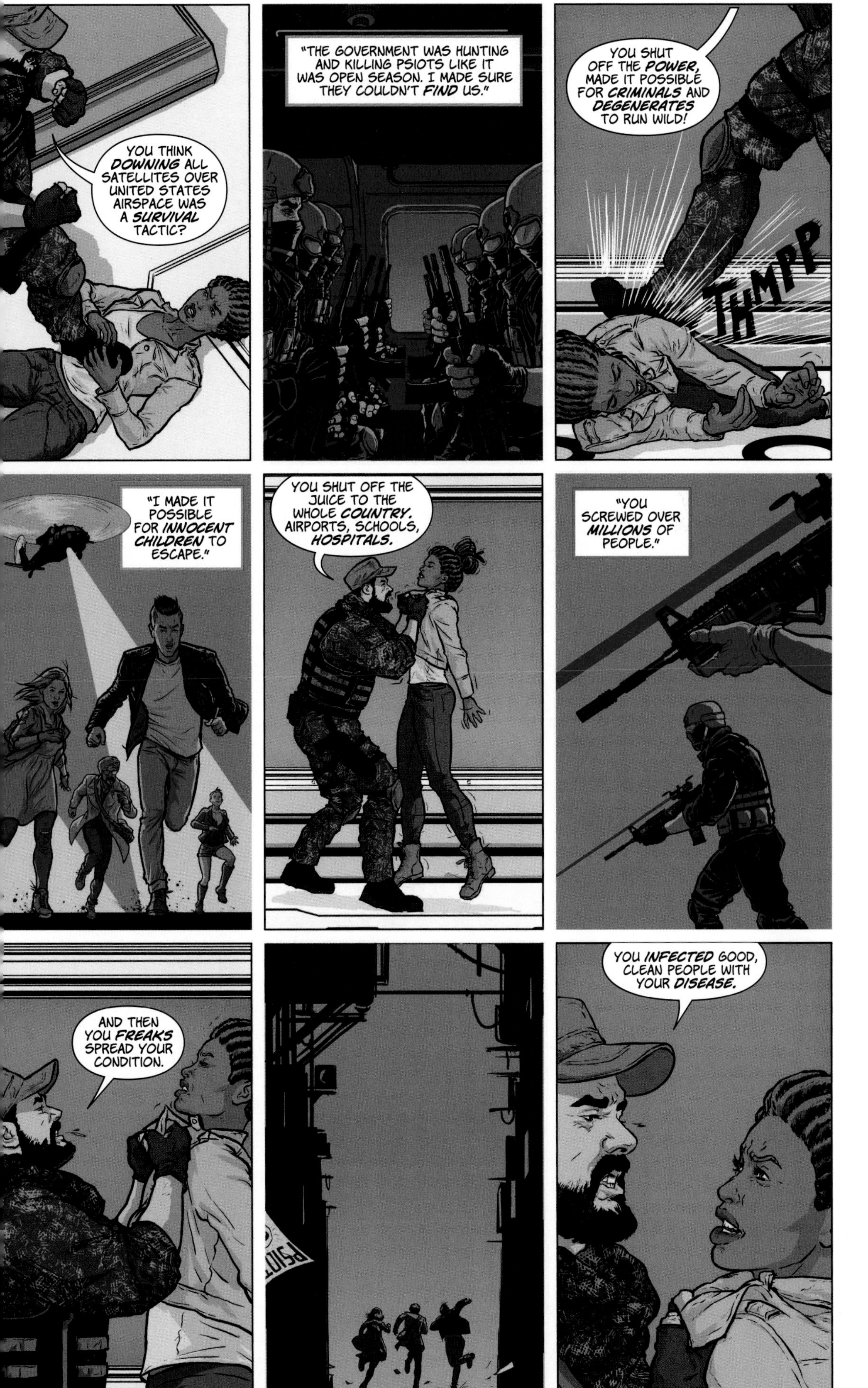
YOU THINK DOWNING ALL SATELLITES OVER UNITED STATES AIRSPACE WAS A SURVIVAL TACTIC?
"THE GOVERNMENT WAS HUNTING AND KILLING PSIOTS LIKE IT WAS OPEN SEASON. I MADE SURE THEY COULDN'T FIND US."
YOU SHUT OFF THE POWER, MADE IT POSSIBLE FOR CRIMINALS AND DEGENERATES TO RUN WILD!
THMPP
"I MADE IT POSSIBLE FOR INNOCENT CHILDREN TO ESCAPE."
YOU SHUT OFF THE JUICE TO THE WHOLE COUNTRY. AIRPORTS, SCHOOLS, HOSPITALS.
"YOU SCREWED OVER MILLIONS OF PEOPLE."
AND THEN YOU FREAKS SPREAD YOUR CONDITION.
YOU INFECTED GOOD, CLEAN PEOPLE WITH YOUR DISEASE.

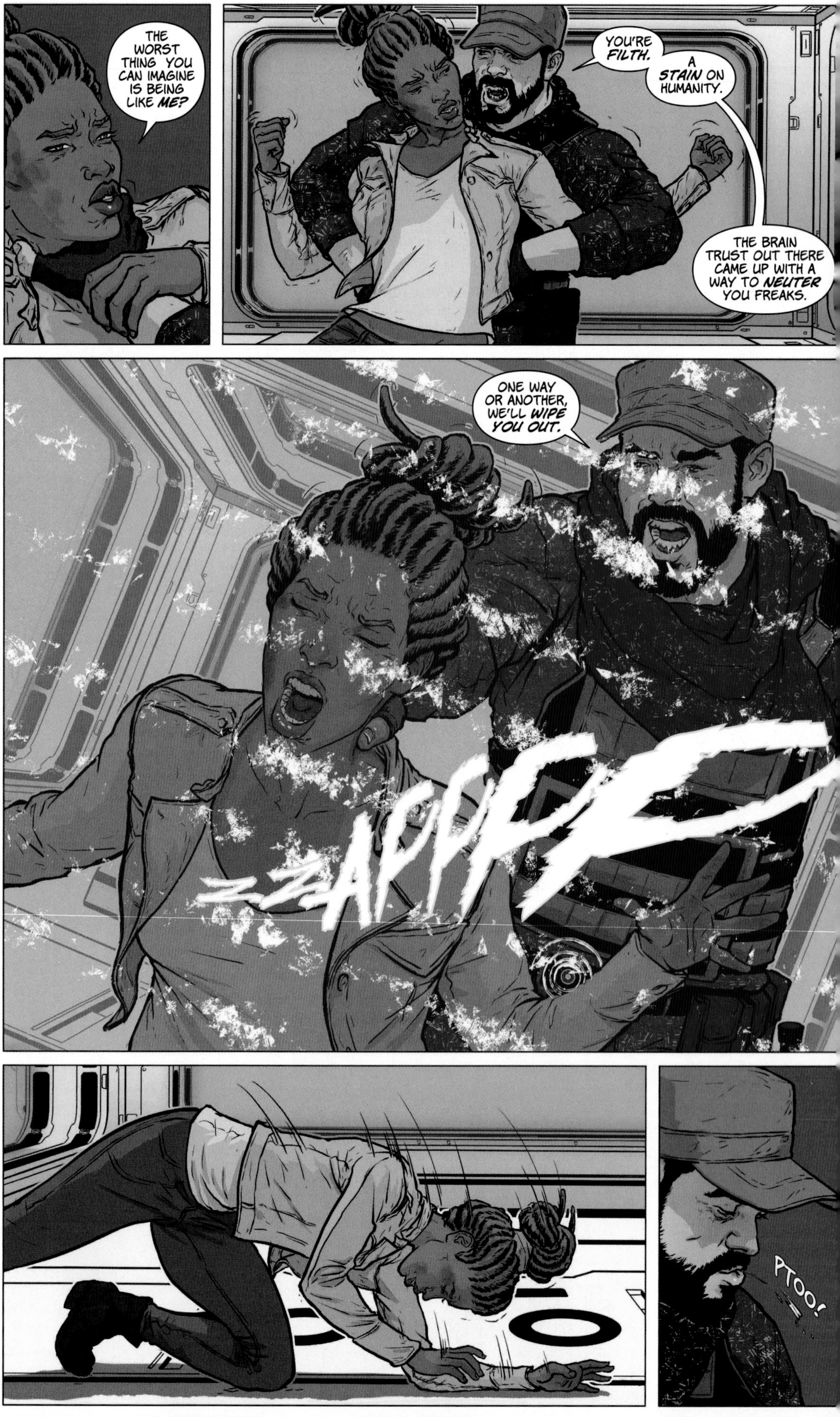
THE WORST THING YOU CAN IMAGINE IS BEING LIKE *ME?*
YOU'RE *FILTH.*
A *STAIN* ON HUMANITY.
THE BRAIN TRUST OUT THERE CAME UP WITH A WAY TO *NEUTER* YOU FREAKS.
ONE WAY OR ANOTHER, WE'LL *WIPE YOU OUT.*
Z-Z-ZAPPFF
PTOO!

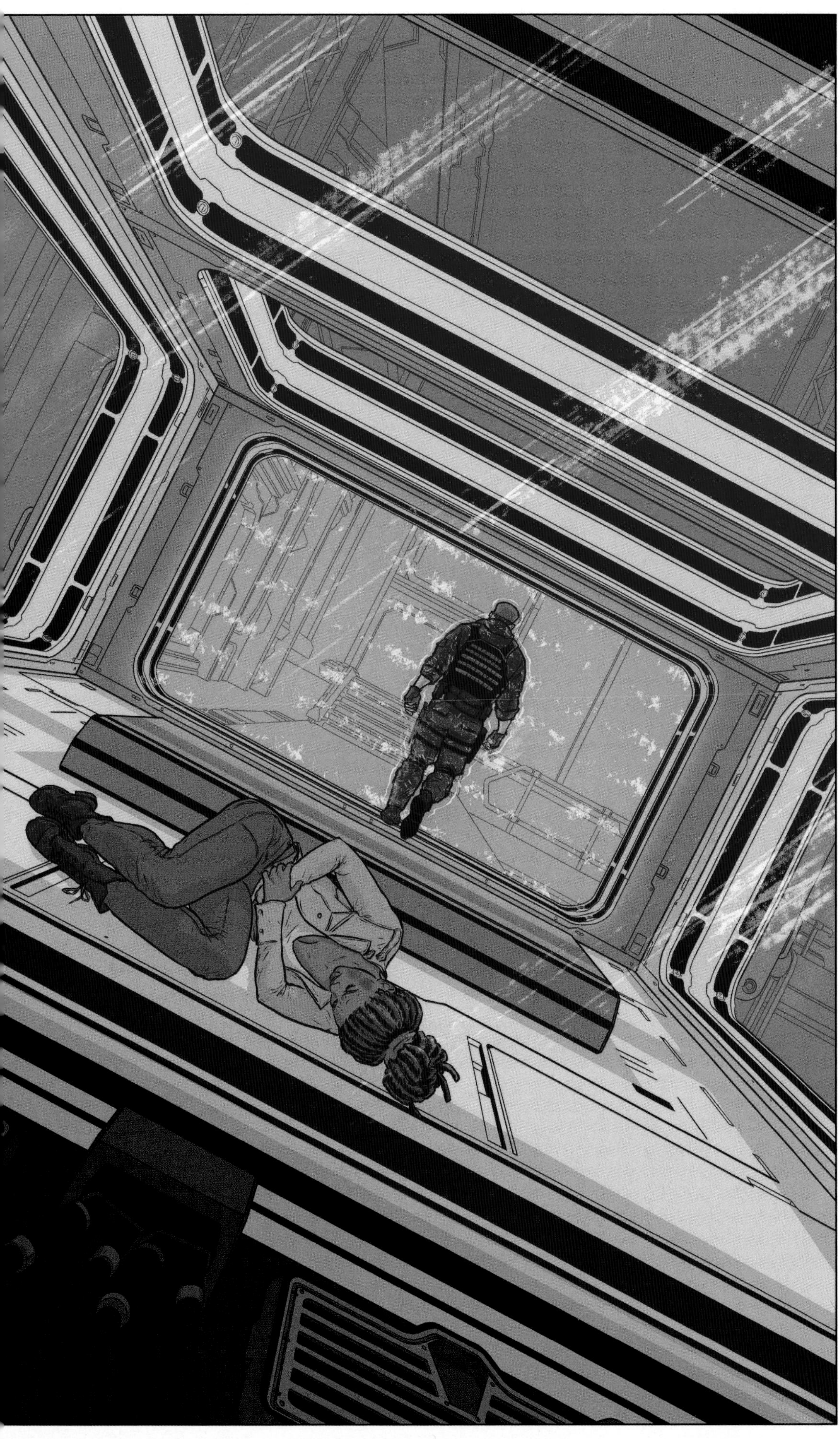

WHAT ARE YOU GOING TO DO TO ME?

ESSENTIALLY WE'RE INSTALLING SOME EXPERIMENTAL HARDWARE THAT WILL PERMANENTLY DAMPEN YOUR POWERS. IT INTERACTS *DIRECTLY* WITH YOUR BRAIN.

WE HAVE A GOVERNMENT CONTRACT TO DEVELOP THIS ANTI-PSIOT TECH.

IF THIS WORKS, WE'LL HAVE ALL THE FUNDING WE COULD EVER WANT.

THINGS LIKE *THESE* ARE EXACTLY WHAT LED ME TO THE *SHUT DOWN.*

PEOPLE LIKE *YOU* MADE THE *FIGHT* NECESSARY.

YOU SHUTTING DOWN THE *POWER GRID* IS WHY WE EVEN *GOT* THIS CONTRACT.

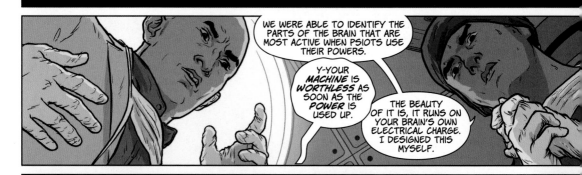

WE WERE ABLE TO IDENTIFY THE PARTS OF THE BRAIN THAT ARE MOST ACTIVE WHEN PSIOTS USE THEIR POWERS.

Y-YOUR *MACHINE* IS *WORTHLESS* AS SOON AS THE *POWER* IS USED UP.

THE BEAUTY OF IT IS, IT RUNS ON YOUR BRAIN'S OWN ELECTRICAL CHARGE. I DESIGNED THIS MYSELF.

TRY TO RELAX, ALRIGHT? IT'LL MAKE THINGS EASIER FOR YOU.

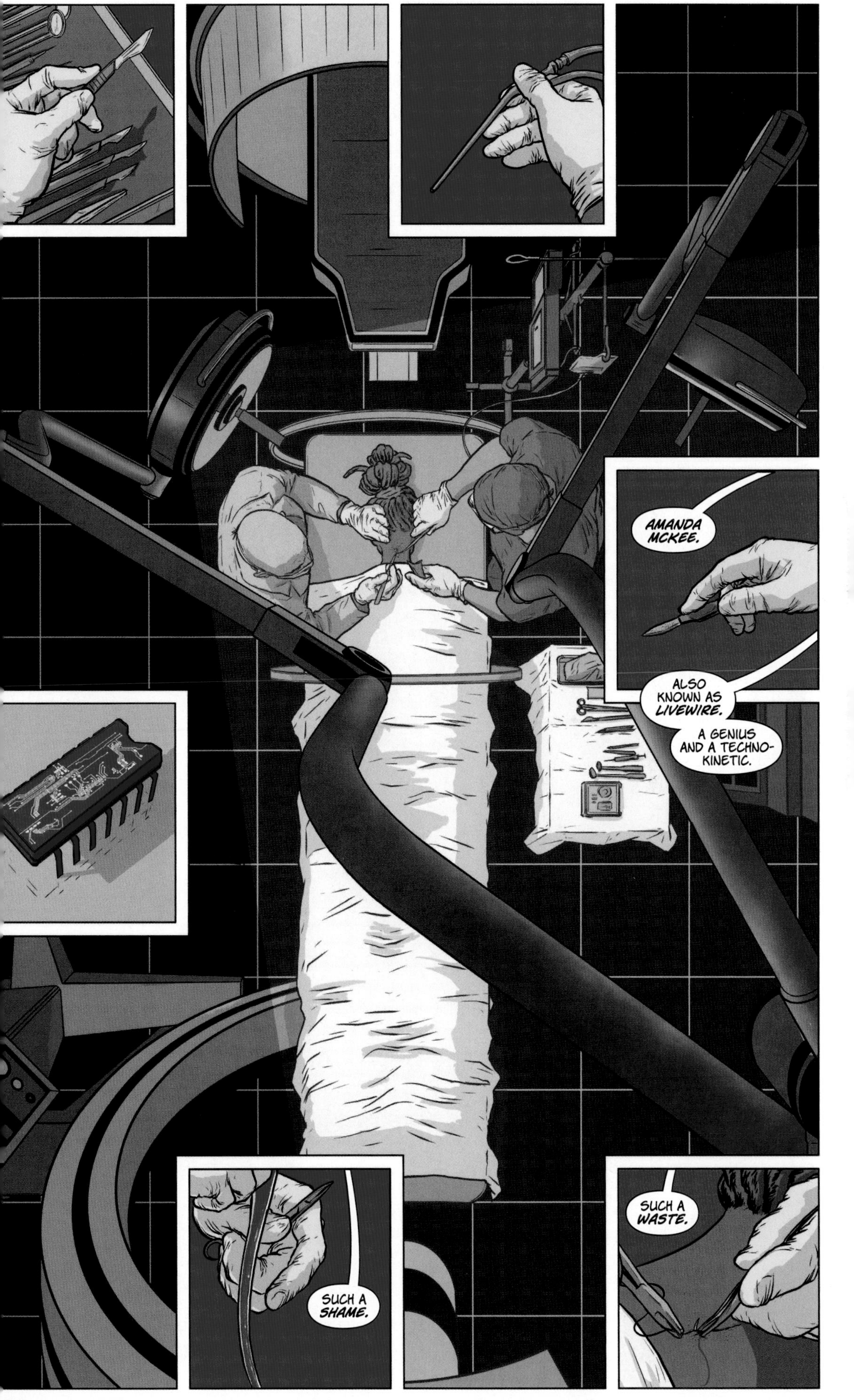
AMANDA MCKEE.
ALSO KNOWN AS LIVEWIRE.
A GENIUS AND A TECHNO-KINETIC.
SUCH A SHAME.
SUCH A WASTE.

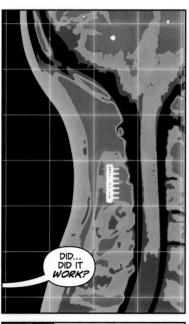

DID... DID IT *WORK?*

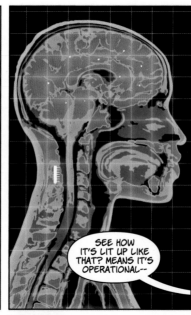

SEE HOW IT'S LIT UP LIKE THAT? MEANS IT'S OPERATIONAL--

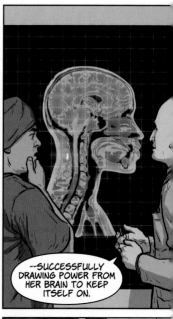

--SUCCESSFULLY DRAWING POWER FROM HER BRAIN TO KEEP ITSELF ON.

HOOKING INTO THE POWER SOURCE WAS THE REAL QUESTION.

IT'S SMOOTH SAILING FROM HERE...

...THE MACHINE WILL SHUT DOWN MAYBE FIVE SECONDS BEFORE COMPLETE BRAIN DEATH.

FIVE SECONDS ISN'T MUCH TIME TO DO MUCH OF *ANYTHING,* I RECKON.

≼GASP≽

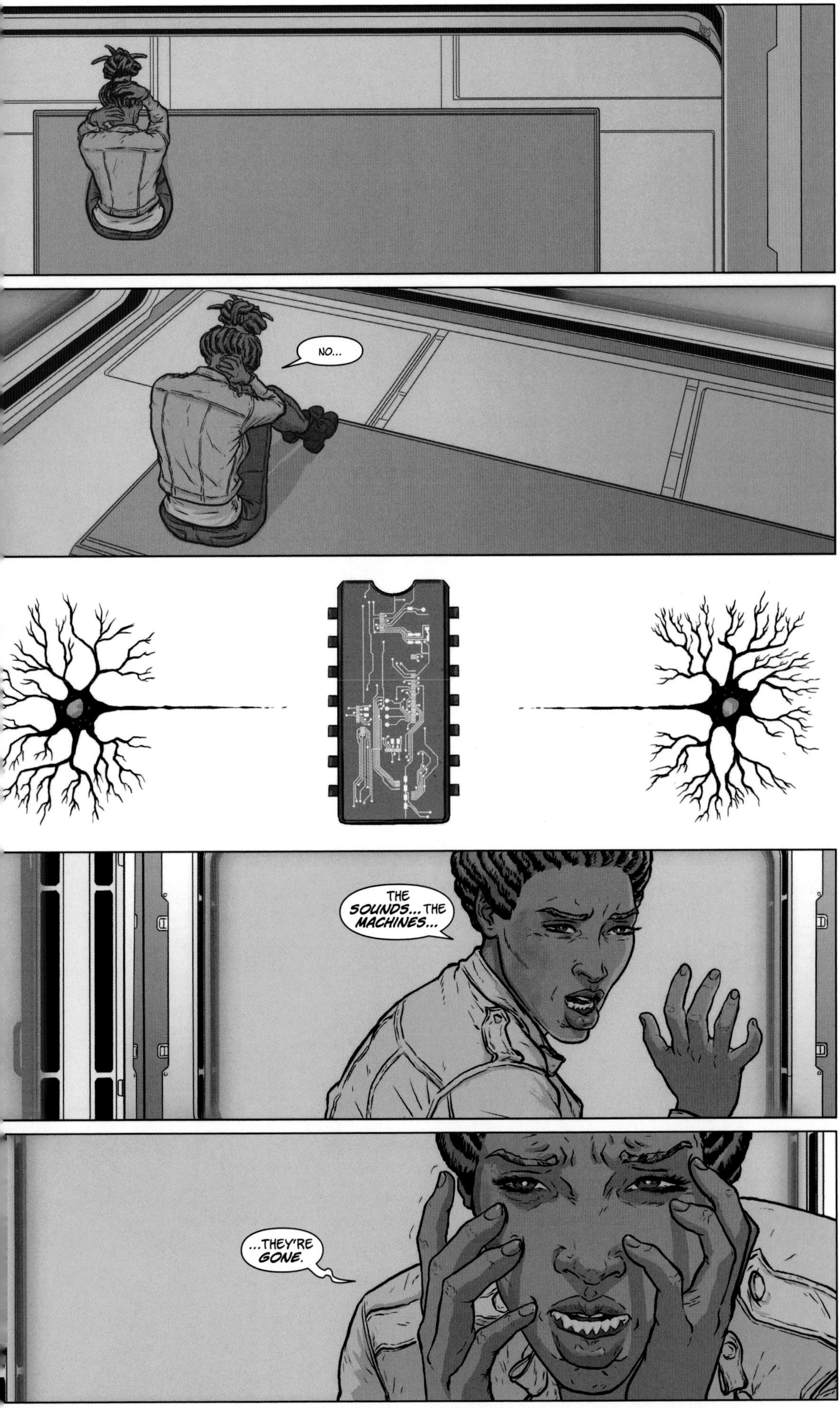
NO...
THE SOUNDS... THE MACHINES...
...THEY'RE GONE.

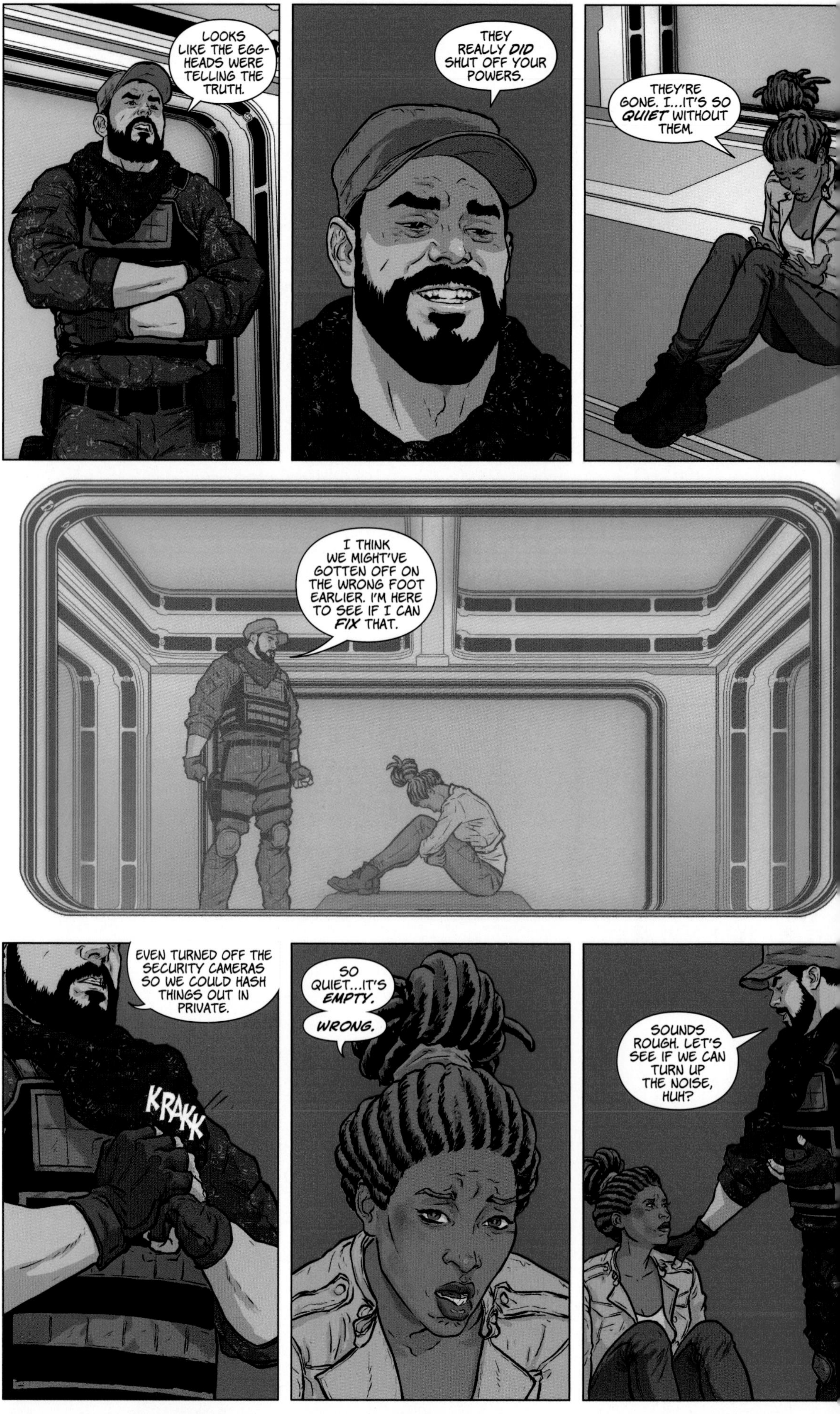
LOOKS LIKE THE EGG-HEADS WERE TELLING THE TRUTH.
THEY REALLY DID SHUT OFF YOUR POWERS.
THEY'RE GONE. I...IT'S SO QUIET WITHOUT THEM.
I THINK WE MIGHT'VE GOTTEN OFF ON THE WRONG FOOT EARLIER. I'M HERE TO SEE IF I CAN FIX THAT.
EVEN TURNED OFF THE SECURITY CAMERAS SO WE COULD HASH THINGS OUT IN PRIVATE.
KRAKK
SO QUIET...IT'S EMPTY.
WRONG.
SOUNDS ROUGH. LET'S SEE IF WE CAN TURN UP THE NOISE, HUH?

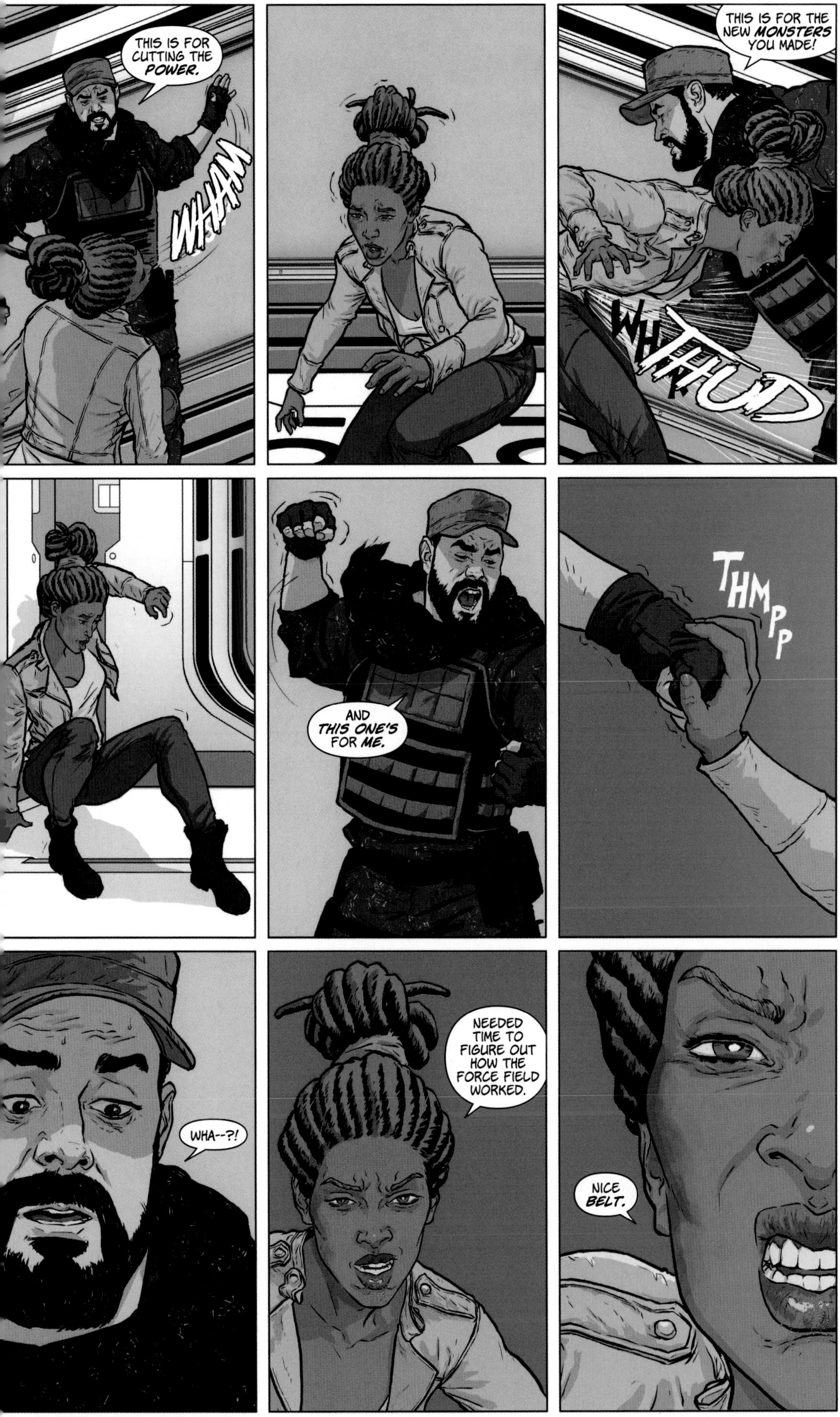
THIS IS FOR CUTTING THE POWER.
WHAM
THIS IS FOR THE NEW MONSTERS YOU MADE!
WHTHUD
AND THIS ONE'S FOR ME.
THMPP
WHA--?!
NEEDED TIME TO FIGURE OUT HOW THE FORCE FIELD WORKED.
NICE BELT.

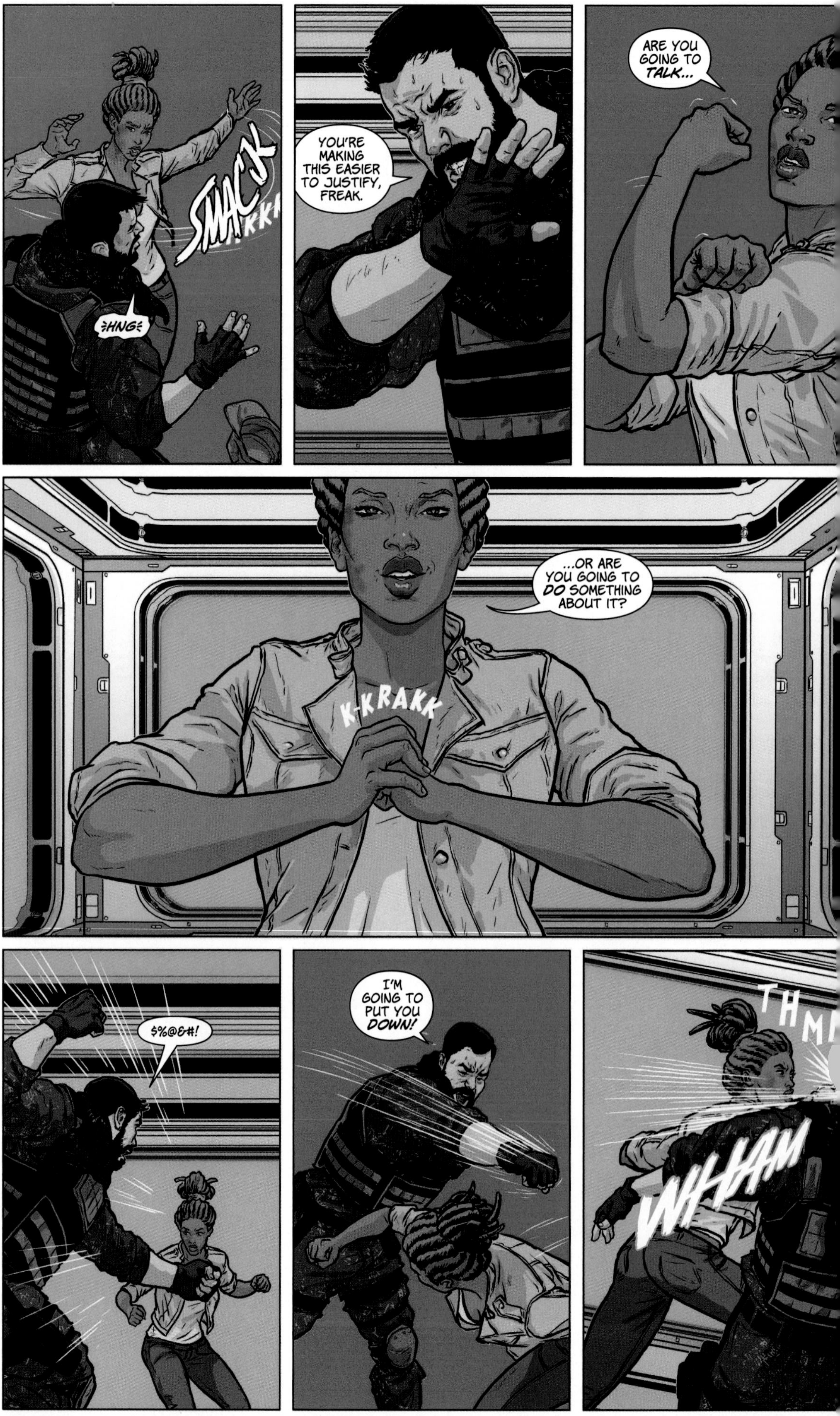
SMACK
HNG
YOU'RE MAKING THIS EASIER TO JUSTIFY, FREAK.
ARE YOU GOING TO *TALK*...
...OR ARE YOU GOING TO *DO* SOMETHING ABOUT IT?
K-KRAKK
$%@&#!
I'M GOING TO PUT YOU *DOWN!*
WHAM

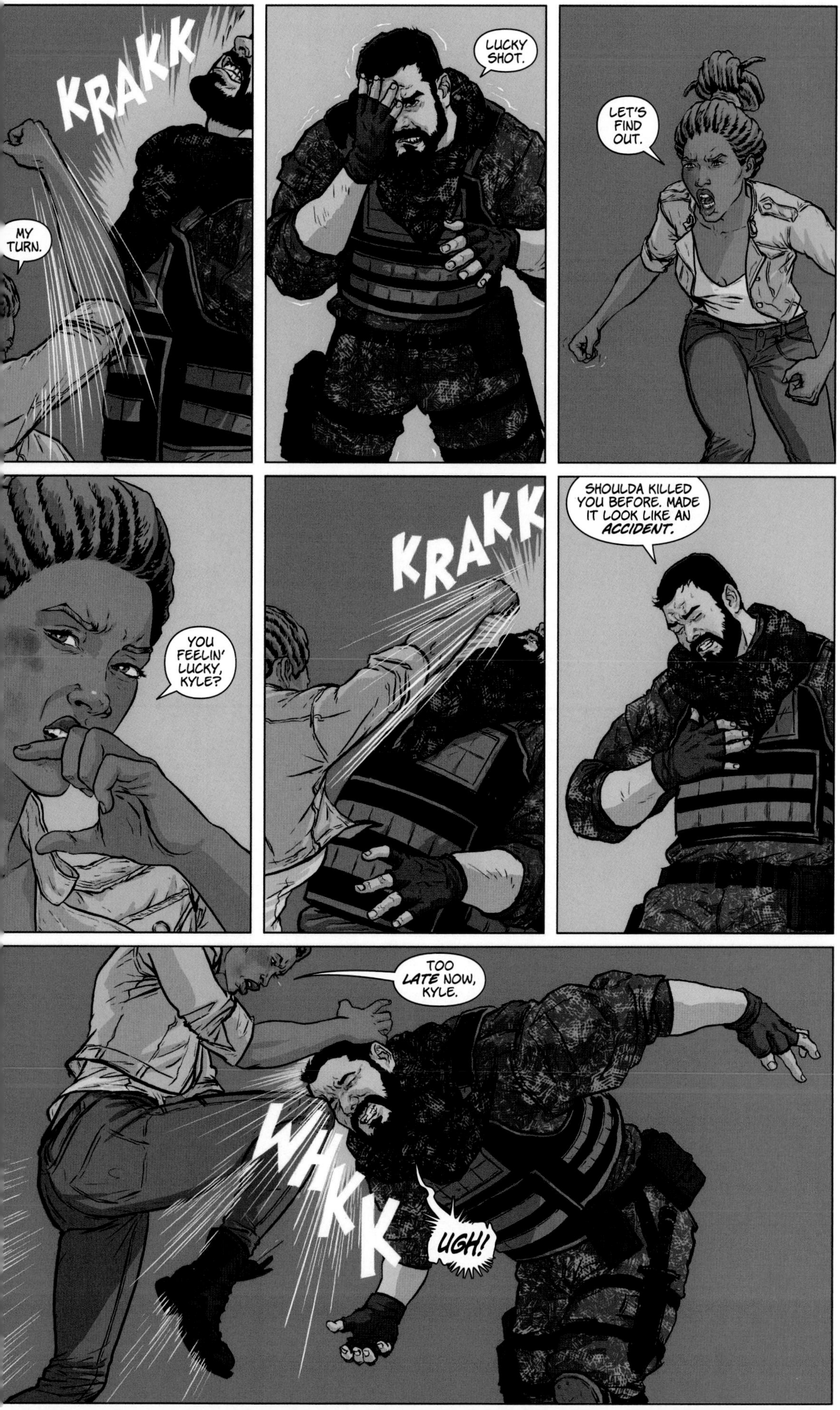
KRAKK
MY TURN.
LUCKY SHOT.
LET'S FIND OUT.
YOU FEELIN' LUCKY, KYLE?
KRAKK
SHOULDA KILLED YOU BEFORE. MADE IT LOOK LIKE AN *ACCIDENT*.
TOO *LATE* NOW, KYLE.
WHKK
UGH!

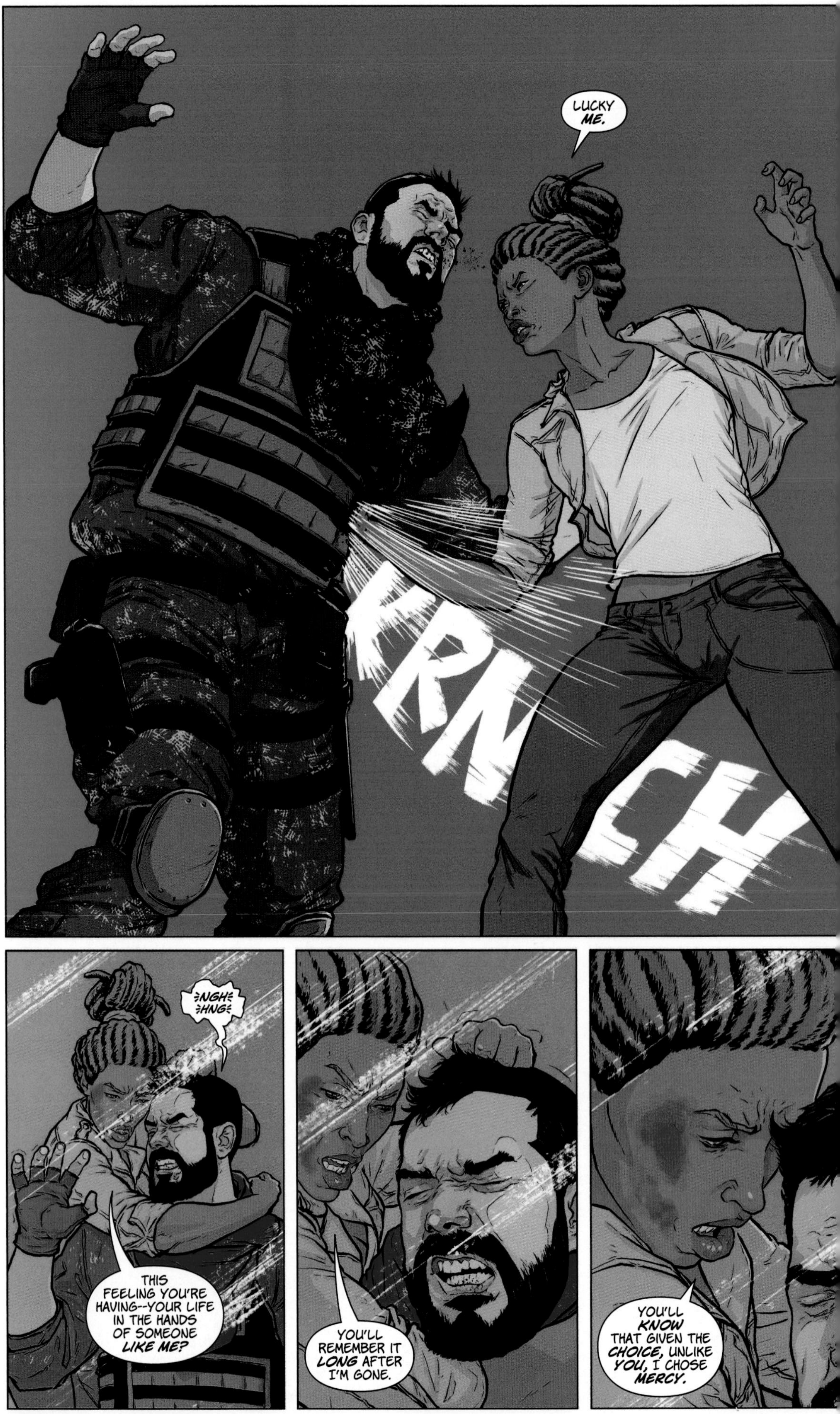
LUCKY ME.
KRNCH
NGH HNG
THIS FEELING YOU'RE HAVING--YOUR LIFE IN THE HANDS OF SOMEONE LIKE ME?
YOU'LL REMEMBER IT LONG AFTER I'M GONE.
YOU'LL KNOW THAT GIVEN THE CHOICE, UNLIKE YOU, I CHOSE MERCY.

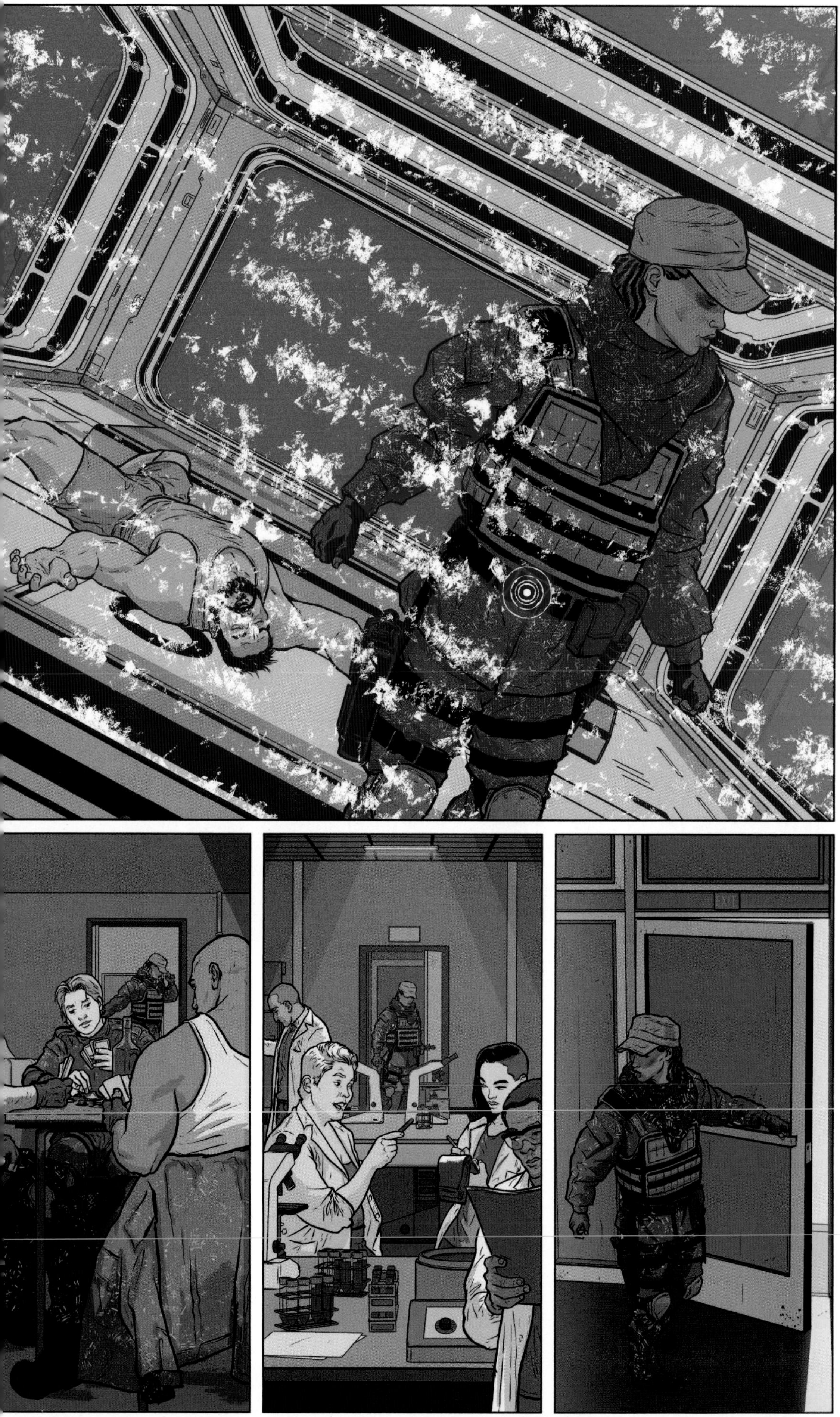
EXIT

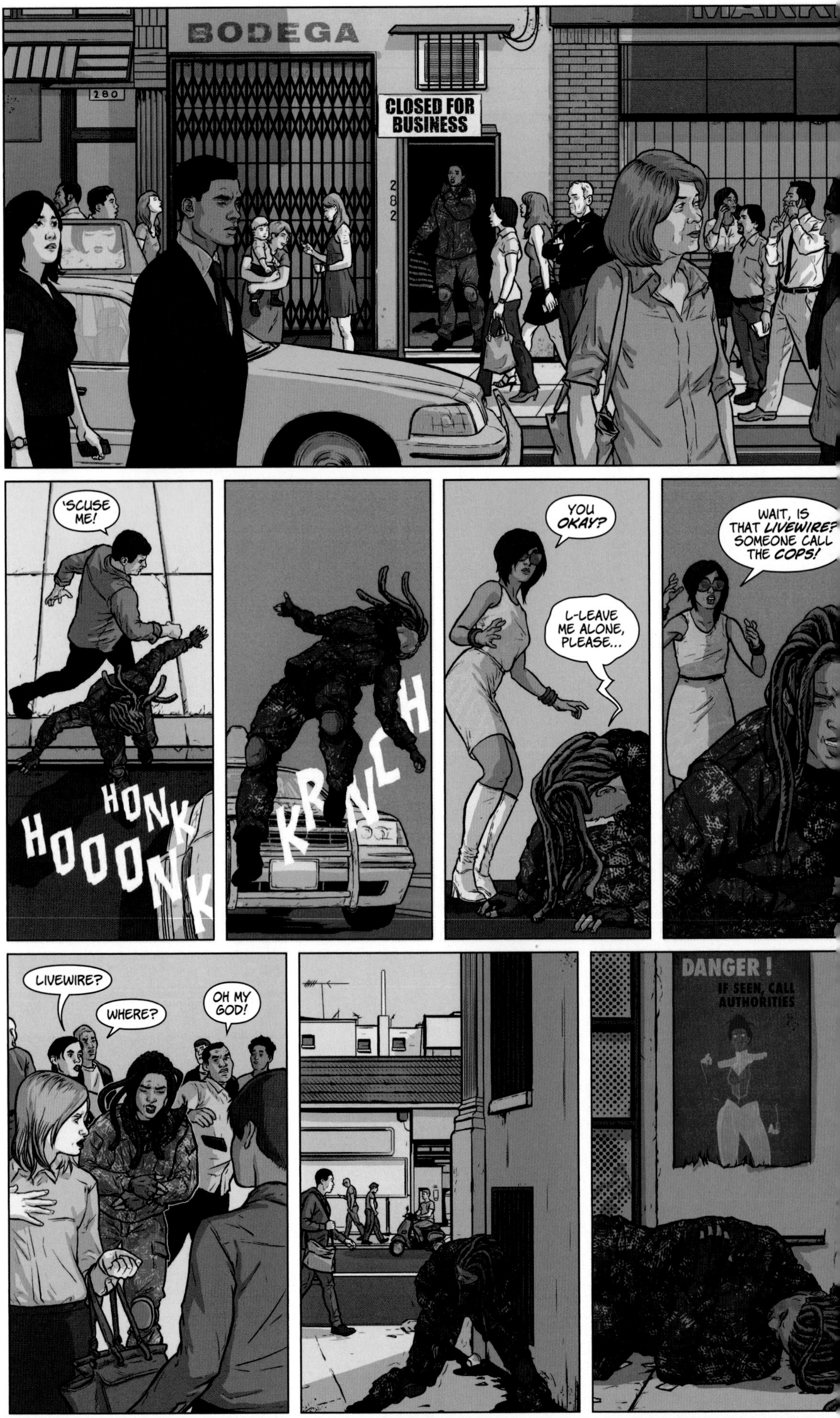
BODEGA
280
CLOSED FOR BUSINESS
282
'SCUSE ME!
HOOOONK HONK
KRNCH
YOU OKAY?
L-LEAVE ME ALONE, PLEASE...
WAIT, IS THAT LIVEWIRE? SOMEONE CALL THE COPS!
LIVEWIRE?
WHERE?
OH MY GOD!
DANGER !
IF SEEN, CALL AUTHORITIES

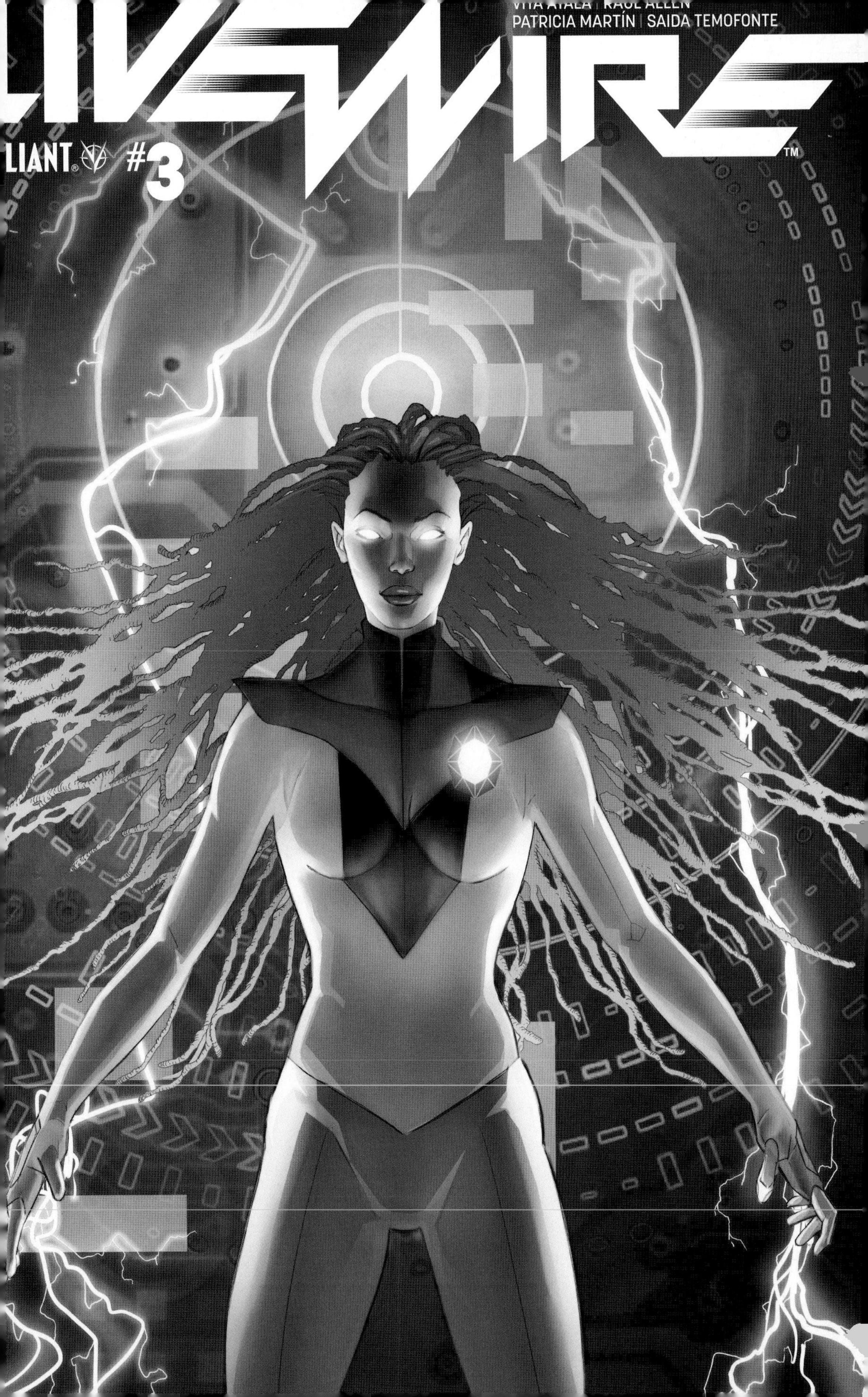
PATRICIA MARTÍN | SAIDA TEMOFONTE
#3

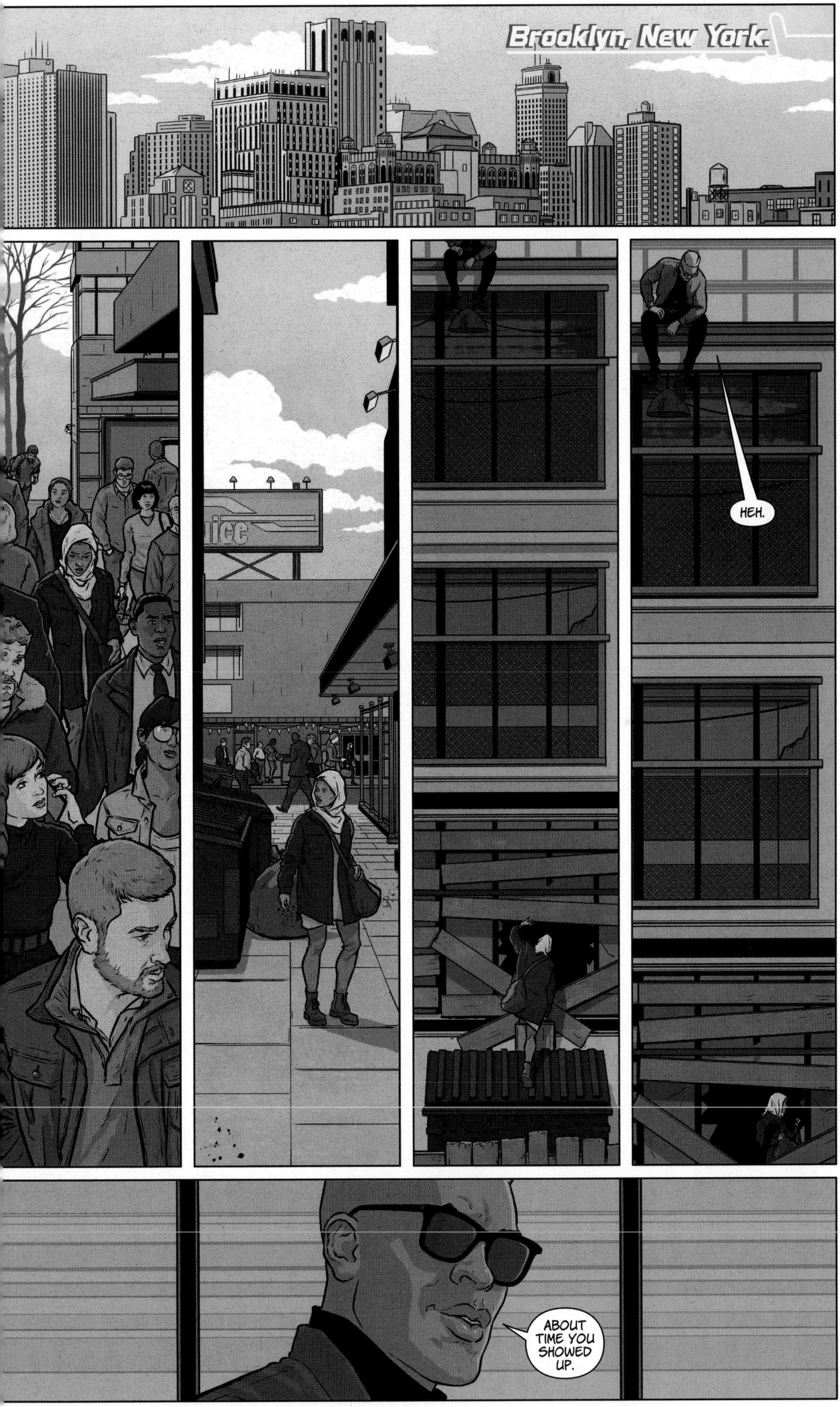
Brooklyn, New York.
HEH.
ABOUT TIME YOU SHOWED UP.

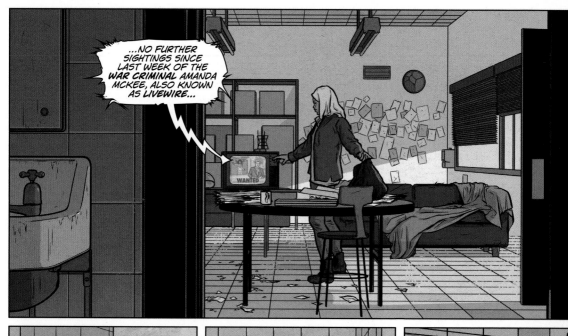

...NO FURTHER SIGHTINGS SINCE LAST WEEK OF THE *WAR CRIMINAL* AMANDA MCKEE, ALSO KNOWN AS *LIVEWIRE*...

≥SIGH≥

WELCOME HOME, AMANDA.

CLINK

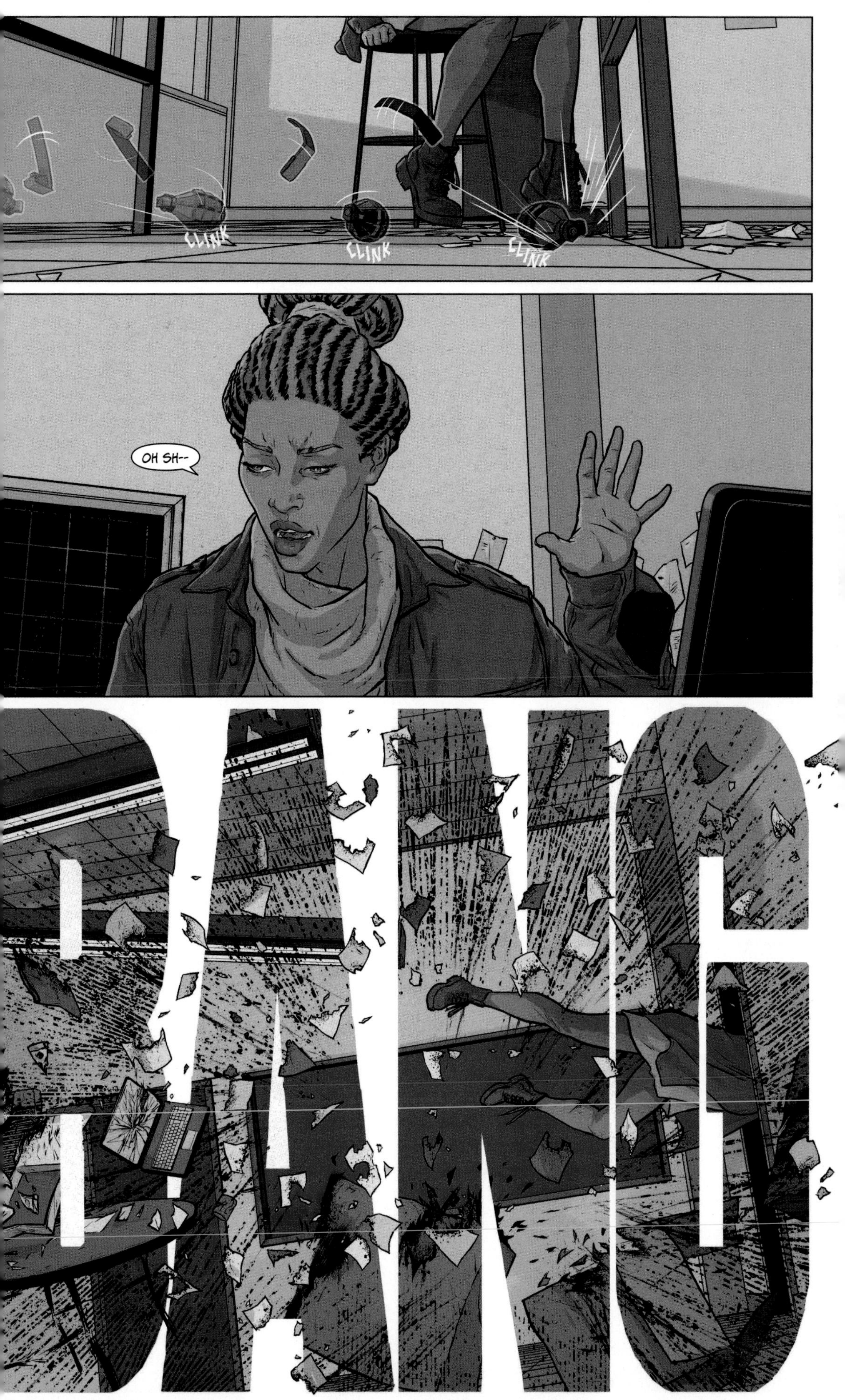
CLINK
CLINK
CLINK
OH SH--
BANG

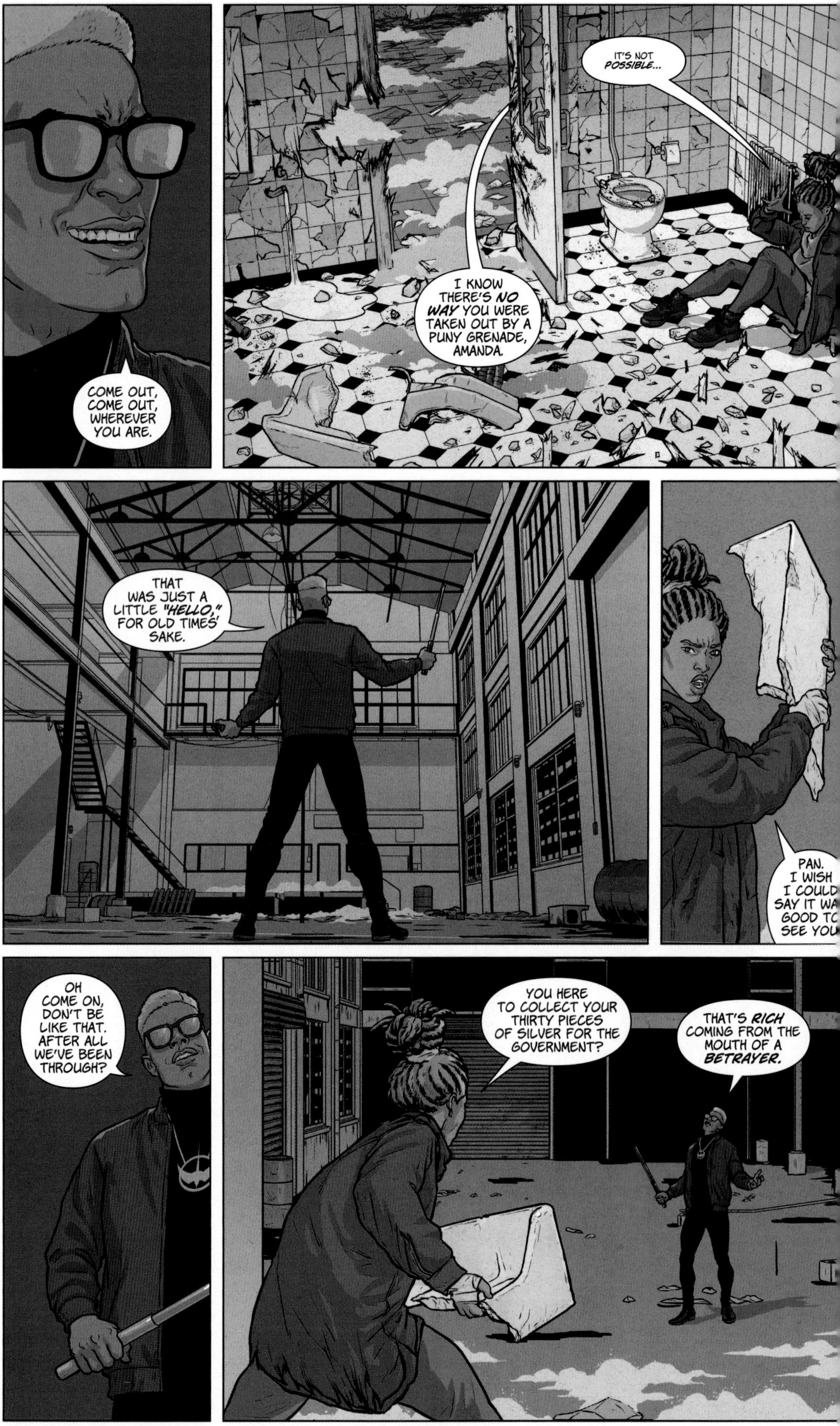
COME OUT, COME OUT, WHEREVER YOU ARE.
IT'S NOT POSSIBLE...
I KNOW THERE'S NO WAY YOU WERE TAKEN OUT BY A PUNY GRENADE, AMANDA.
THAT WAS JUST A LITTLE "HELLO," FOR OLD TIMES' SAKE.
PAN. I WISH I COULD SAY IT WA GOOD TO SEE YOU
OH COME ON, DON'T BE LIKE THAT. AFTER ALL WE'VE BEEN THROUGH?
YOU HERE TO COLLECT YOUR THIRTY PIECES OF SILVER FOR THE GOVERNMENT?
THAT'S RICH COMING FROM THE MOUTH OF A BETRAYER.

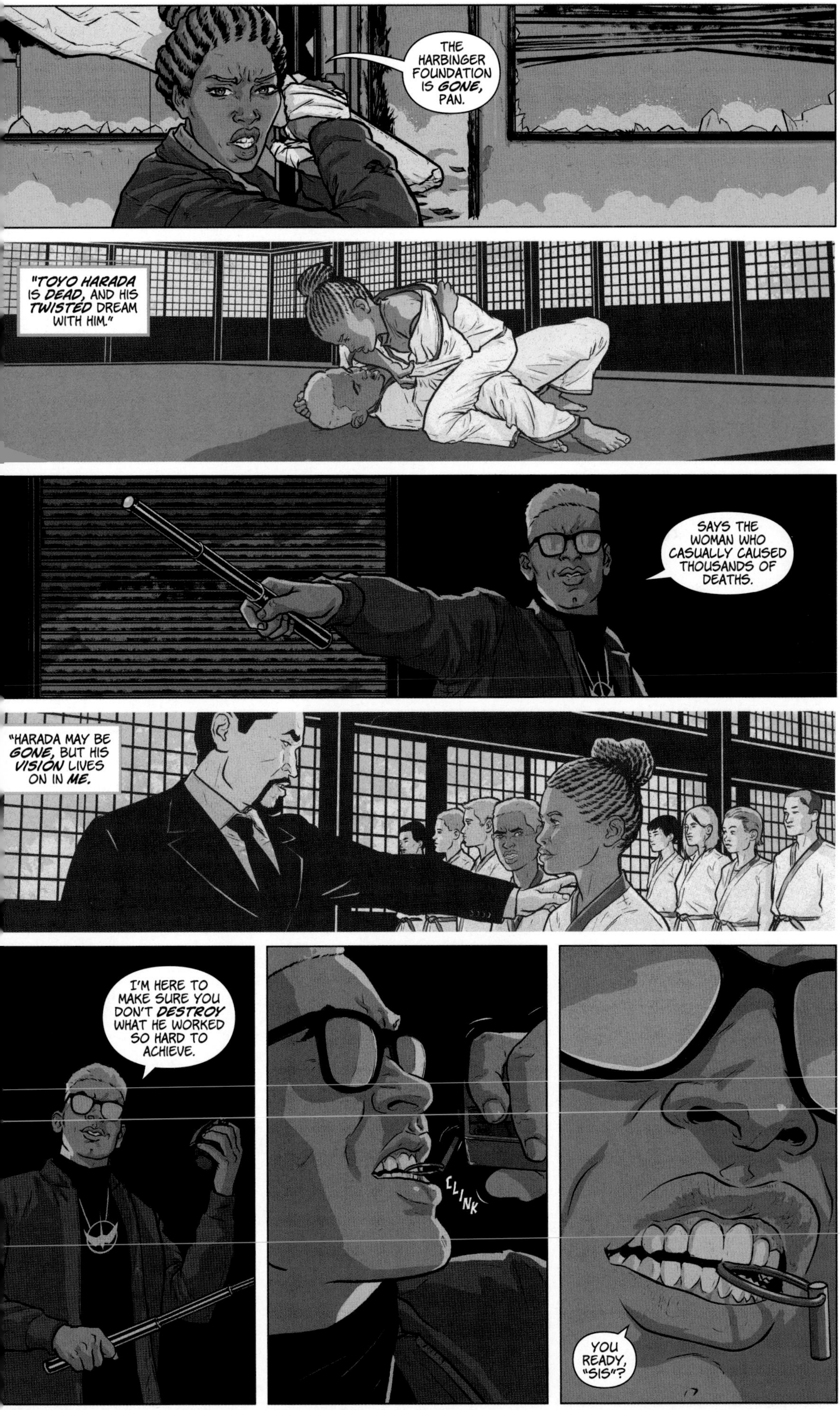
THE HARBINGER FOUNDATION IS *GONE,* PAN.
"*TOYO HARADA* IS *DEAD,* AND HIS *TWISTED* DREAM WITH HIM."
SAYS THE WOMAN WHO CASUALLY CAUSED THOUSANDS OF DEATHS.
"HARADA MAY BE *GONE,* BUT HIS *VISION* LIVES ON IN *ME.*
I'M HERE TO MAKE SURE YOU DON'T *DESTROY* WHAT HE WORKED SO HARD TO ACHIEVE.
CLINK
YOU READY, "SIS"?

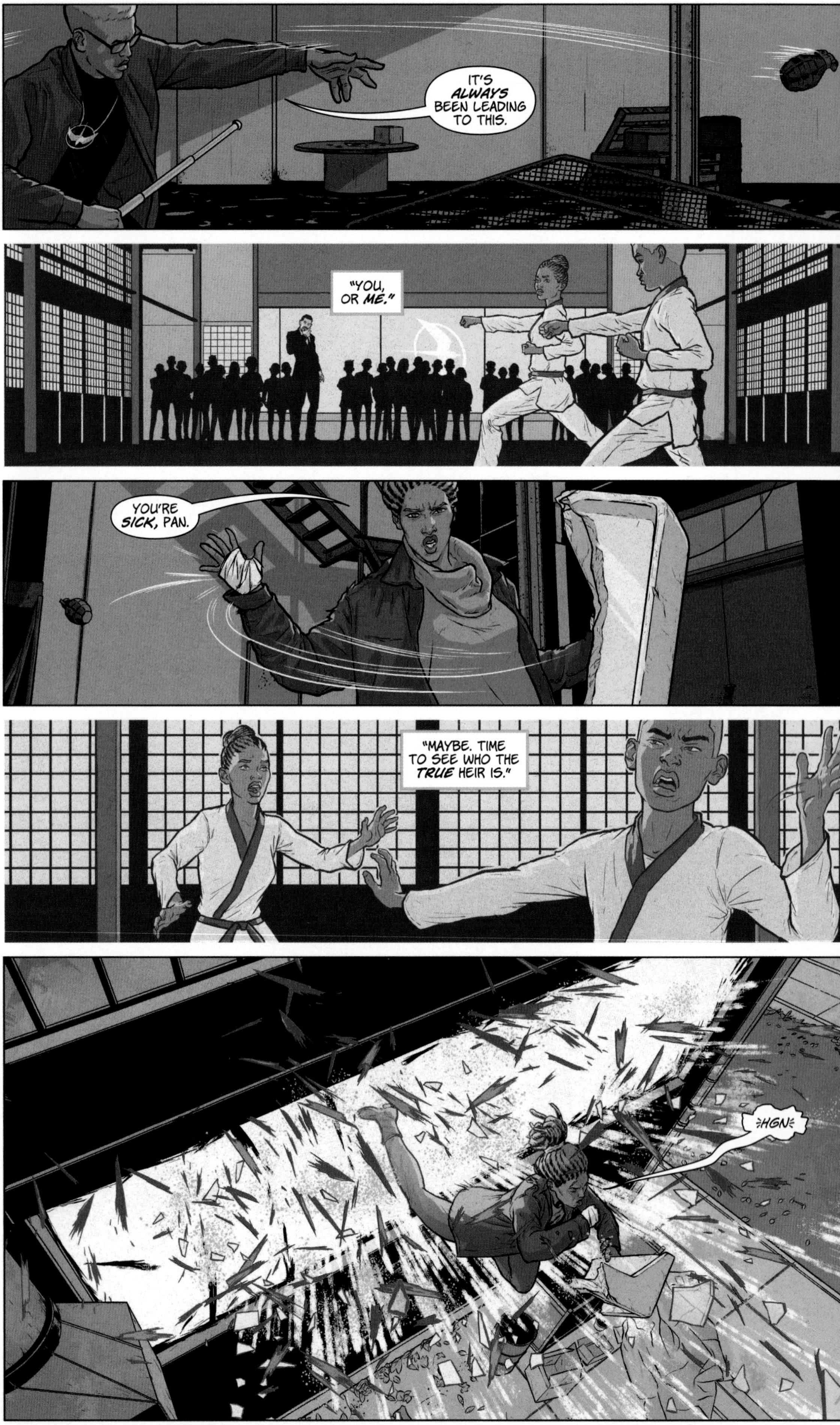
IT'S ALWAYS BEEN LEADING TO THIS.
"YOU, OR ME."
YOU'RE SICK, PAN.
"MAYBE. TIME TO SEE WHO THE TRUE HEIR IS."
HGN

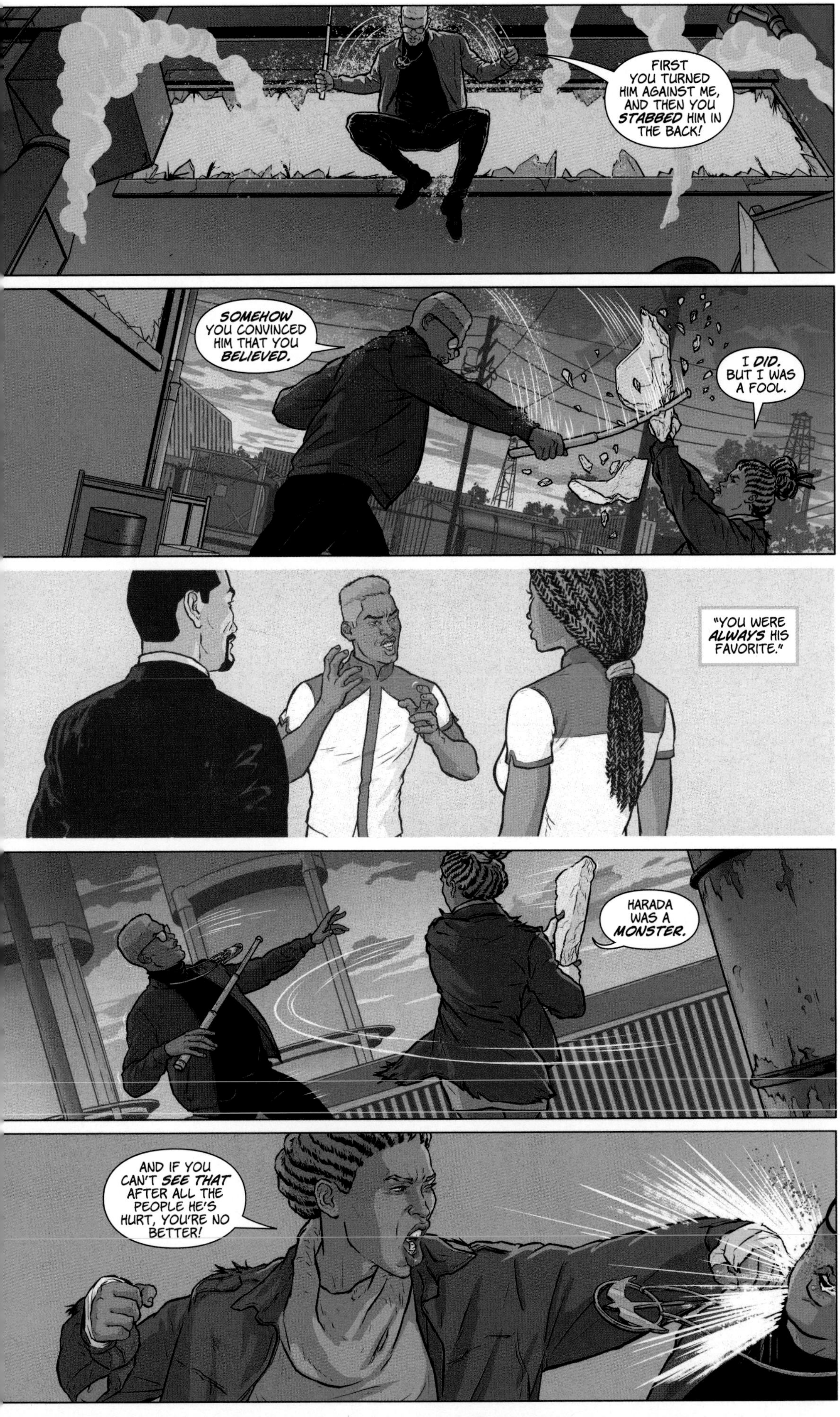

FIRST YOU TURNED HIM AGAINST ME, AND THEN YOU STABBED HIM IN THE BACK!
SOMEHOW YOU CONVINCED HIM THAT YOU BELIEVED.
I DID. BUT I WAS A FOOL.
"YOU WERE ALWAYS HIS FAVORITE."
HARADA WAS A MONSTER.
AND IF YOU CAN'T SEE THAT AFTER ALL THE PEOPLE HE'S HURT, YOU'RE NO BETTER!

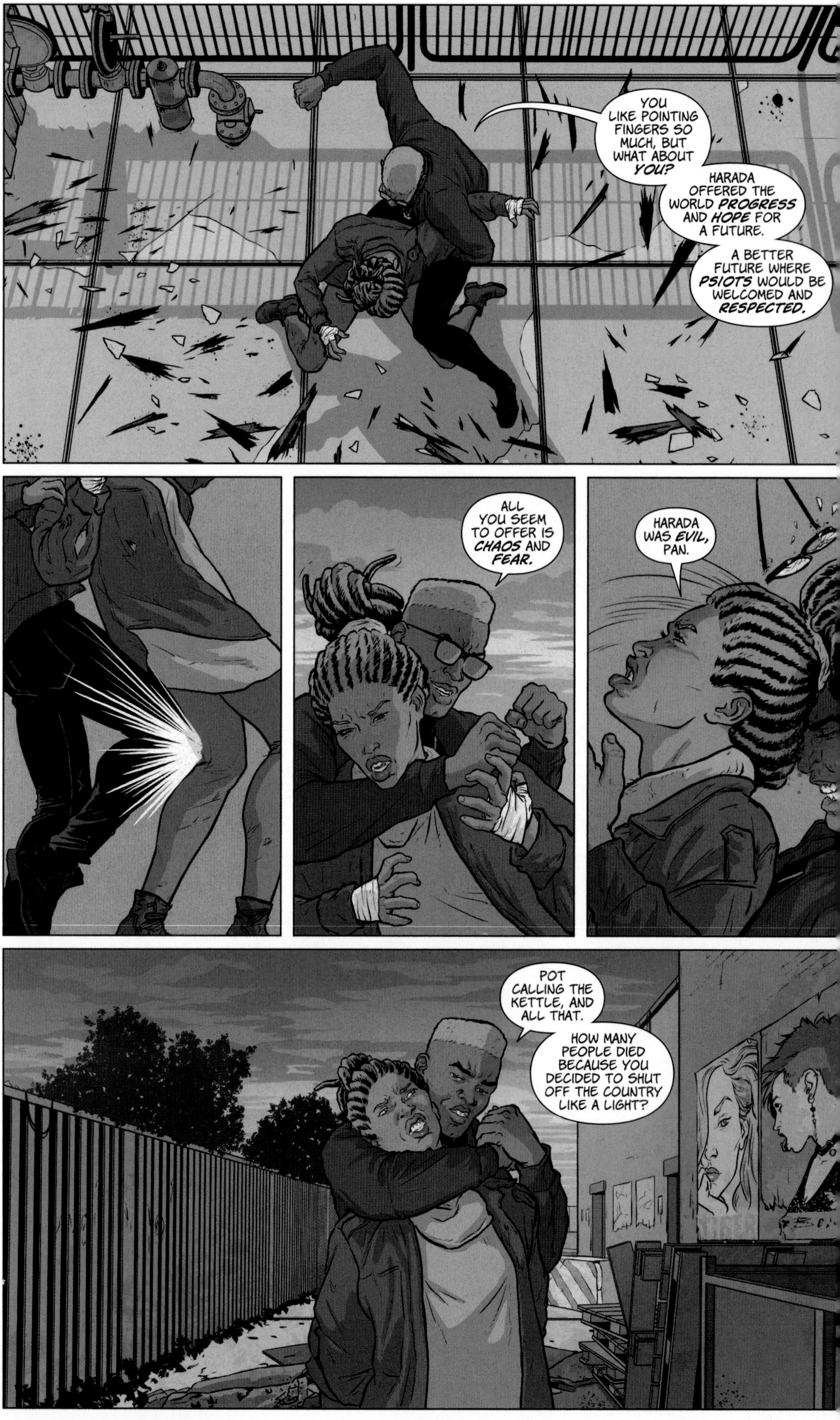

YOU LIKE POINTING FINGERS SO MUCH, BUT WHAT ABOUT *YOU?*
HARADA OFFERED THE WORLD *PROGRESS* AND *HOPE* FOR A FUTURE.
A BETTER FUTURE WHERE *PSIOTS* WOULD BE WELCOMED AND *RESPECTED.*
ALL YOU SEEM TO OFFER IS *CHAOS* AND *FEAR.*
HARADA WAS *EVIL,* PAN.
POT CALLING THE KETTLE, AND ALL THAT.
HOW MANY PEOPLE DIED BECAUSE YOU DECIDED TO SHUT OFF THE COUNTRY LIKE A LIGHT?

I HAD *NO* CHOICE!

THEY WERE *HUNTING* PSIOTS--HUNTING AND KILLING *CHILDREN.*

I THOUGHT THERE WERE *ALWAYS* CHOICES?

GOTTA *RISE ABOVE,* RIGHT?

YOU LOSE ALL *GOOD GUY* CRED WHEN YOU PLAY *GOD,* AMANDA.

AND I'M STARTING TO *FORGET* WHAT EXACTLY MADE *YOU* WORTHY OF BEING HARADA'S RIGHT HAND.

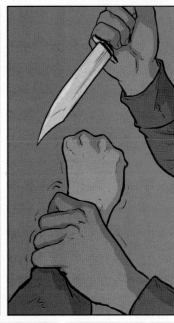

≈HRUK≈

ARE YOU EVEN *CURIOUS* HOW I FOUND YOU?

YOU WERE *SO CAREFUL,* AND YET HERE I AM TO RUIN YOUR DAY.

HERE, LET ME *SHOW YOU.*

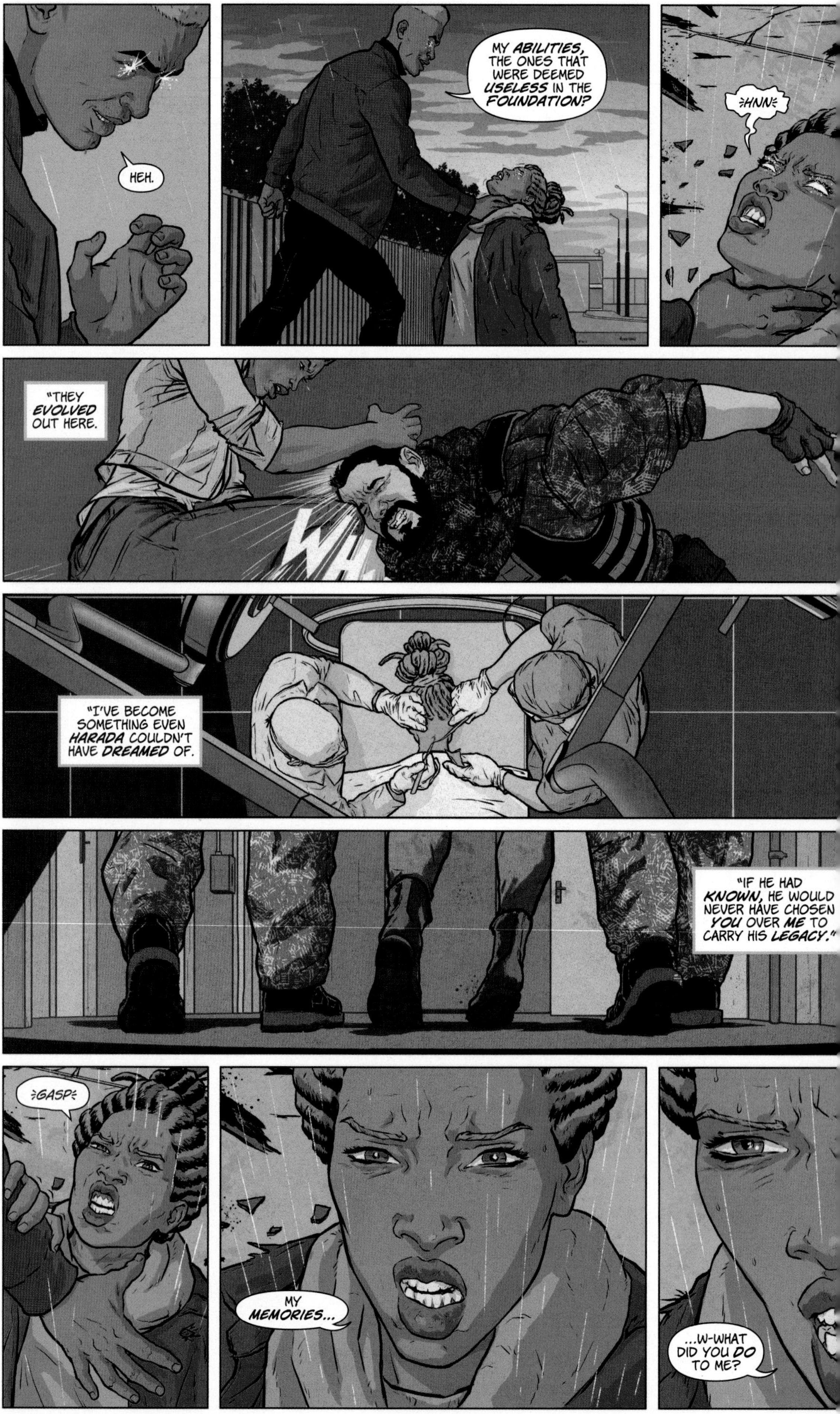

HEH.
MY ABILITIES, THE ONES THAT WERE DEEMED USELESS IN THE FOUNDATION?
HNN
"THEY EVOLVED OUT HERE.
WH
"I'VE BECOME SOMETHING EVEN HARADA COULDN'T HAVE DREAMED OF.
"IF HE HAD KNOWN, HE WOULD NEVER HAVE CHOSEN YOU OVER ME TO CARRY HIS LEGACY."
GASP
MY MEMORIES...
...W-WHAT DID YOU DO TO ME?

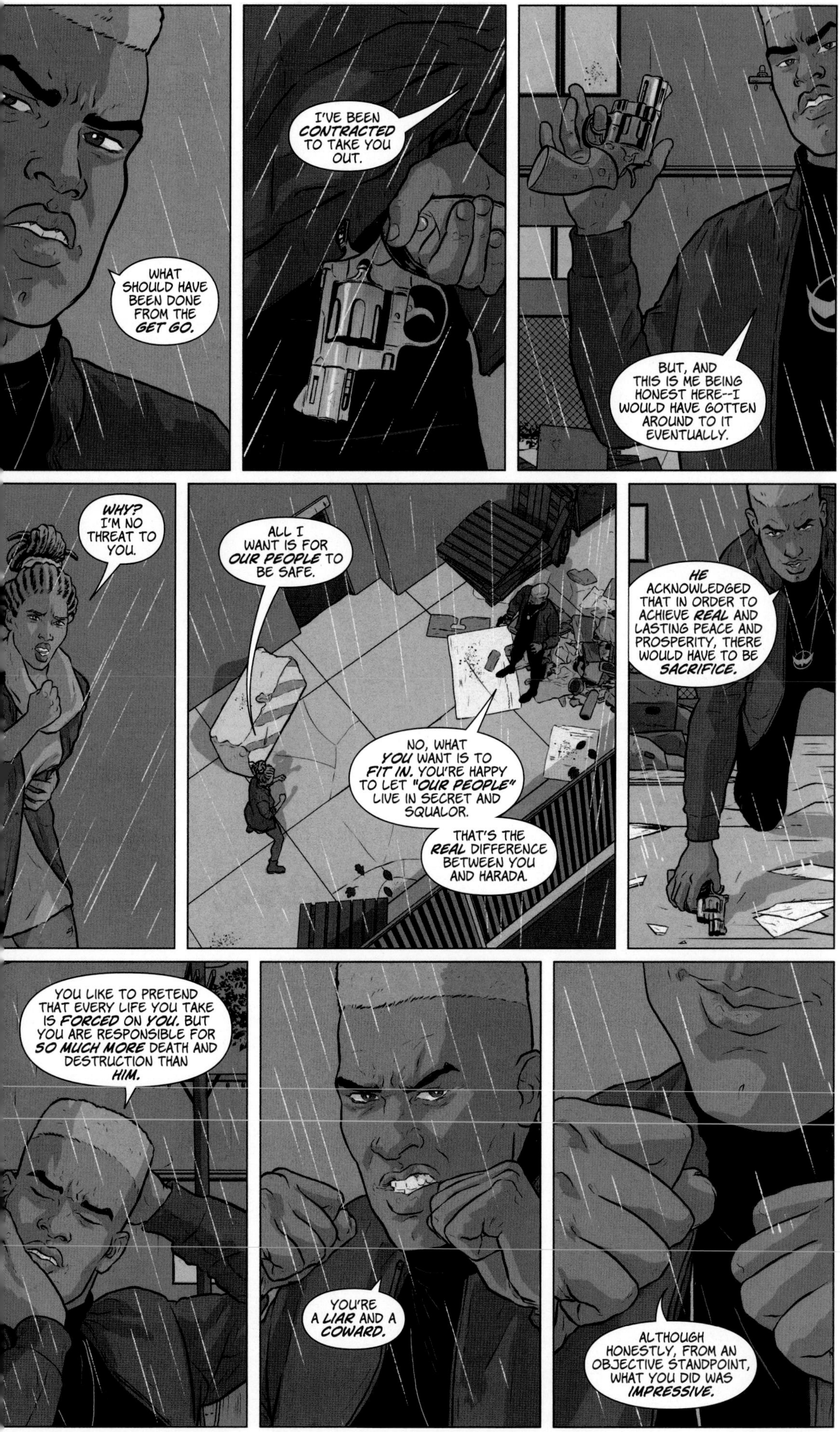
WHAT SHOULD HAVE BEEN DONE FROM THE GET GO.
I'VE BEEN CONTRACTED TO TAKE YOU OUT.
BUT, AND THIS IS ME BEING HONEST HERE--I WOULD HAVE GOTTEN AROUND TO IT EVENTUALLY.
WHY? I'M NO THREAT TO YOU.
ALL I WANT IS FOR OUR PEOPLE TO BE SAFE.
NO, WHAT YOU WANT IS TO FIT IN. YOU'RE HAPPY TO LET "OUR PEOPLE" LIVE IN SECRET AND SQUALOR.
THAT'S THE REAL DIFFERENCE BETWEEN YOU AND HARADA.
HE ACKNOWLEDGED THAT IN ORDER TO ACHIEVE REAL AND LASTING PEACE AND PROSPERITY, THERE WOULD HAVE TO BE SACRIFICE.
YOU LIKE TO PRETEND THAT EVERY LIFE YOU TAKE IS FORCED ON YOU. BUT YOU ARE RESPONSIBLE FOR SO MUCH MORE DEATH AND DESTRUCTION THAN HIM.
YOU'RE A LIAR AND A COWARD.
ALTHOUGH HONESTLY, FROM AN OBJECTIVE STANDPOINT, WHAT YOU DID WAS IMPRESSIVE.

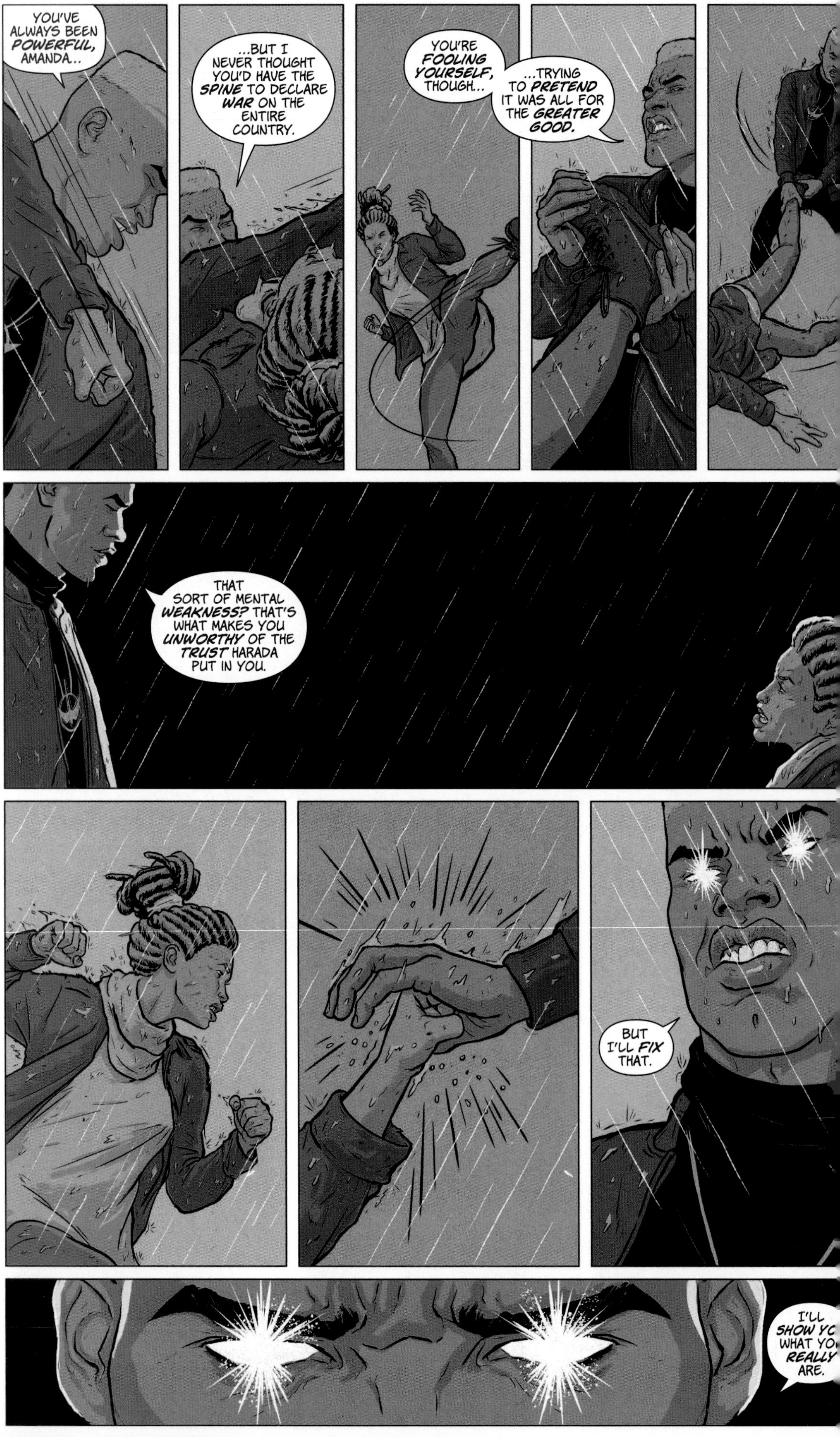
YOU'VE ALWAYS BEEN POWERFUL, AMANDA...
...BUT I NEVER THOUGHT YOU'D HAVE THE SPINE TO DECLARE WAR ON THE ENTIRE COUNTRY.
YOU'RE FOOLING YOURSELF, THOUGH...
...TRYING TO PRETEND IT WAS ALL FOR THE GREATER GOOD.
THAT SORT OF MENTAL WEAKNESS? THAT'S WHAT MAKES YOU UNWORTHY OF THE TRUST HARADA PUT IN YOU.
BUT I'LL FIX THAT.

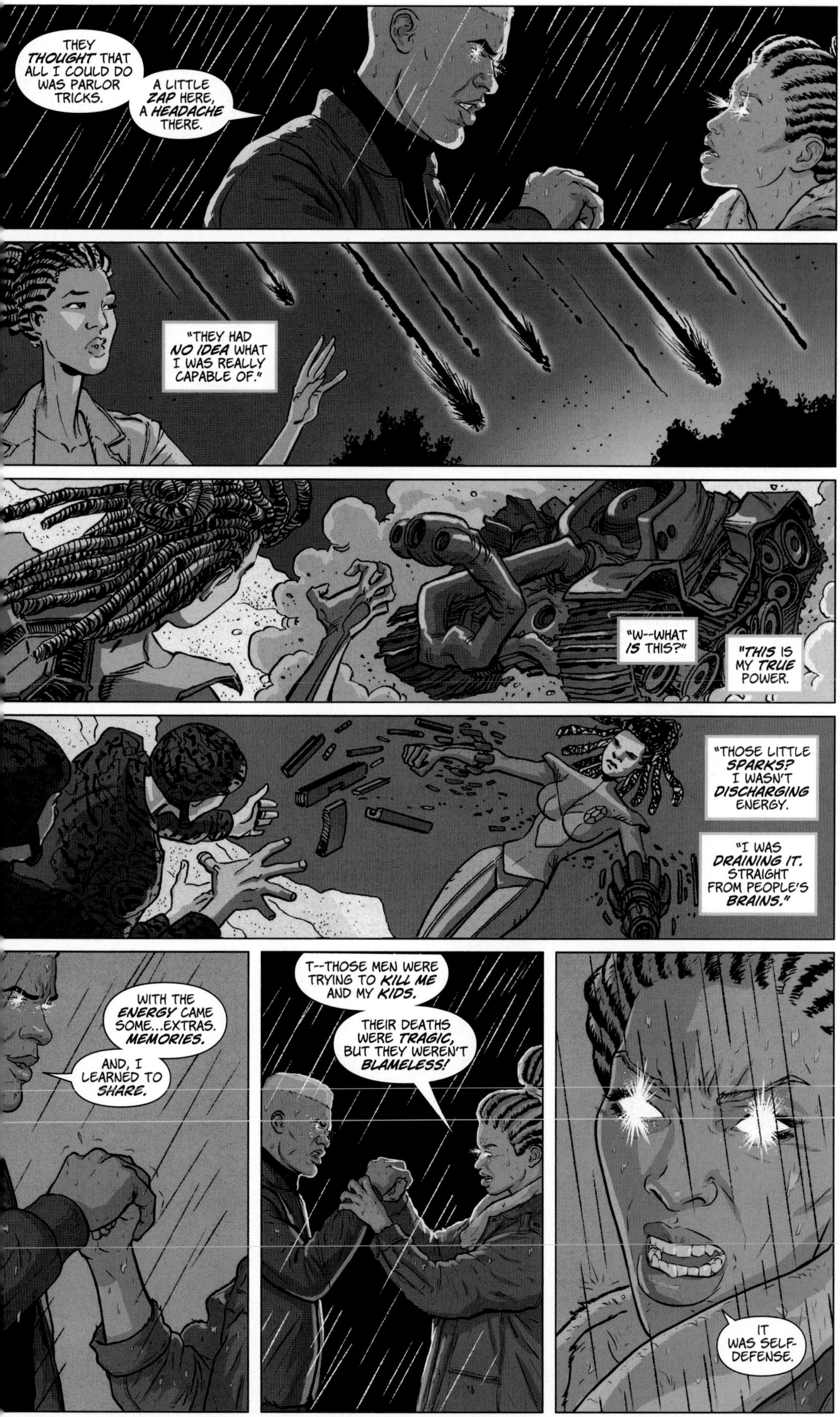
THEY THOUGHT THAT ALL I COULD DO WAS PARLOR TRICKS.
A LITTLE ZAP HERE, A HEADACHE THERE.
"THEY HAD NO IDEA WHAT I WAS REALLY CAPABLE OF."
"W--WHAT IS THIS?"
"THIS IS MY TRUE POWER.
"THOSE LITTLE SPARKS? I WASN'T DISCHARGING ENERGY.
"I WAS DRAINING IT. STRAIGHT FROM PEOPLE'S BRAINS."
WITH THE ENERGY CAME SOME...EXTRAS. MEMORIES.
AND, I LEARNED TO SHARE.
T--THOSE MEN WERE TRYING TO KILL ME AND MY KIDS.
THEIR DEATHS WERE TRAGIC, BUT THEY WEREN'T BLAMELESS!
IT WAS SELF-DEFENSE.

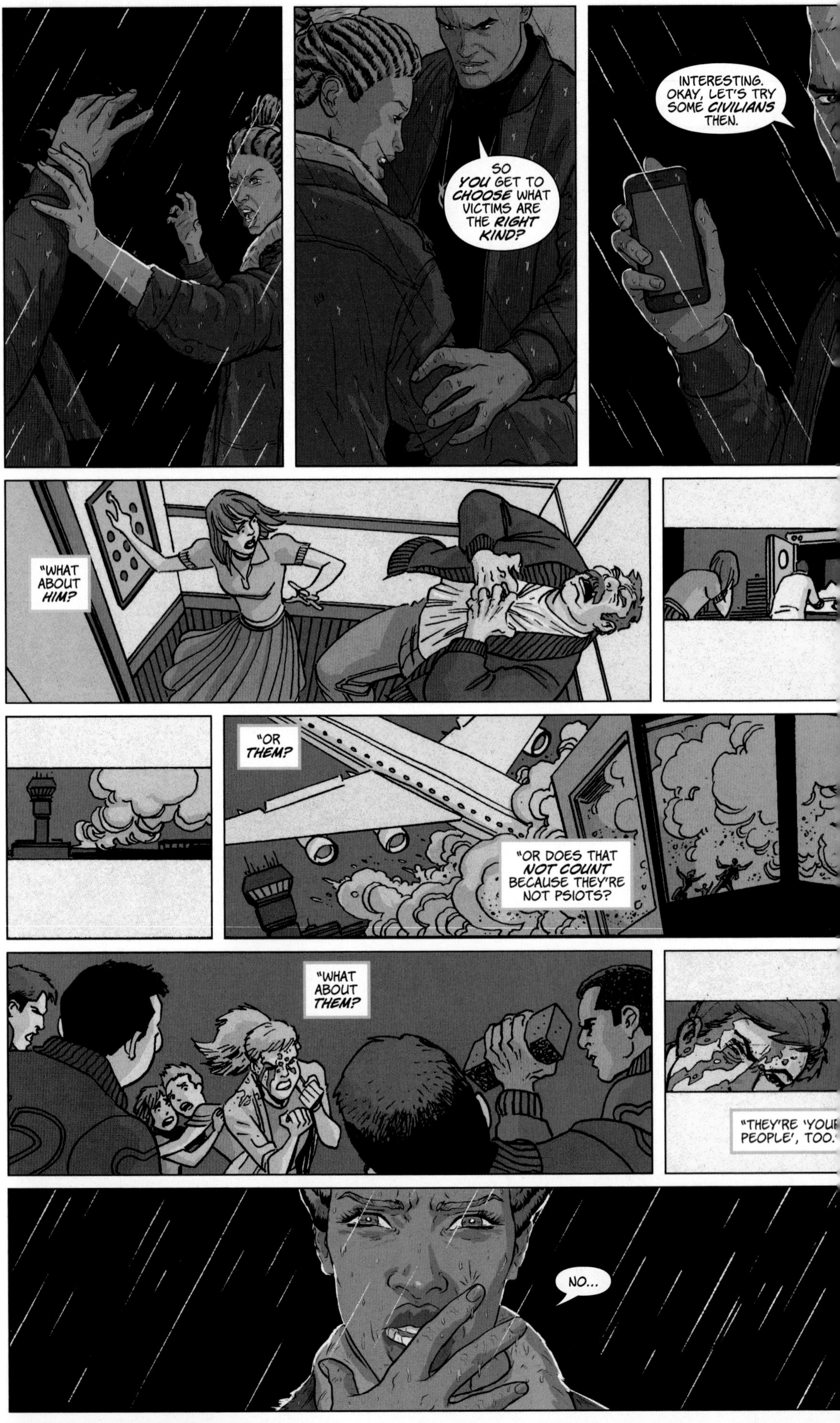
SO *YOU* GET TO *CHOOSE* WHAT VICTIMS ARE THE *RIGHT KIND?*
INTERESTING. OKAY, LET'S TRY SOME *CIVILIANS* THEN.
"WHAT ABOUT *HIM?*
"OR *THEM?*
"OR DOES THAT *NOT COUNT* BECAUSE THEY'RE NOT PSIOTS?
"WHAT ABOUT *THEM?*
"THEY'RE 'YOUR PEOPLE', TOO.
NO...

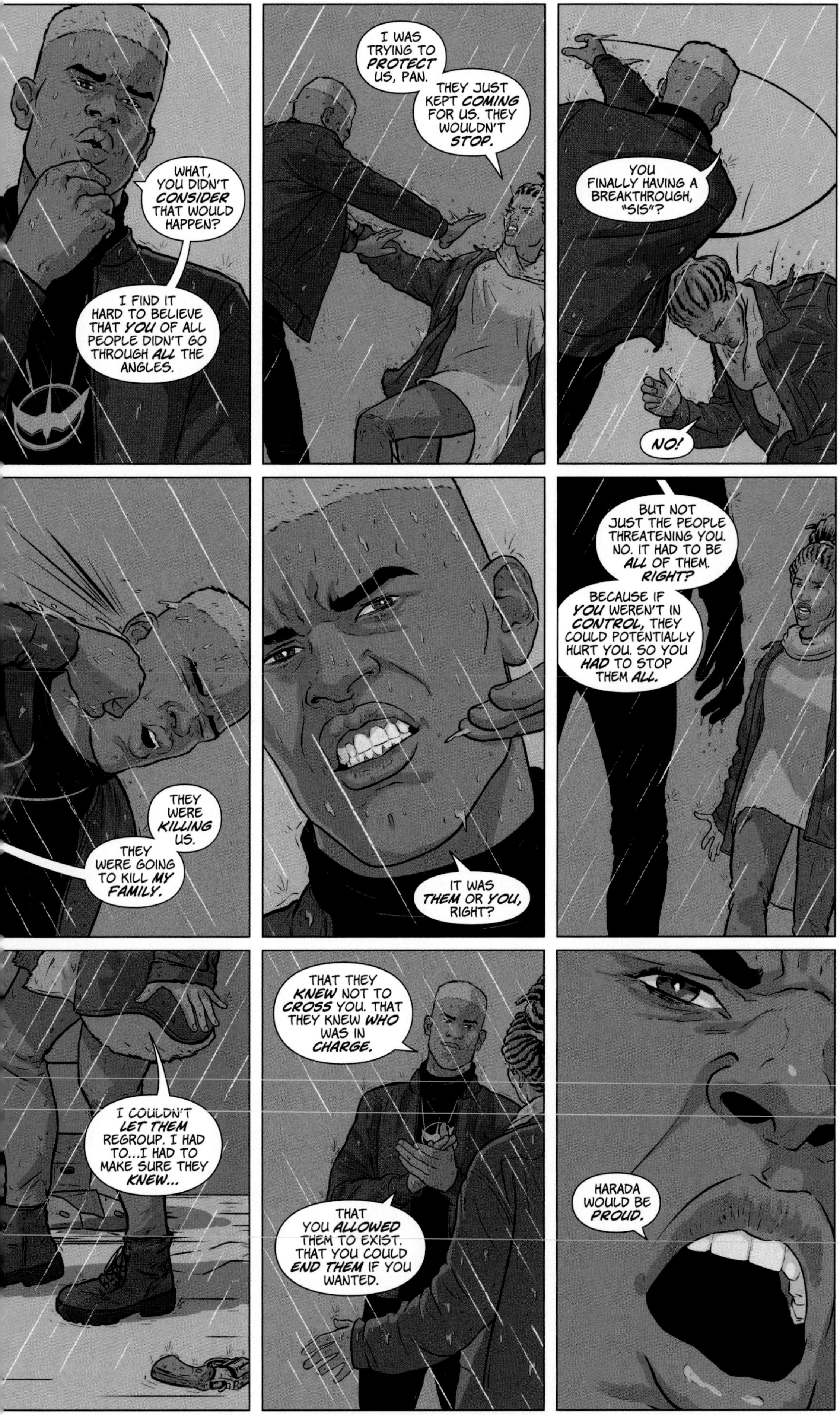

WHAT, YOU DIDN'T CONSIDER THAT WOULD HAPPEN?
I FIND IT HARD TO BELIEVE THAT YOU OF ALL PEOPLE DIDN'T GO THROUGH ALL THE ANGLES.
I WAS TRYING TO PROTECT US, PAN.
THEY JUST KEPT COMING FOR US. THEY WOULDN'T STOP.
YOU FINALLY HAVING A BREAKTHROUGH, "SIS"?
NO!
THEY WERE KILLING US.
THEY WERE GOING TO KILL MY FAMILY.
IT WAS THEM OR YOU, RIGHT?
BUT NOT JUST THE PEOPLE THREATENING YOU. NO. IT HAD TO BE ALL OF THEM. RIGHT?
BECAUSE IF YOU WEREN'T IN CONTROL, THEY COULD POTENTIALLY HURT YOU. SO YOU HAD TO STOP THEM ALL.
I COULDN'T LET THEM REGROUP. I HAD TO...I HAD TO MAKE SURE THEY KNEW...
THAT THEY KNEW NOT TO CROSS YOU. THAT THEY KNEW WHO WAS IN CHARGE.
THAT YOU ALLOWED THEM TO EXIST. THAT YOU COULD END THEM IF YOU WANTED.
HARADA WOULD BE PROUD.

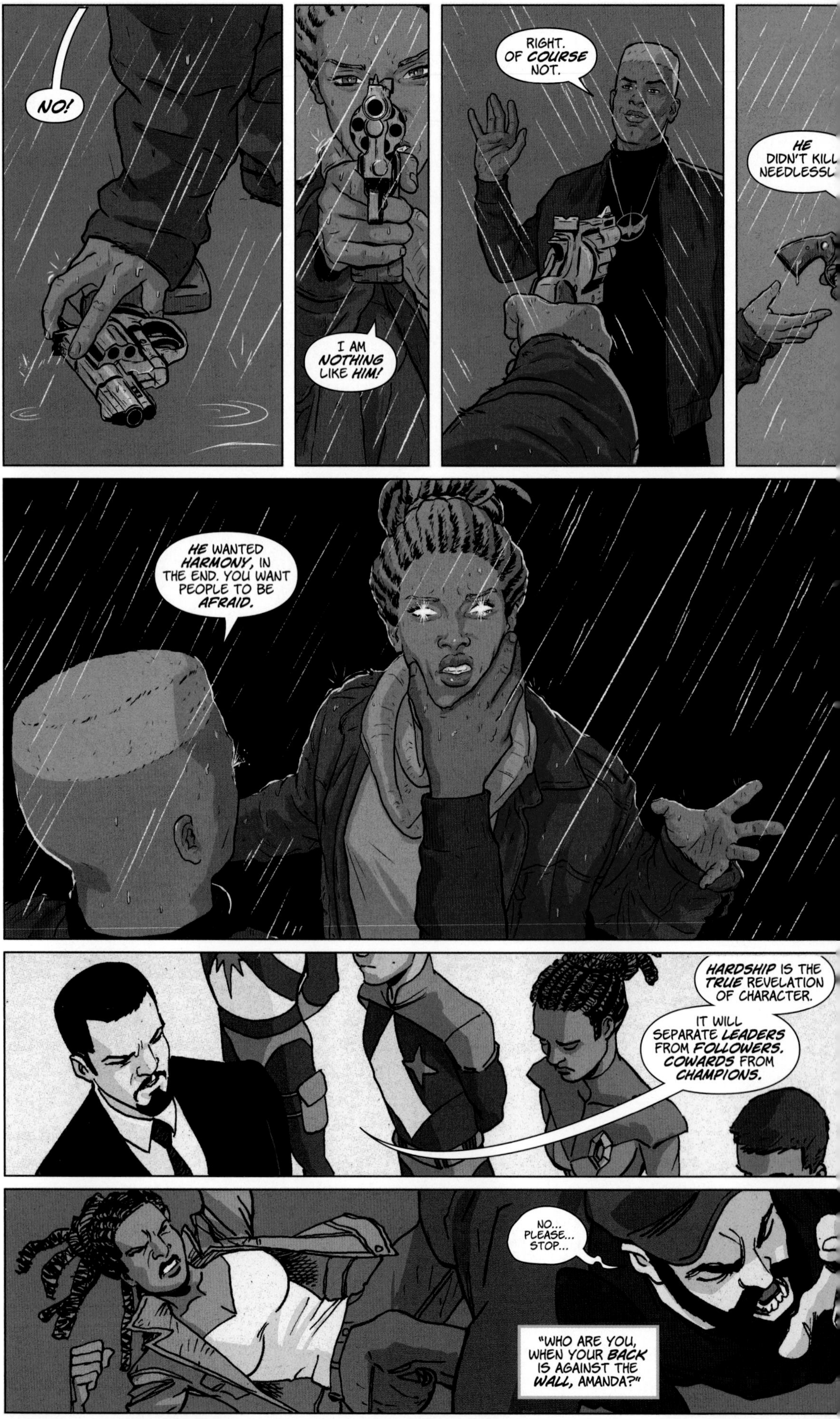
NO!
I AM NOTHING LIKE HIM!
RIGHT. OF COURSE NOT.
HE DIDN'T KILL NEEDLESSL
HE WANTED HARMONY, IN THE END. YOU WANT PEOPLE TO BE AFRAID.
HARDSHIP IS THE TRUE REVELATION OF CHARACTER.
IT WILL SEPARATE LEADERS FROM FOLLOWERS. COWARDS FROM CHAMPIONS.
NO... PLEASE... STOP...
"WHO ARE YOU, WHEN YOUR BACK IS AGAINST THE WALL, AMANDA?"

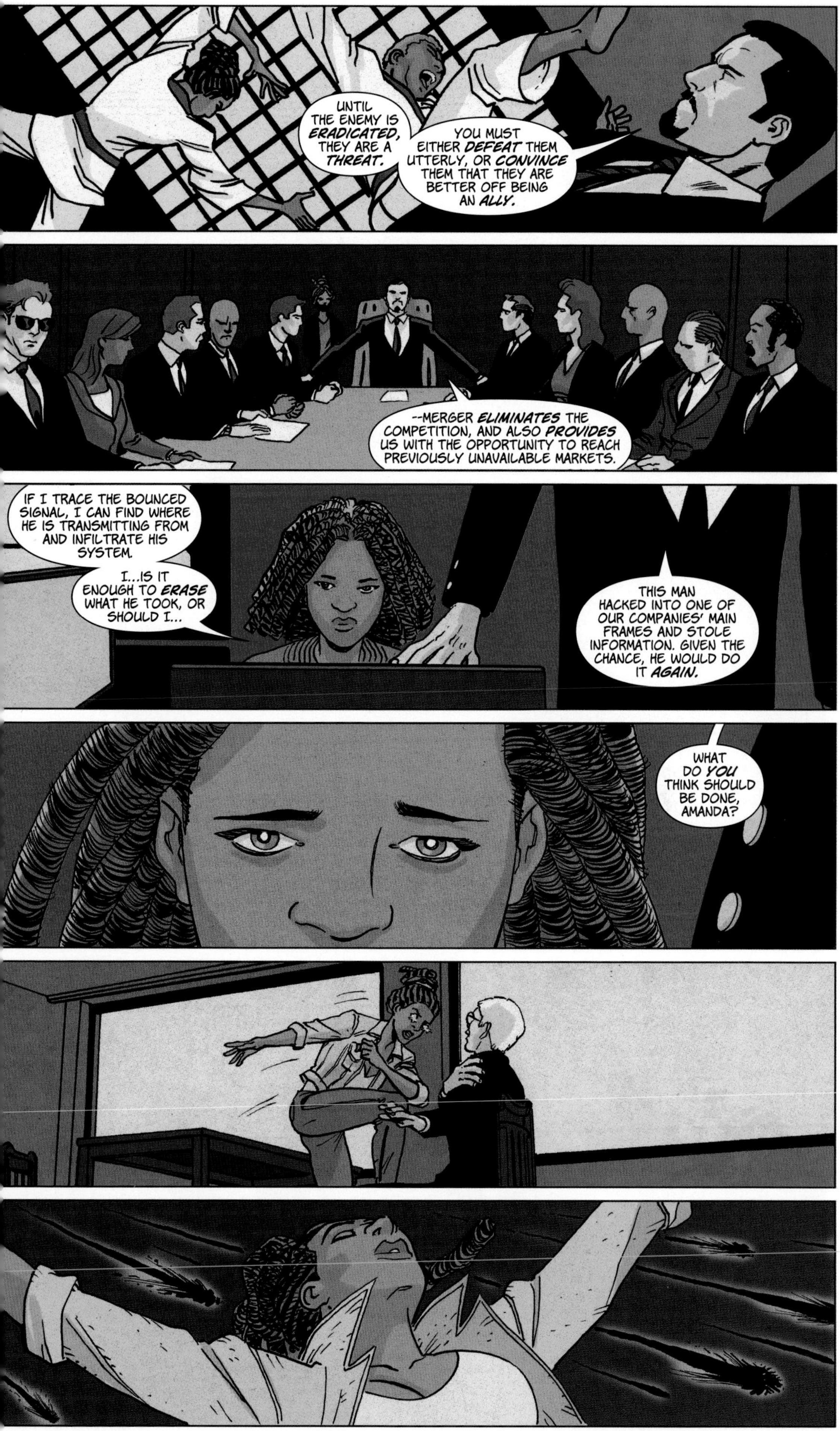
UNTIL THE ENEMY IS ERADICATED, THEY ARE A THREAT.
YOU MUST EITHER DEFEAT THEM UTTERLY, OR CONVINCE THEM THAT THEY ARE BETTER OFF BEING AN ALLY.
--MERGER ELIMINATES THE COMPETITION, AND ALSO PROVIDES US WITH THE OPPORTUNITY TO REACH PREVIOUSLY UNAVAILABLE MARKETS.
IF I TRACE THE BOUNCED SIGNAL, I CAN FIND WHERE HE IS TRANSMITTING FROM AND INFILTRATE HIS SYSTEM.
I...IS IT ENOUGH TO ERASE WHAT HE TOOK, OR SHOULD I...
THIS MAN HACKED INTO ONE OF OUR COMPANIES' MAIN FRAMES AND STOLE INFORMATION. GIVEN THE CHANCE, HE WOULD DO IT AGAIN.
WHAT DO YOU THINK SHOULD BE DONE, AMANDA?

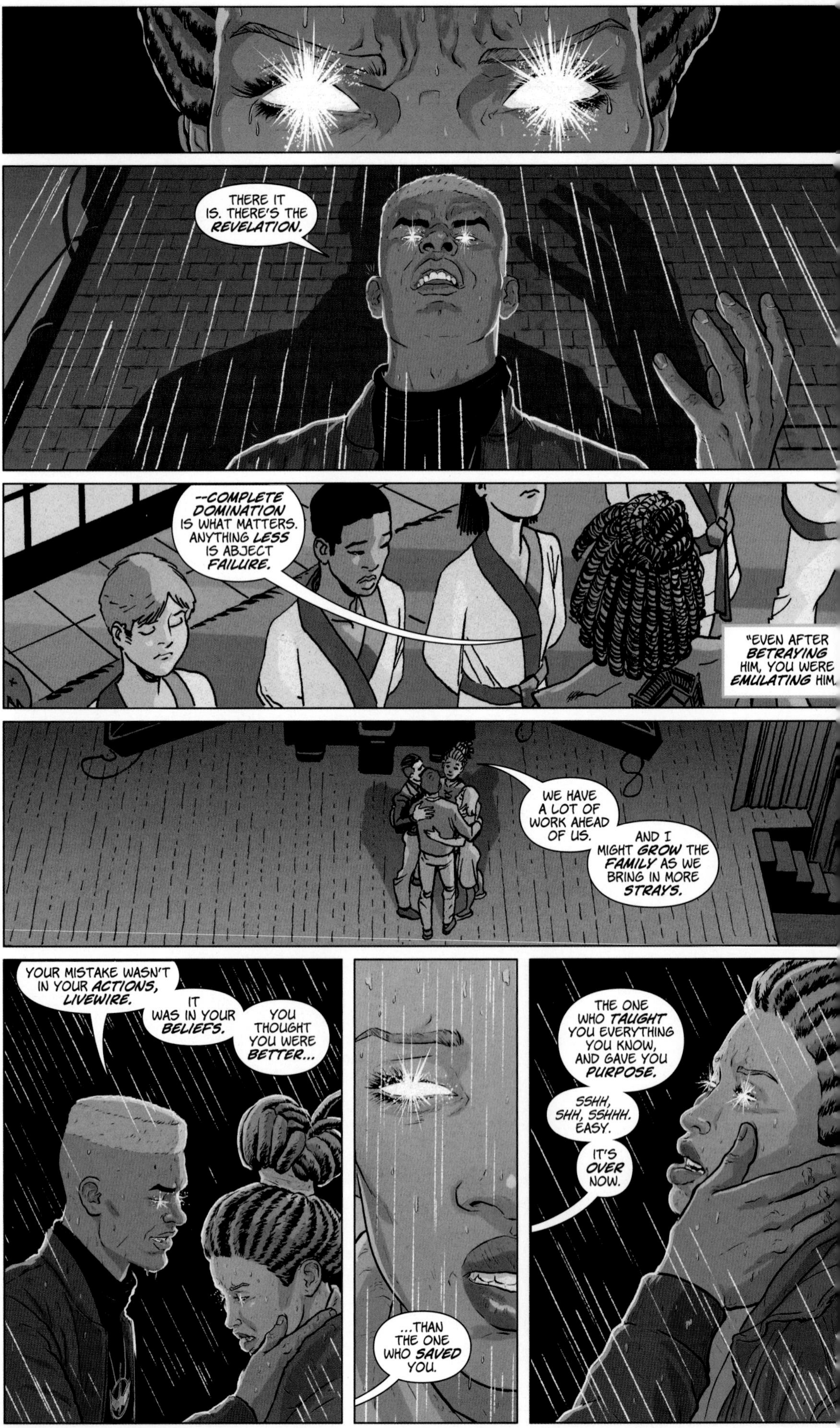
THERE IT IS. THERE'S THE REVELATION.
--COMPLETE DOMINATION IS WHAT MATTERS. ANYTHING LESS IS ABJECT FAILURE.
"EVEN AFTER BETRAYING HIM, YOU WERE EMULATING HIM.
WE HAVE A LOT OF WORK AHEAD OF US.
AND I MIGHT GROW THE FAMILY AS WE BRING IN MORE STRAYS.
YOUR MISTAKE WASN'T IN YOUR ACTIONS, LIVEWIRE.
IT WAS IN YOUR BELIEFS.
YOU THOUGHT YOU WERE BETTER...
...THAN THE ONE WHO SAVED YOU.
THE ONE WHO TAUGHT YOU EVERYTHING YOU KNOW, AND GAVE YOU PURPOSE.
SSHH, SHH, SSHHH. EASY.
IT'S OVER NOW.

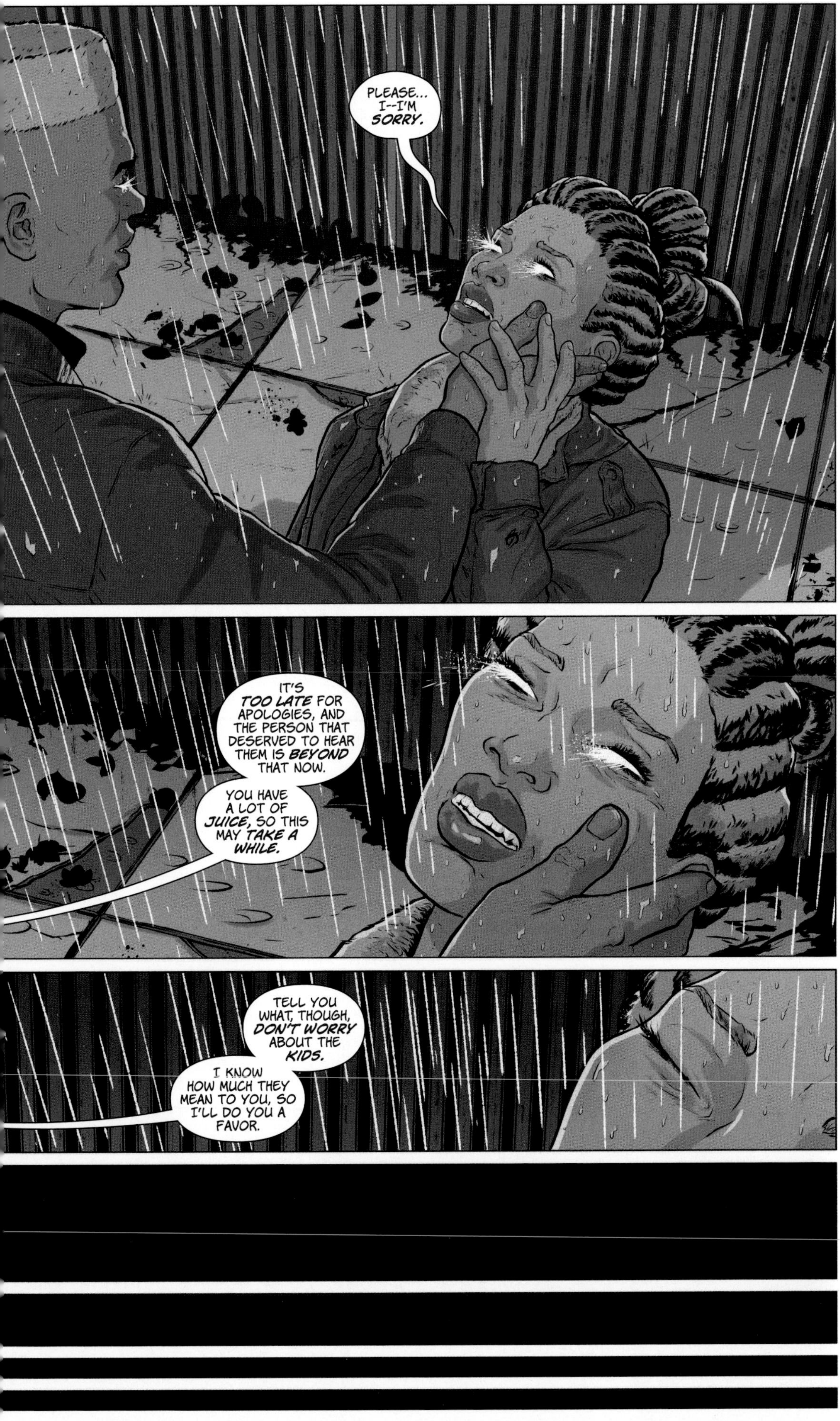
PLEASE... I--I'M SORRY.
IT'S TOO LATE FOR APOLOGIES, AND THE PERSON THAT DESERVED TO HEAR THEM IS BEYOND THAT NOW.
YOU HAVE A LOT OF JUICE, SO THIS MAY TAKE A WHILE.
TELL YOU WHAT, THOUGH, DON'T WORRY ABOUT THE KIDS.
I KNOW HOW MUCH THEY MEAN TO YOU, SO I'LL DO YOU A FAVOR.

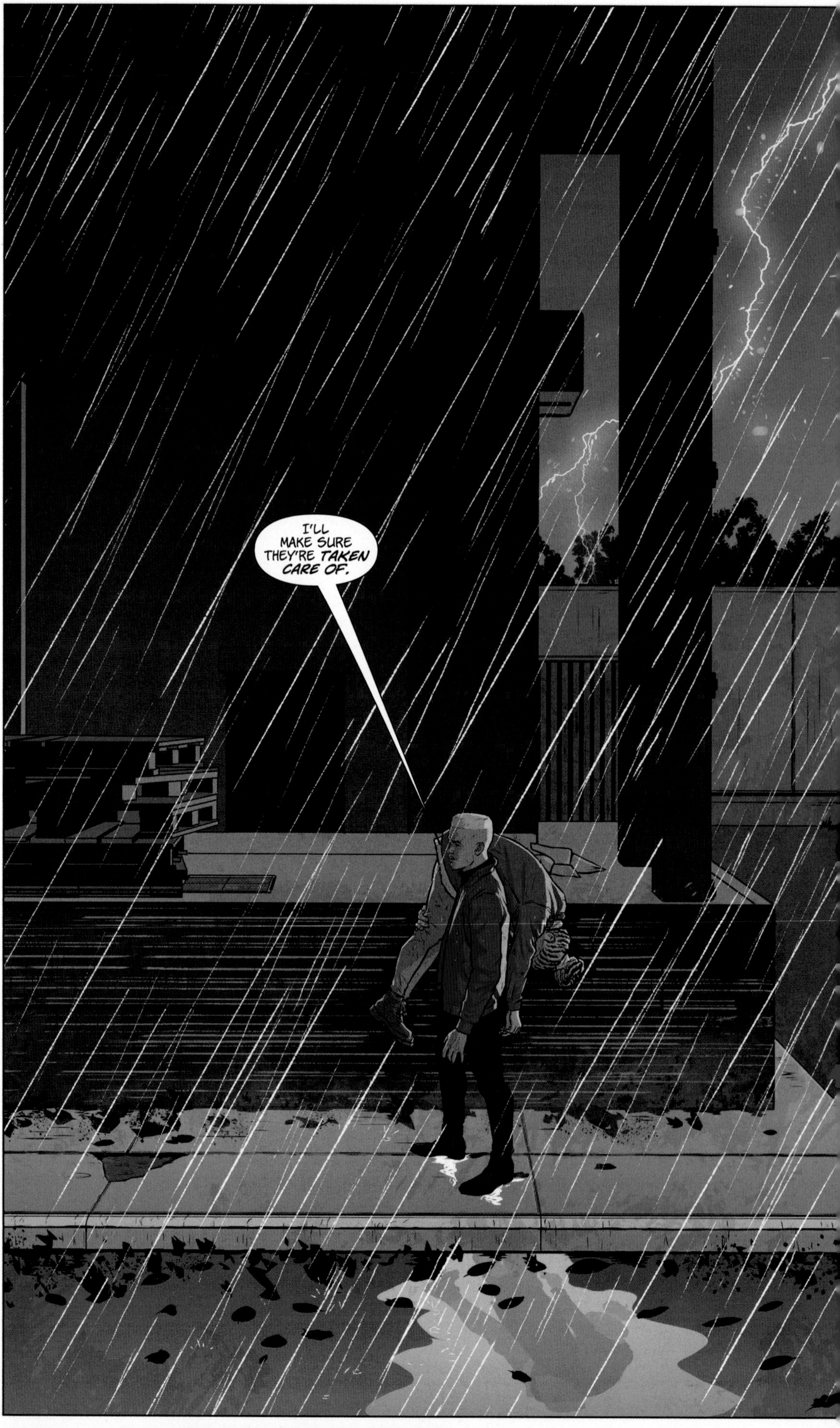
I'LL MAKE SURE THEY'RE *TAKEN CARE OF.*

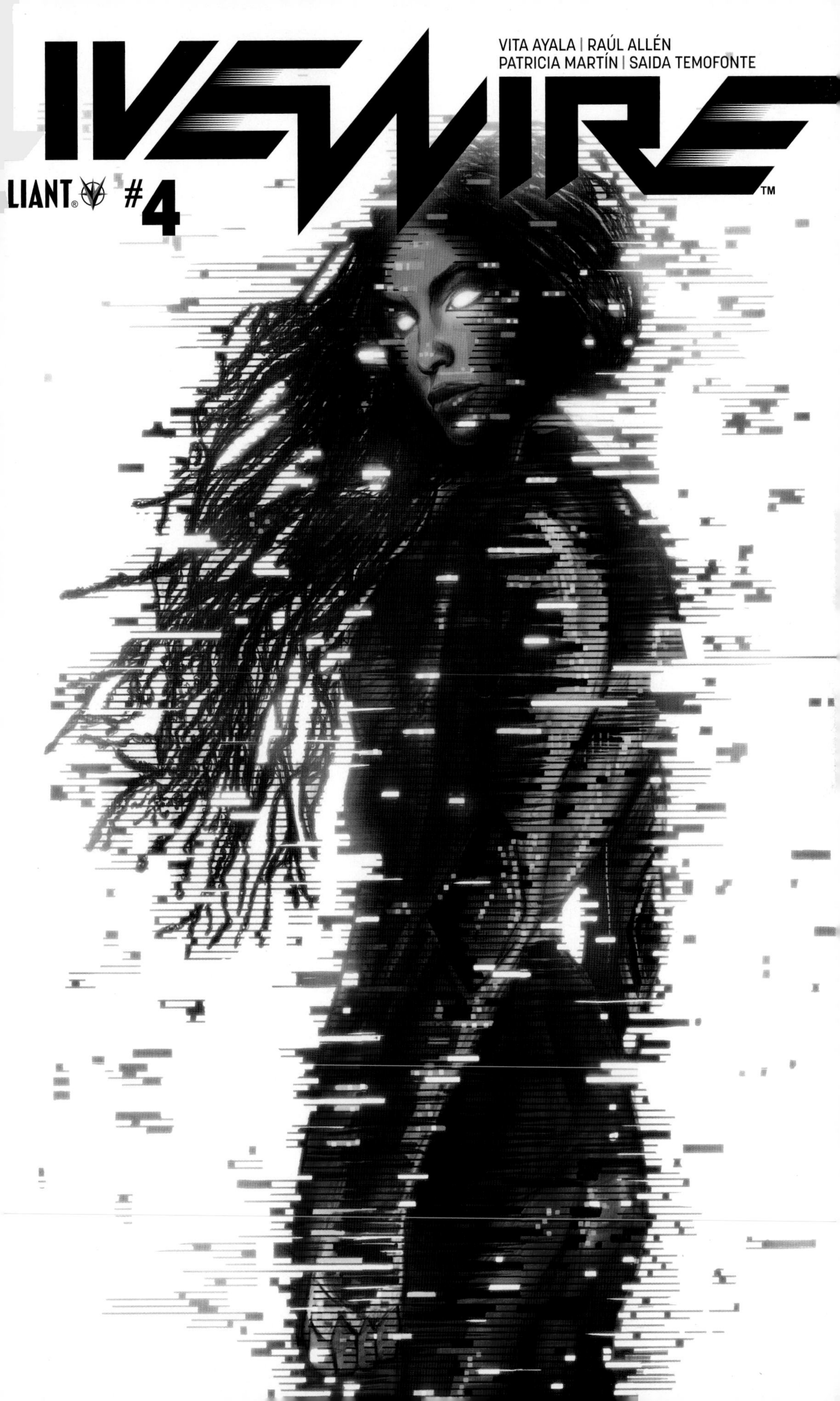
VITA AYALA | RAÚL ALLÉN
PATRICIA MARTÍN | SAIDA TEMOFONTE
LIVEWIRE™
LIANT®
#4

THIS IS WHAT YOU DESERVE, LIVEWIRE.

MILLIONS SUFFERED, ALL BECAUSE I LET MY CONTROL LAPSE.

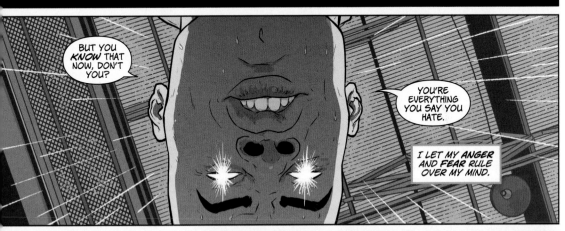

BUT YOU KNOW THAT NOW, DON'T YOU?

YOU'RE EVERYTHING YOU SAY YOU HATE.

I LET MY ANGER AND FEAR RULE OVER MY MIND.

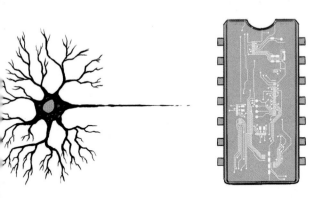
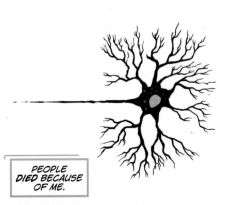

PEOPLE DIED BECAUSE OF ME.

THIS IS WHAT I DESERVE.

≶GASP≷

≥HNNH≤

SHH, SHH, IT'S OKAY. THE PAIN FADES.

IF YOU DON'T FIGHT IT, IT'S ALMOST LIKE GOING TO SLEEP.

LET THE *MEMORIES* WASH OVER YOU.

HEY AMANDA? THANKS. FOR, UH... *EVERYTHING.*

SQUAWK!

ALWAYS, NIKKI.

THEY *TRUSTED* ME TO CARE FOR THEM.

ENOUGH, PAN...I DON'T *WANT* TO SEE ANYMORE.

YOU DON'T GET A *CHOICE* HERE, *AMANDA.*

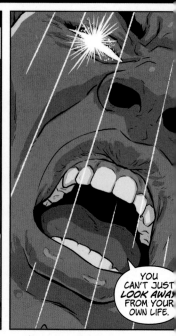

YOU CAN'T JUST *LOOK AWAY* FROM YOUR OWN LIFE.

"THESE ARE *OUR* MEMORIES-- *OUR* MISTAKES."

IT'S *OVER* FOR YOU NOW, YOU KNOW THAT DON'T YOU?

THE GAME'S *JUST BEGUN,* AVI. YOU'VE PUT YOUR *QUEEN* IN THE LINE OF FIRE.

HOW CAN YOU BASICALLY *BE* THE INTERNET, AND *SUCK* SO BAD AT THIS?

I DON'T APPRECIATE THE *TRASH TALK,* OWEN.

...OU LET YOURSELF ...T *DISTRACTED* BY ...ANDFUL, WHEN YOU ...OULD HAVE BEEN UNITING *ALL* OUR KIND.

THE NEEDS OF THE *MANY* OVER THE NEEDS OF THE *FEW,* AMANDA. THAT IS *FOUNDATIONAL.*

YOU LET SOMETHING AS *SUBJECTIVE* AND *FOOLISH* AS *LOVE* GET IN THE WAY OF THAT.

HOW COULD *YOU* SAY THAT? THAT'S WHY *HARADA* ABANDONED *YOU.*

HE CHOSE *YOU* AS HEIR. I WAS CAST ASIDE BECAUSE OF *YOU.*

"IF HE HAD *KNOWN* HOW *POWERFUL* I WOULD BECOME, HE WOULDN'T HAVE GIVEN YOU A SECOND GLANCE."

I WAS *WRONG* IN WHAT I DID, I *SEE THAT* NOW.

BUT *LOVING* AND *PROTECTING* THOSE KIDS WILL *NEVER* BE A WASTE OF TIME.

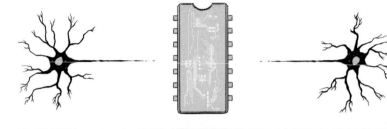

THOUGHT WE BROKE *THROUGH* YOUR DELUSIONS, "SIS."

ALL THAT *EMPATHY* AND COMPASSION NONSENSE IS *SHORT-SIGHTED.* IT'S WHAT GOT YOU WHERE YOU ARE RIGHT NOW.

NO.

NO.

I *UNDERSTAND* THAT YOU CHOOSE *MERCY* OVER *PREEMPTIVE ACTION,* LIVEWIRE?

THAT... *DISAPPOINTS* ME.

Y-YES, SIR.

SHOULD HE EVER *TROUBLE* US AGAIN, IT WILL BE ON *YOU.*

THAT'S...NOT *RIGHT. THEY'RE* NOT RIGHT.

IT'S *NOT FAIR.* YOU DON'T EVEN *WANT* TO BE TEAM CAPTAIN!

HARADA CHOSE ME BECAUSE I AM *MORE POWERFUL.*

WANT MY *SPOT?* BE *STRONGER.* BE *BETTER.* THEN HE *MIGHT* SEE YOU AS WORTH HIS TIME.

ALL THOSE TIMES I *PUSHED* YOU TO BE COLDER-- TO SWALLOW YOUR SADNESS AND JOY. I WAS *WRONG.*

THE *MISSION* WAS NEVER MORE IMPORTANT THAN *YOU,* THAN *US.*

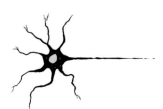

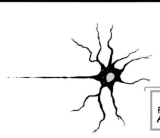

"I'M SORRY... FOR MY PART... *HURTING YOU.*

YOU... DESERVED... BETT...

FINALLY.

"I WAS GETTING TIRED OF YOUR MOUTH."

AMANDA MCKEE. THE *MIGHTY LIVEWIRE.*

TCH.

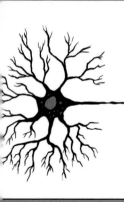

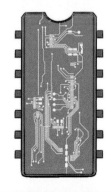

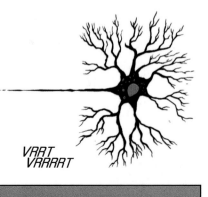

VRRT
VRRRRT

YEAH. IT'S D--

THE F--?!

THEY'LL HAVE TO CALL YOU BACK.

WELL AIN'T *THIS* A $%&#@?

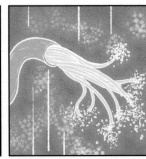

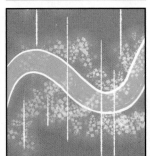

I WAS *WRONG* IN WHAT I *DID.*

WE COVERED THAT ALREADY.

I AM RESPONSIBLE FOR ALL THE PEOPLE THAT WERE *HURT,* THAT *DIED* BECAUSE I LOST CONTROL.

BUT *YOU'RE* WRONG, TOO.

I WASN'T *WEAK* BECAUSE I *CARED* ABOUT PEOPLE, PAN.

I *FAILED* THEM BECAUSE I *STOPPED* CARING WHO GOT HURT, FOR JUST A *SECOND.*

THAT'S *ALL* IT TOOK.

YOU REALLY HAVE TO LEARN TO *LEAN INTO* YOUR CONVICTIONS, AMANDA.

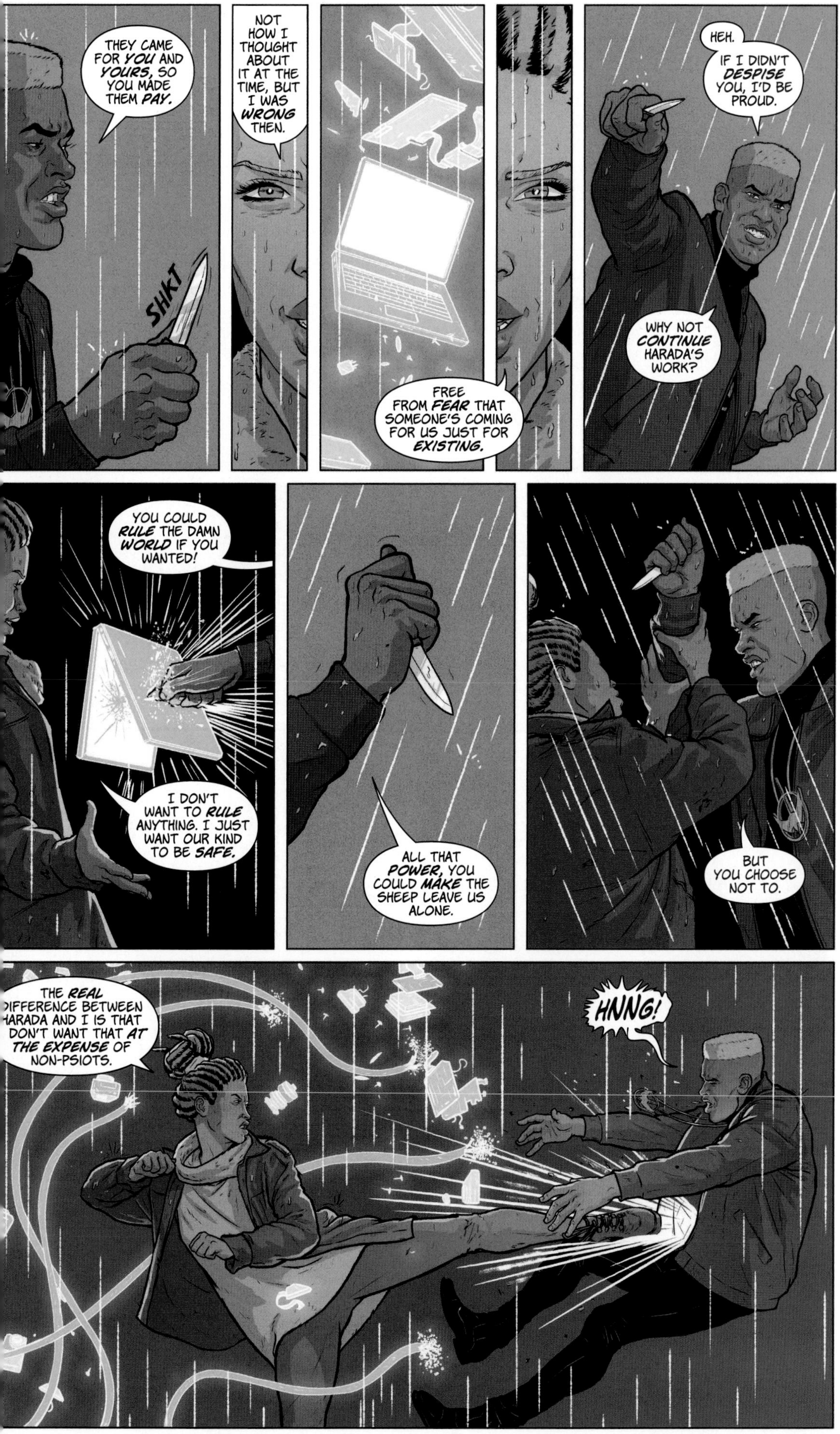

THEY CAME FOR YOU AND YOURS, SO YOU MADE THEM PAY.
SHKT
NOT HOW I THOUGHT ABOUT IT AT THE TIME, BUT I WAS WRONG THEN.
FREE FROM FEAR THAT SOMEONE'S COMING FOR US JUST FOR EXISTING.
HEH.
IF I DIDN'T DESPISE YOU, I'D BE PROUD.
WHY NOT CONTINUE HARADA'S WORK?
YOU COULD RULE THE DAMN WORLD IF YOU WANTED!
I DON'T WANT TO RULE ANYTHING. I JUST WANT OUR KIND TO BE SAFE.
ALL THAT POWER, YOU COULD MAKE THE SHEEP LEAVE US ALONE.
BUT YOU CHOOSE NOT TO.
THE REAL DIFFERENCE BETWEEN HARADA AND I IS THAT I DON'T WANT THAT AT THE EXPENSE OF NON-PSIOTS.
HNNG!

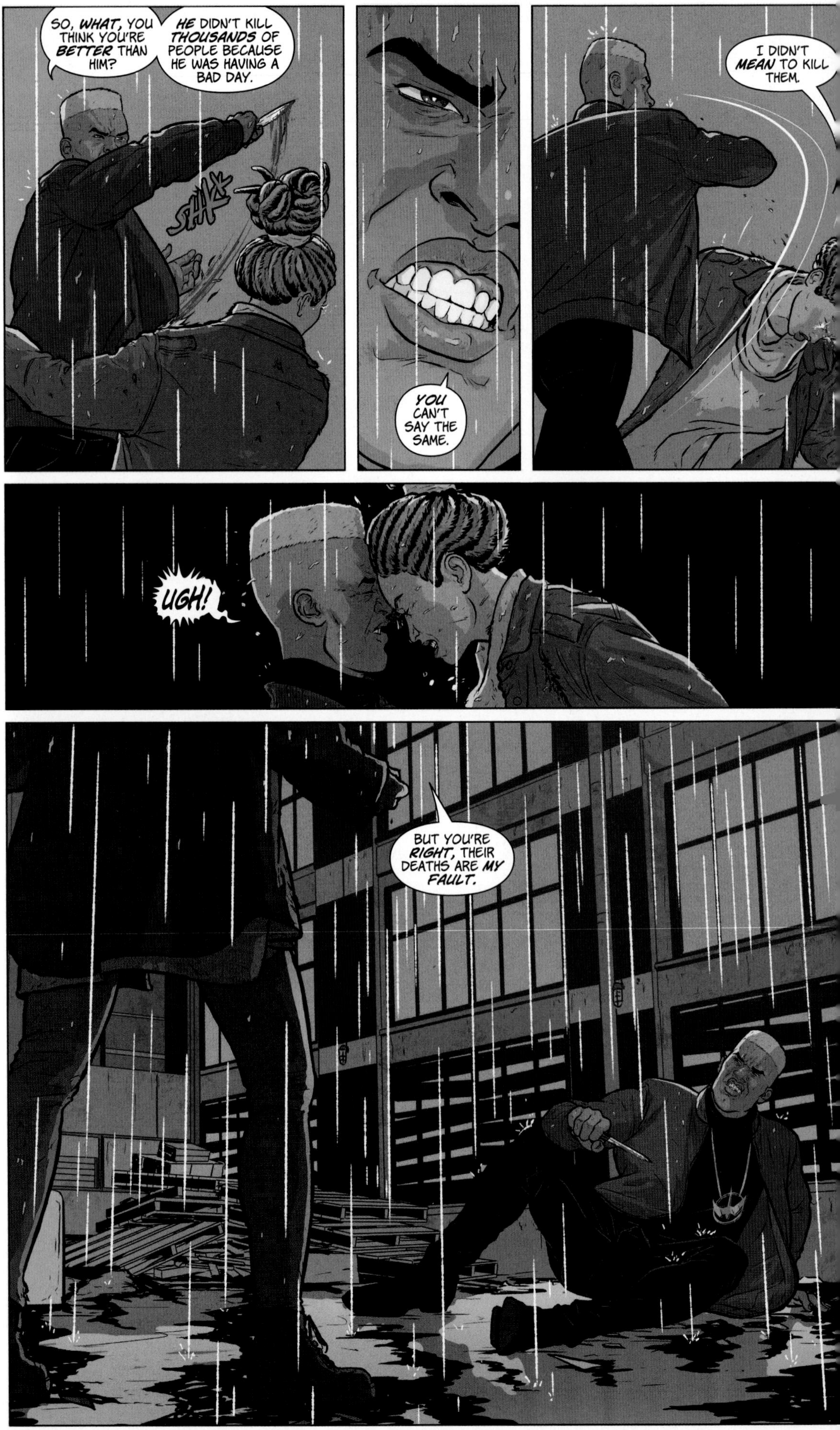
SO, WHAT, YOU THINK YOU'RE BETTER THAN HIM?
HE DIDN'T KILL THOUSANDS OF PEOPLE BECAUSE HE WAS HAVING A BAD DAY.
SHK
YOU CAN'T SAY THE SAME.
I DIDN'T MEAN TO KILL THEM.
UGH!
BUT YOU'RE RIGHT, THEIR DEATHS ARE MY FAULT.

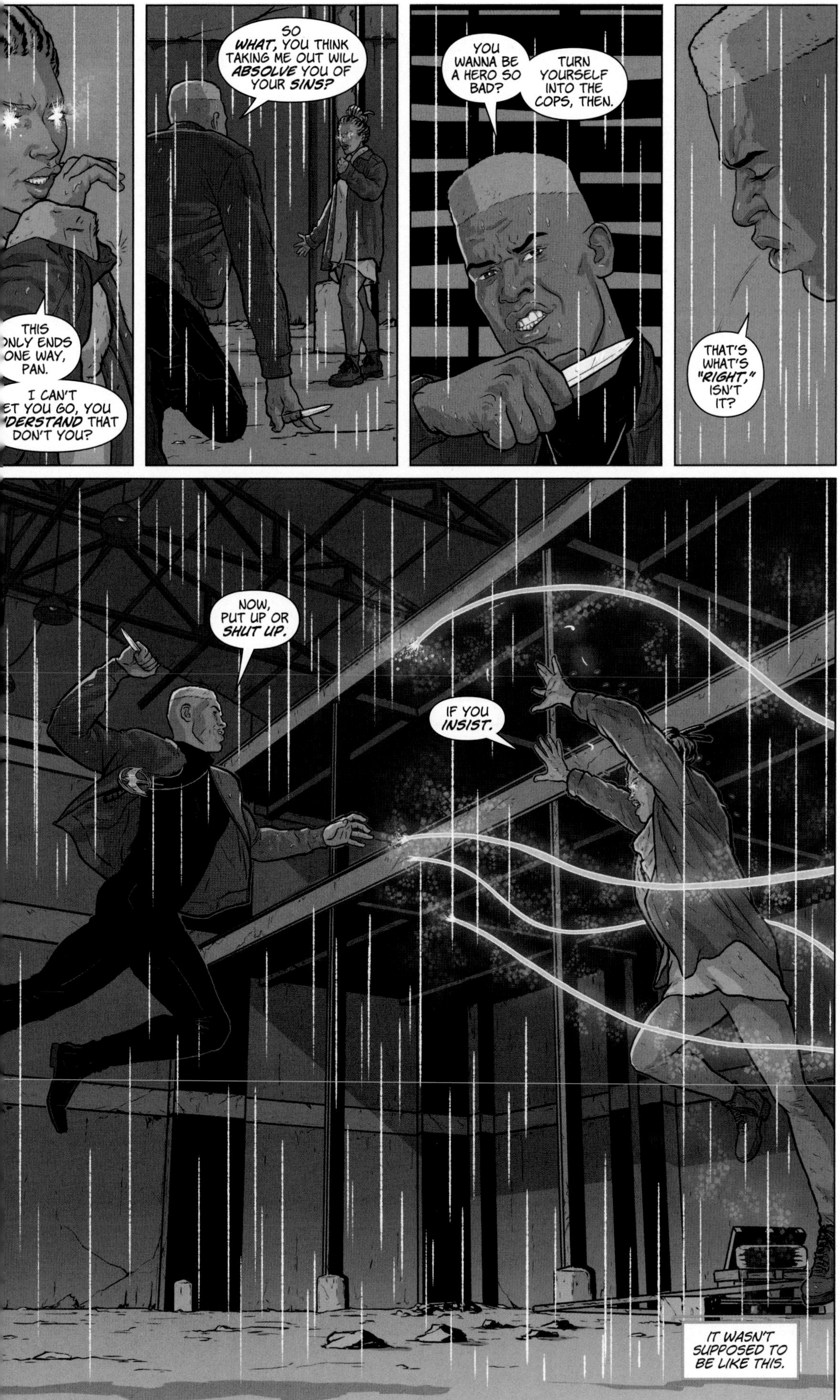

THIS
NLY ENDS
ONE WAY,
PAN.
I CAN'T
ET YOU GO, YOU
IDERSTAND THAT
DON'T YOU?
SO
WHAT, YOU THINK
TAKING ME OUT WILL
ABSOLVE YOU OF
YOUR SINS?
YOU
WANNA BE
A HERO SO
BAD?
TURN
YOURSELF
INTO THE
COPS, THEN.
THAT'S
WHAT'S
"RIGHT,"
ISN'T
IT?
NOW,
PUT UP OR
SHUT UP.
IF YOU
INSIST.
IT WASN'T
SUPPOSED TO
BE LIKE THIS.

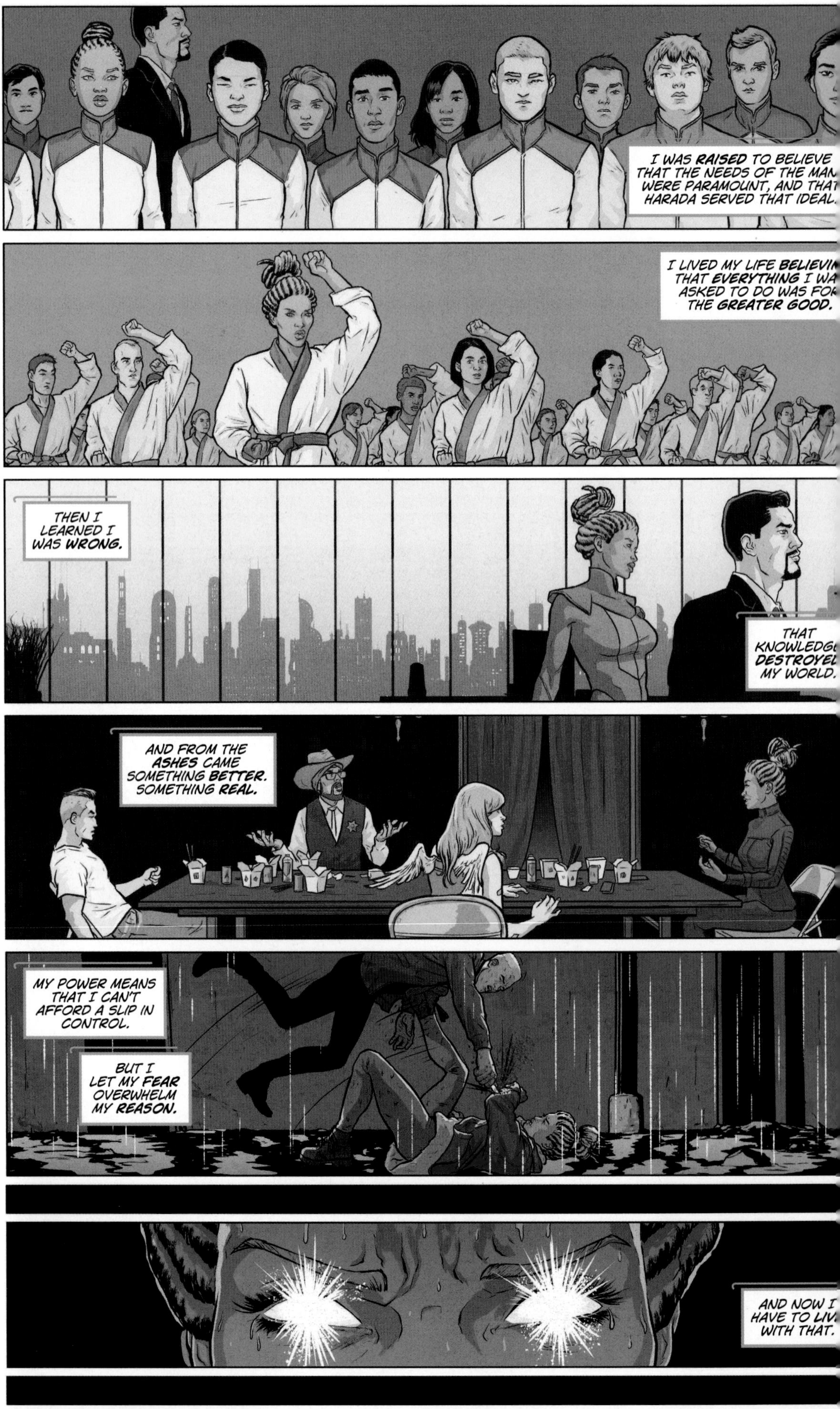
I WAS RAISED TO BELIEVE THAT THE NEEDS OF THE MAN WERE PARAMOUNT, AND THAT HARADA SERVED THAT IDEAL.
I LIVED MY LIFE BELIEVIN THAT EVERYTHING I WA ASKED TO DO WAS FOR THE GREATER GOOD.
THEN I LEARNED I WAS WRONG.
THAT KNOWLEDG DESTROYEL MY WORLD.
AND FROM THE ASHES CAME SOMETHING BETTER. SOMETHING REAL.
MY POWER MEANS THAT I CAN'T AFFORD A SLIP IN CONTROL.
BUT I LET MY FEAR OVERWHELM MY REASON.
AND NOW I HAVE TO LIV WITH THAT.

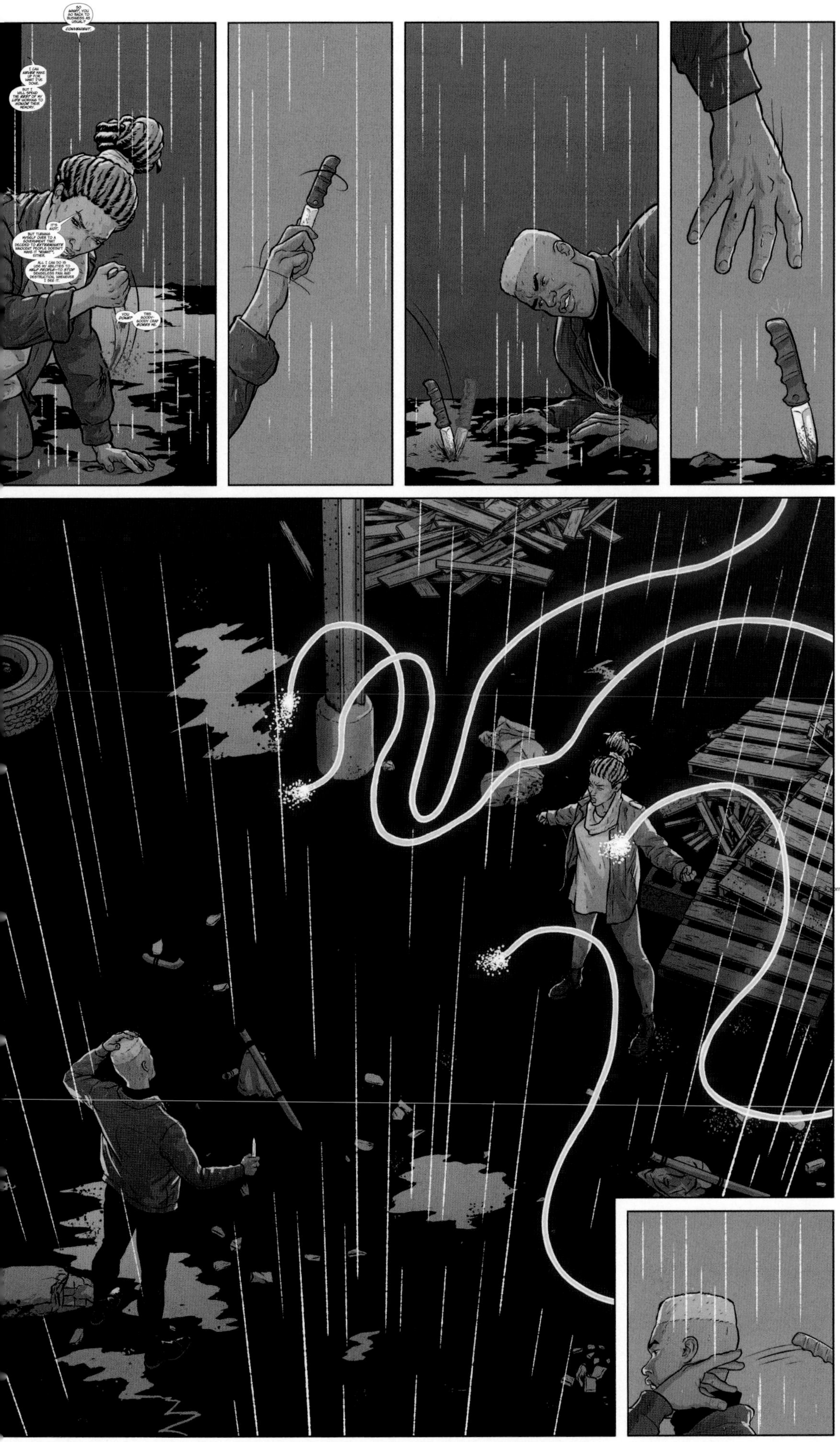

SO WHAT, YOU GO BACK TO BUSINESS AS USUAL?
CONVENIENT.
I CAN NEVER MAKE UP FOR WHAT I'VE DONE.
BUT I WILL SPEND THE REST OF MY LIFE WORKING TO HONOR THEIR MEMORY.
IT'S NOT.
BUT TURNING MYSELF OVER TO A GOVERNMENT THAT DECIDED TO EXTERMINATE INNOCENT PEOPLE DOESN'T MAKE IT "RIGHT", EITHER.
ALL I CAN DO IS USE MY ABILITIES TO HELP PEOPLE—TO STOP SENSELESS PAIN AND DESTRUCTION WHENEVER I SEE IT.
YOU DONE?
THIS GOODY-GOODY CRAP BORES ME.

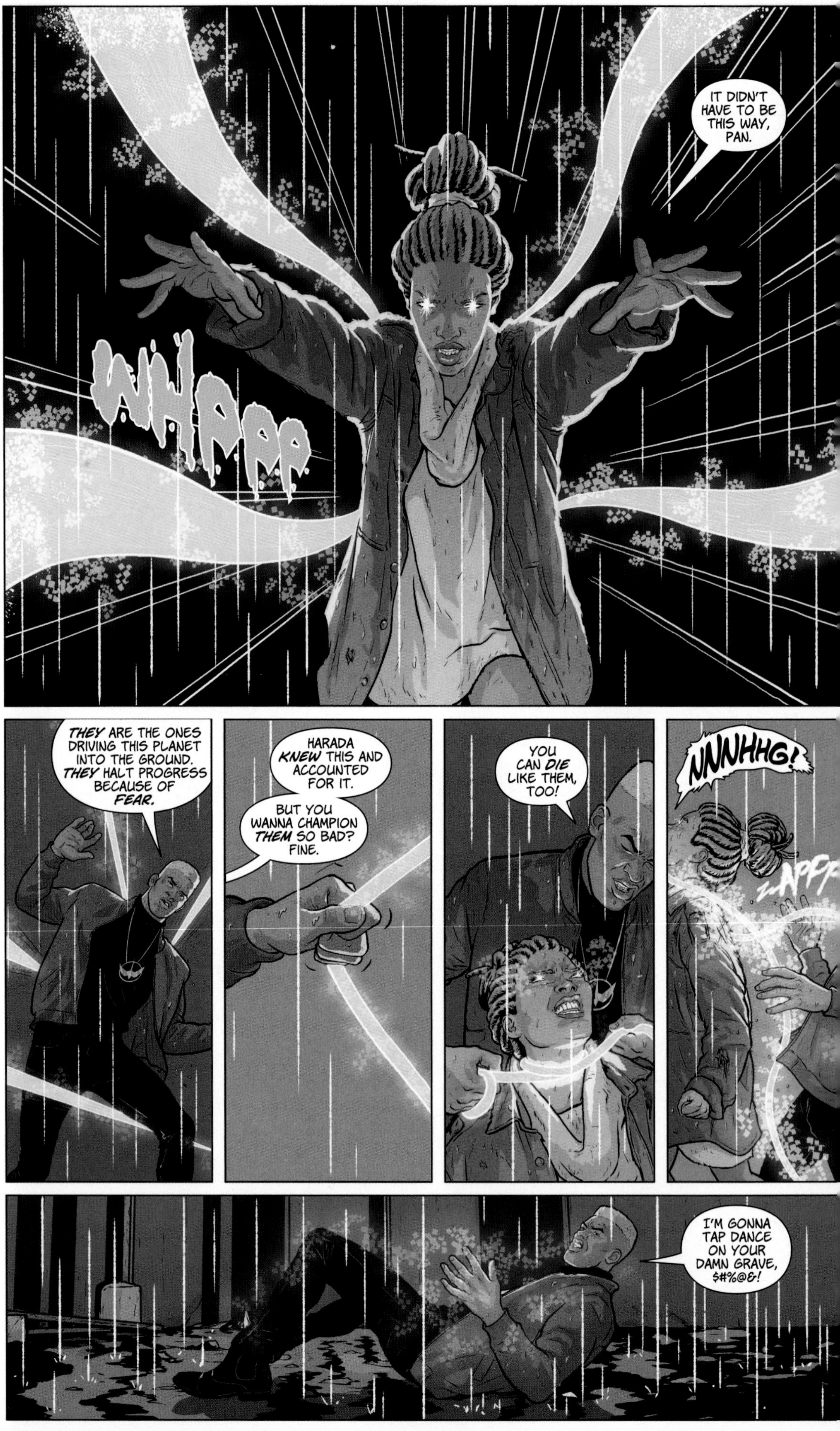
IT DIDN'T HAVE TO BE THIS WAY, PAN.
WHPPP
THEY ARE THE ONES DRIVING THIS PLANET INTO THE GROUND. THEY HALT PROGRESS BECAUSE OF FEAR.
HARADA KNEW THIS AND ACCOUNTED FOR IT.
BUT YOU WANNA CHAMPION THEM SO BAD? FINE.
YOU CAN DIE LIKE THEM, TOO!
NNNHHG!
I'M GONNA TAP DANCE ON YOUR DAMN GRAVE, $#%@&!

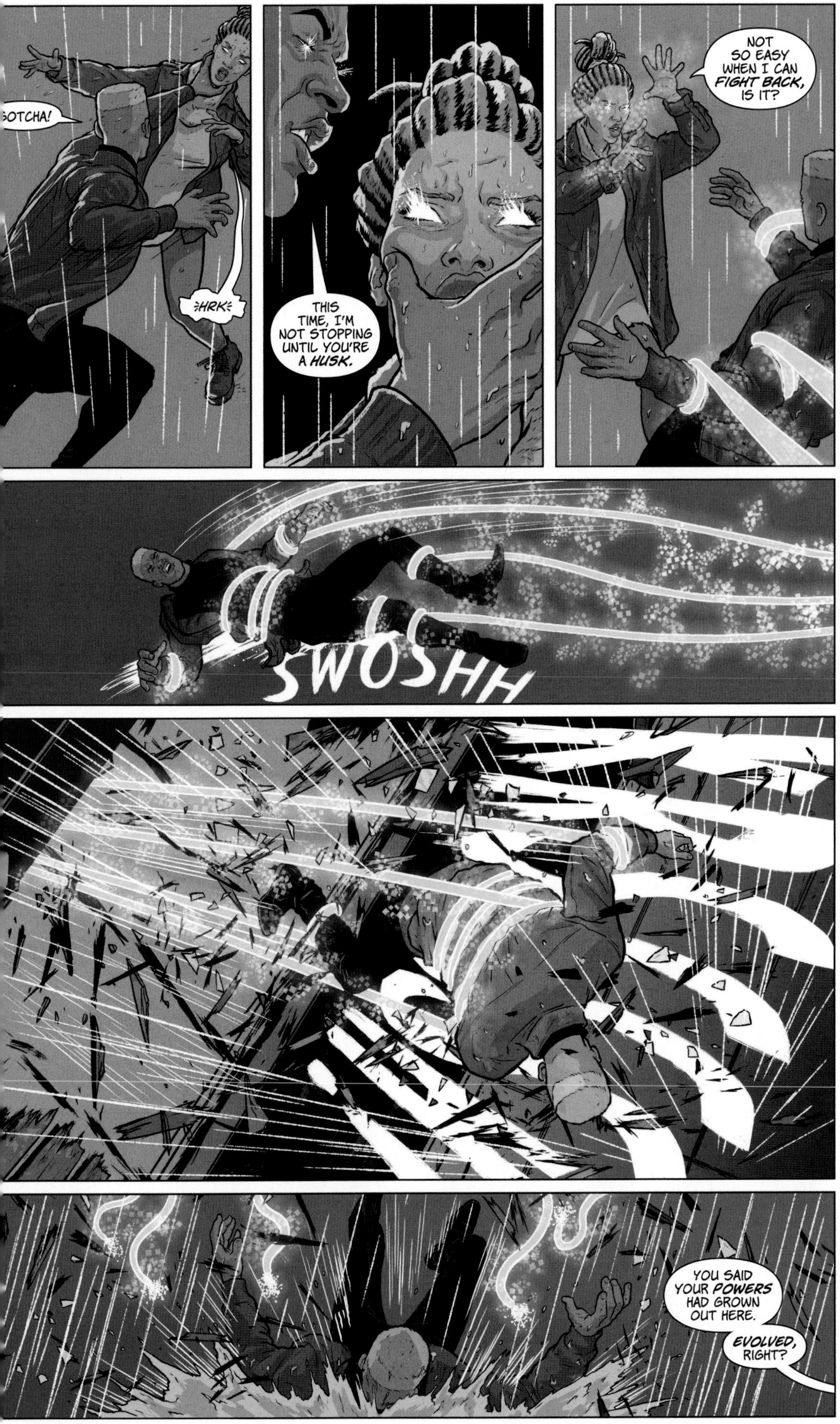
GOTCHA!
HRK
THIS TIME, I'M NOT STOPPING UNTIL YOU'RE A HUSK.
NOT SO EASY WHEN I CAN FIGHT BACK, IS IT?
SWOSHH
YOU SAID YOUR POWERS HAD GROWN OUT HERE.
EVOLVED, RIGHT?

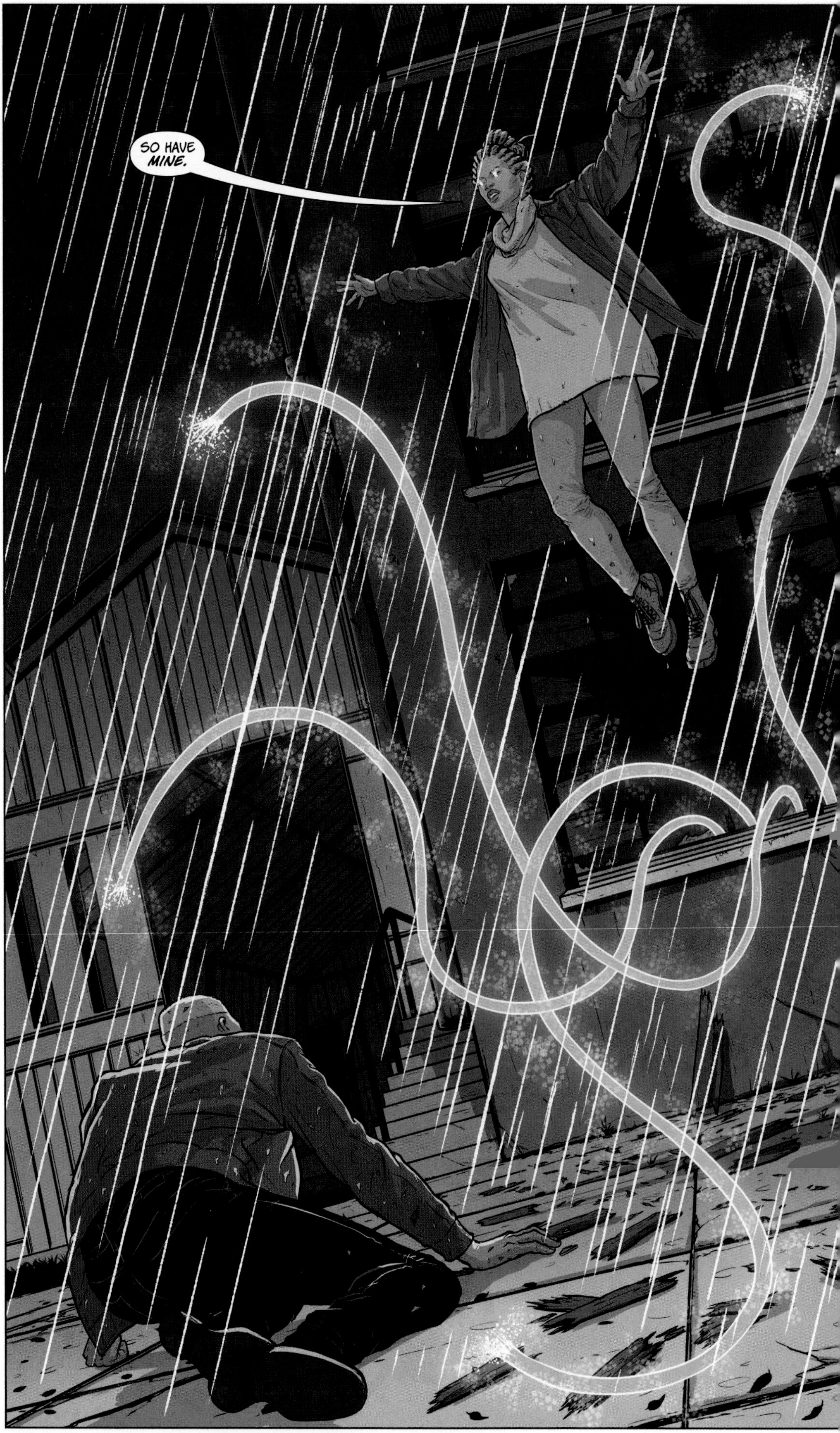
SO HAVE MINE.

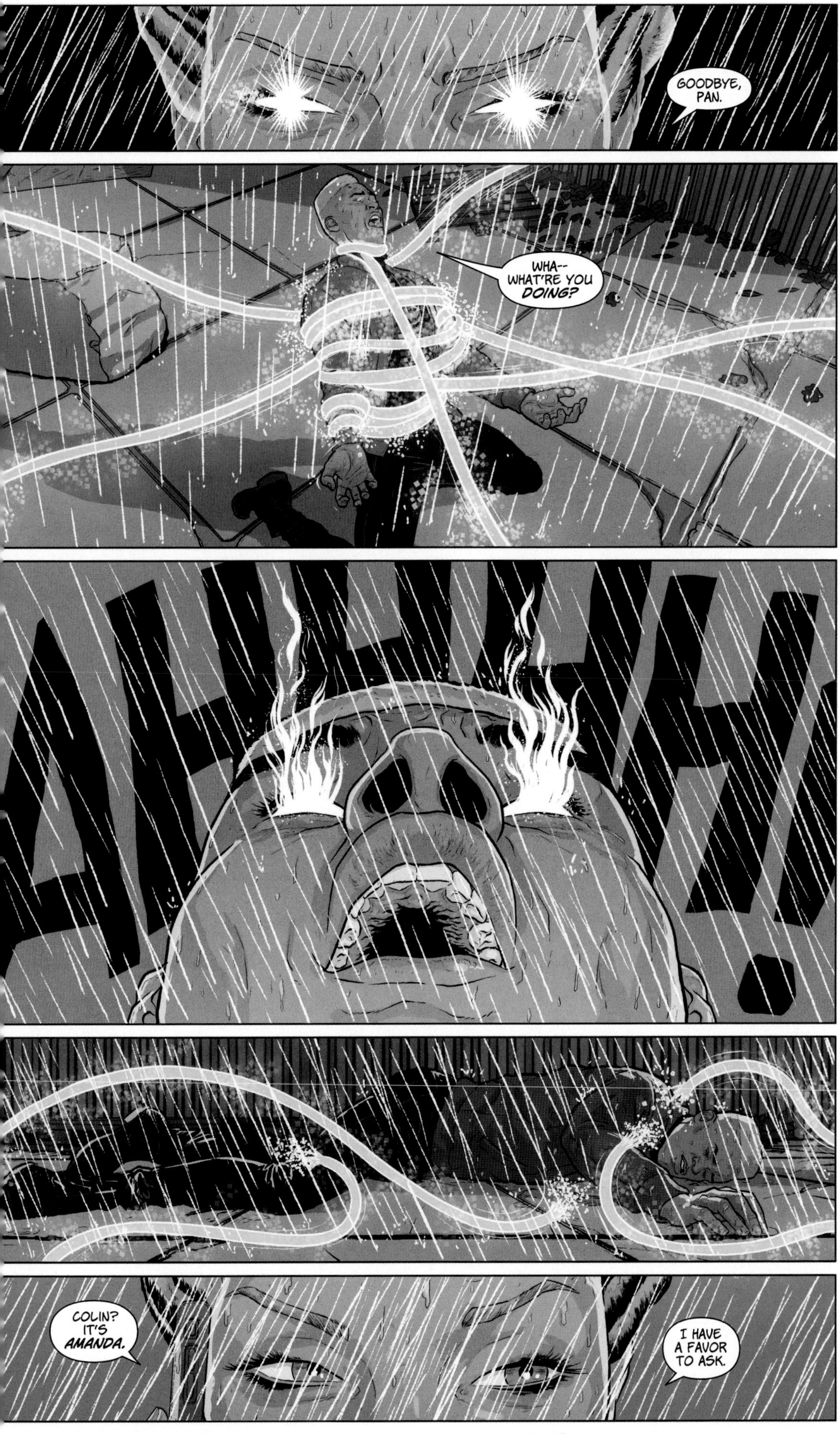
GOODBYE, PAN.
WHA-- WHAT'RE YOU DOING?
AHHHH!
COLIN? IT'S AMANDA.
I HAVE A FAVOR TO ASK.

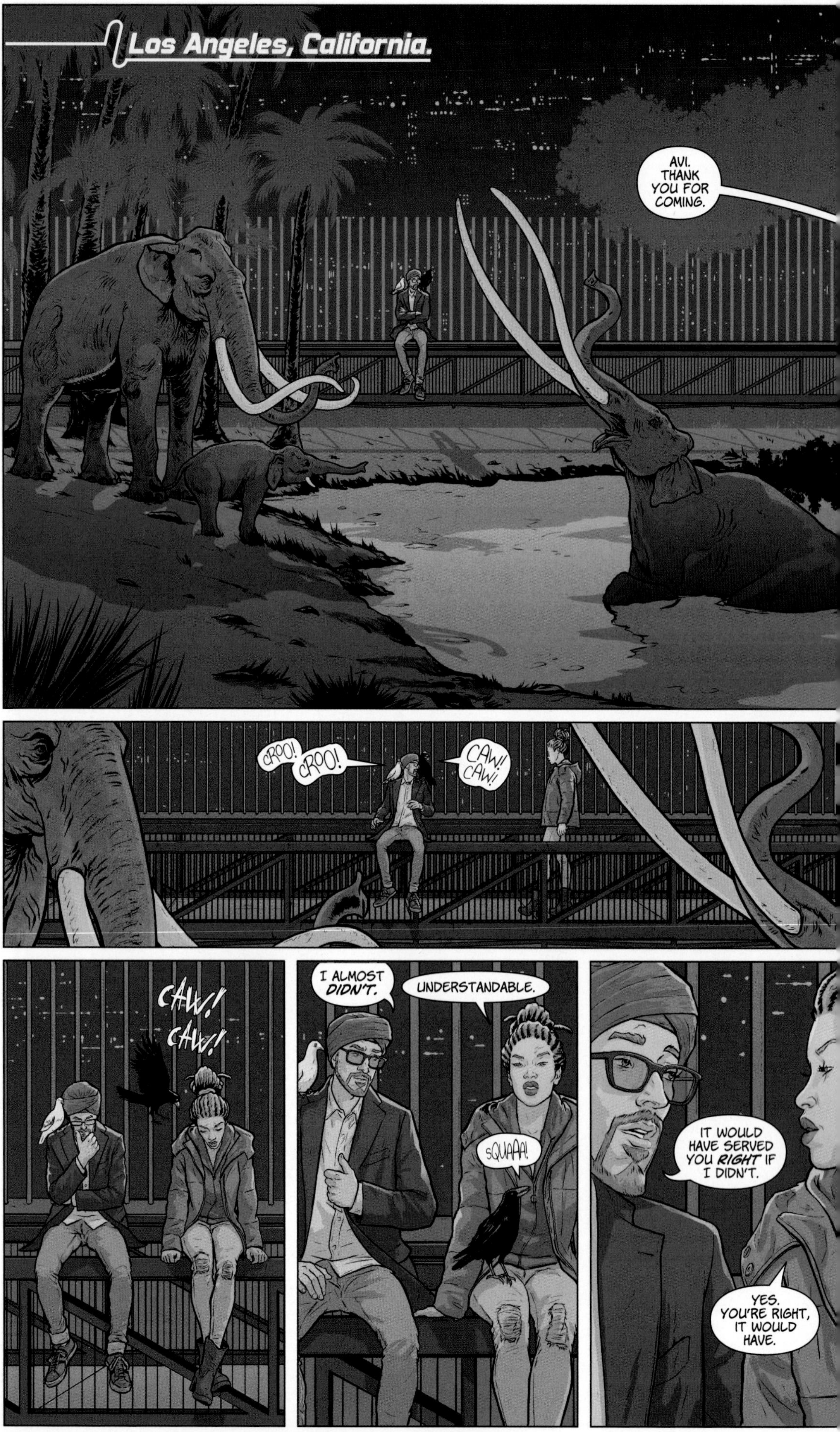
Los Angeles, California.
AVI. THANK YOU FOR COMING.
CROO! CROO!
CAW! CAW!
CAW! CAW!
I ALMOST DIDN'T.
UNDERSTANDABLE.
SQUAAA!
IT WOULD HAVE SERVED YOU RIGHT IF I DIDN'T.
YES. YOU'RE RIGHT, IT WOULD HAVE.

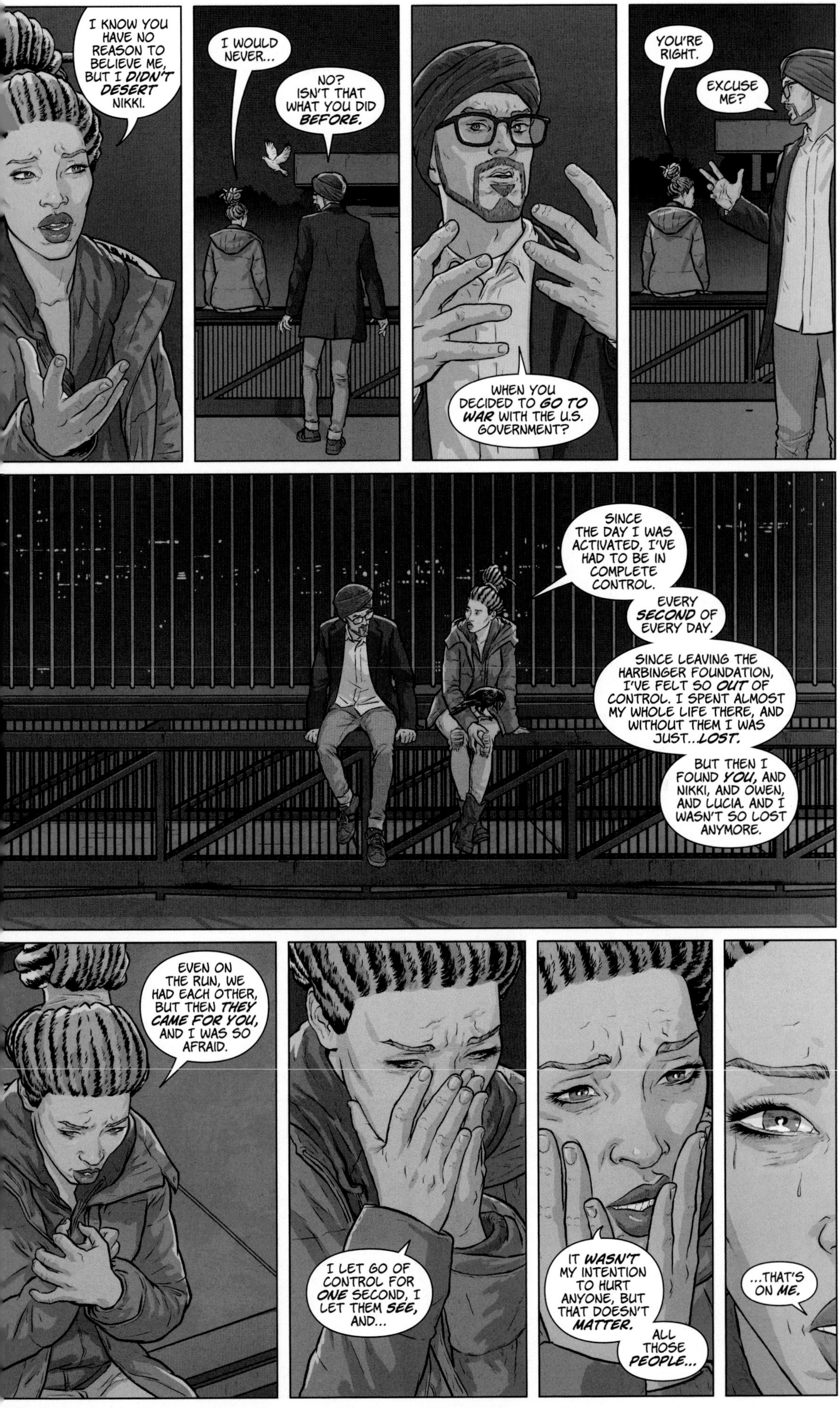
I KNOW YOU HAVE NO REASON TO BELIEVE ME, BUT I *DIDN'T DESERT* NIKKI.
I WOULD NEVER...
NO? ISN'T THAT WHAT YOU DID *BEFORE*.
WHEN YOU DECIDED TO *GO TO WAR* WITH THE U.S. GOVERNMENT?
YOU'RE RIGHT.
EXCUSE ME?
SINCE THE DAY I WAS ACTIVATED, I'VE HAD TO BE IN COMPLETE CONTROL.
EVERY *SECOND* OF EVERY DAY.
SINCE LEAVING THE HARBINGER FOUNDATION, I'VE FELT SO *OUT* OF CONTROL. I SPENT ALMOST MY WHOLE LIFE THERE, AND WITHOUT THEM I WAS JUST...*LOST.*
BUT THEN I FOUND *YOU,* AND NIKKI, AND OWEN, AND LUCIA. AND I WASN'T SO LOST ANYMORE.
EVEN ON THE RUN, WE HAD EACH OTHER, BUT THEN *THEY CAME FOR YOU,* AND I WAS SO AFRAID.
I LET GO OF CONTROL FOR *ONE* SECOND, I LET THEM *SEE,* AND...
IT *WASN'T* MY INTENTION TO HURT ANYONE, BUT THAT DOESN'T *MATTER.*
ALL THOSE *PEOPLE...*
...THAT'S ON *ME.*

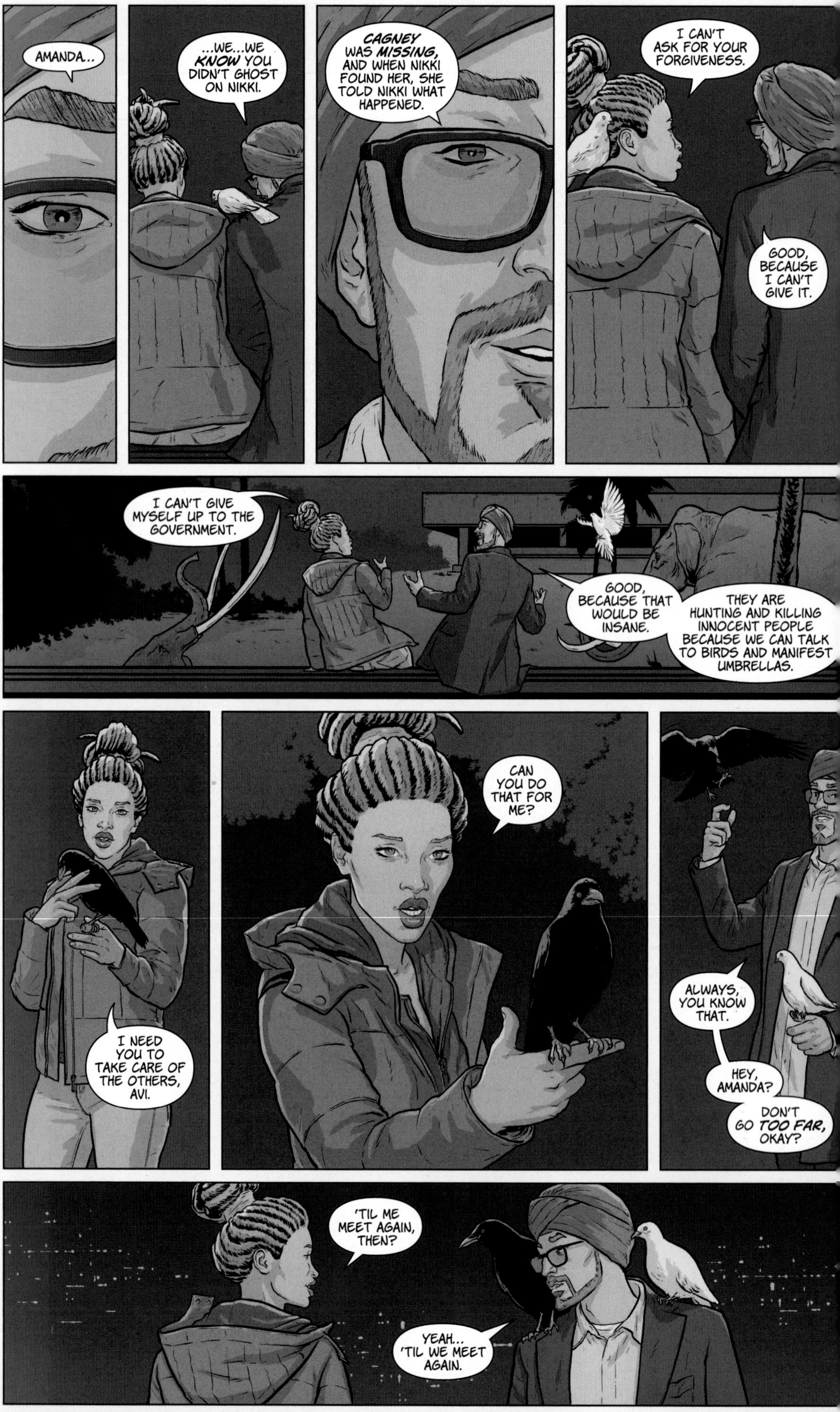
AMANDA...
...WE...WE KNOW YOU DIDN'T GHOST ON NIKKI.
CAGNEY WAS MISSING, AND WHEN NIKKI FOUND HER, SHE TOLD NIKKI WHAT HAPPENED.
I CAN'T ASK FOR YOUR FORGIVENESS.
GOOD, BECAUSE I CAN'T GIVE IT.
I CAN'T GIVE MYSELF UP TO THE GOVERNMENT.
GOOD, BECAUSE THAT WOULD BE INSANE.
THEY ARE HUNTING AND KILLING INNOCENT PEOPLE BECAUSE WE CAN TALK TO BIRDS AND MANIFEST UMBRELLAS.
I NEED YOU TO TAKE CARE OF THE OTHERS, AVI.
CAN YOU DO THAT FOR ME?
ALWAYS, YOU KNOW THAT.
HEY, AMANDA?
DON'T GO TOO FAR, OKAY?
'TIL ME MEET AGAIN, THEN?
YEAH... 'TIL WE MEET AGAIN.

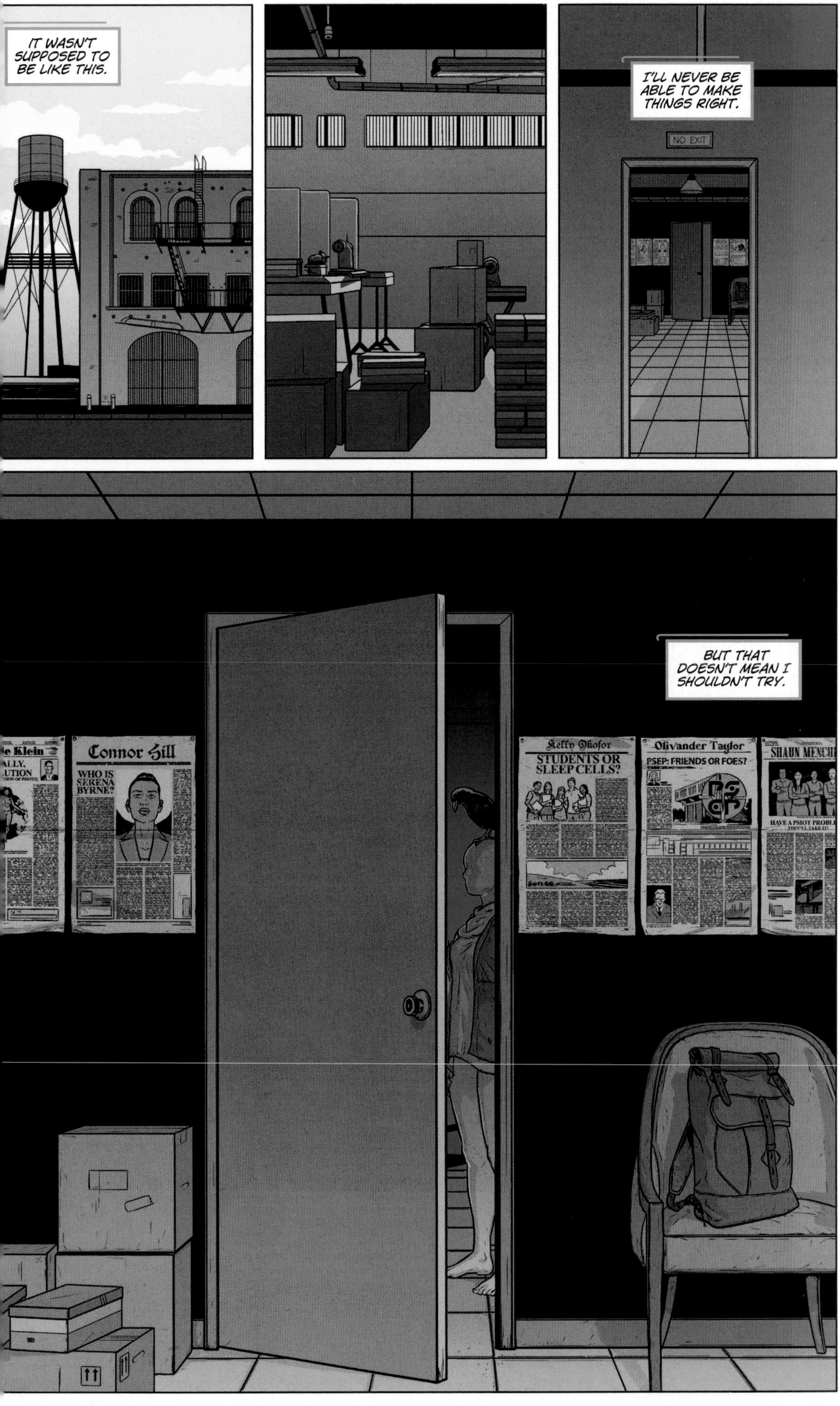
IT WASN'T SUPPOSED TO BE LIKE THIS.
I'LL NEVER BE ABLE TO MAKE THINGS RIGHT.
NO EXIT
BUT THAT DOESN'T MEAN I SHOULDN'T TRY.
Connor Hill
WHO IS SERENA BYRNE?
Kelly Okofor
STUDENTS OR SLEEP CELLS?
Olivander Taylor
PSEP: FRIENDS OR FOES?

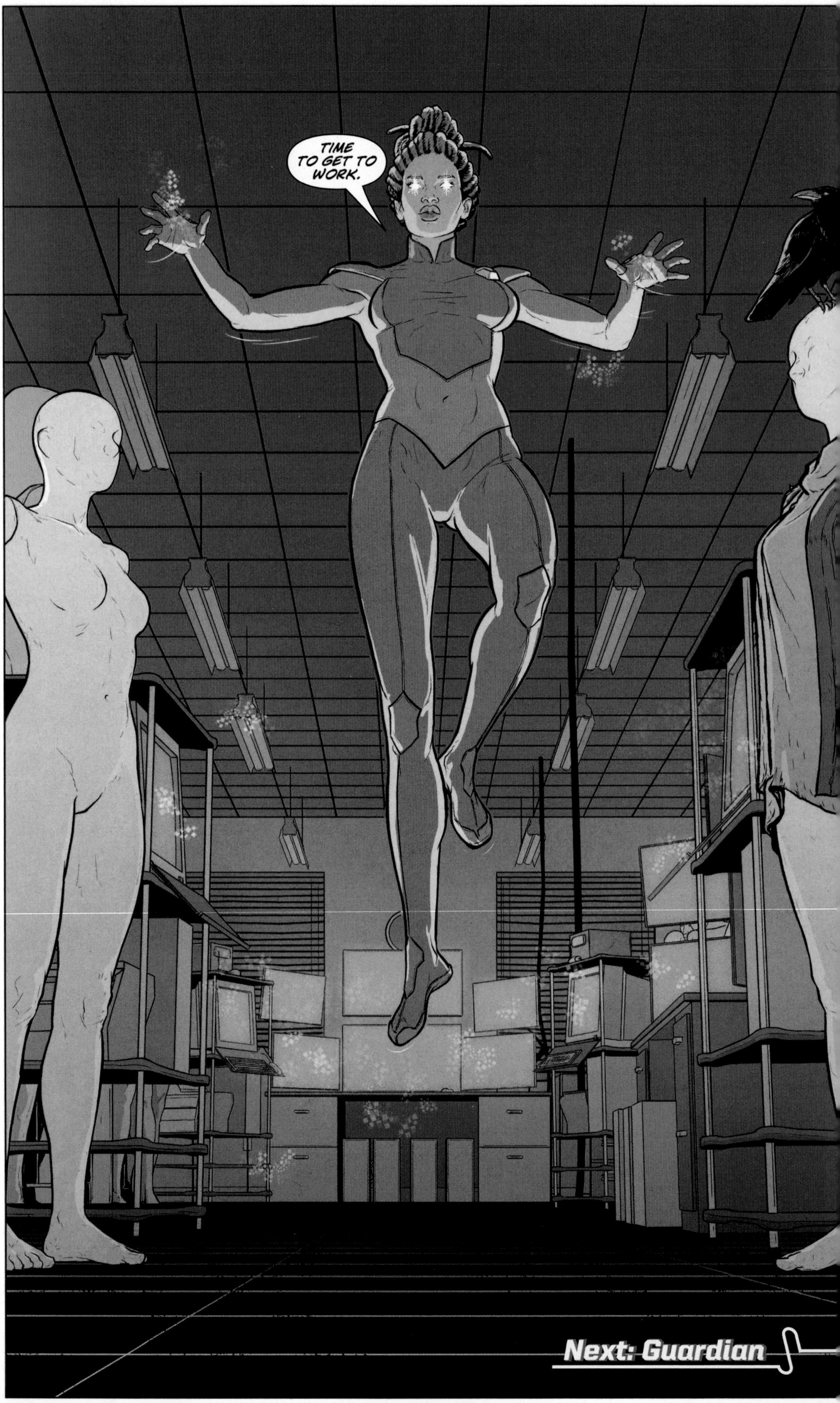
TIME TO GET TO WORK.
Next: Guardian

BEHIND THE SCENES

PAGE BY PAGE COMMENTARY WITH SERIES WRITER VITA AYALA

One of the things that I love about Amanda is her power set. Her powers have such a broad scope - she is both a hammer and a scalpel - and her reach is massive. I thought it would be good to orient the readers (new and old) in that right up front.

I thought the first three panels would be smaller, taking up the upper part of the page, and that the fourth panel would be a half page splash. I wanted to set the scene some, but wanted to still have the impact of the crash be intense.

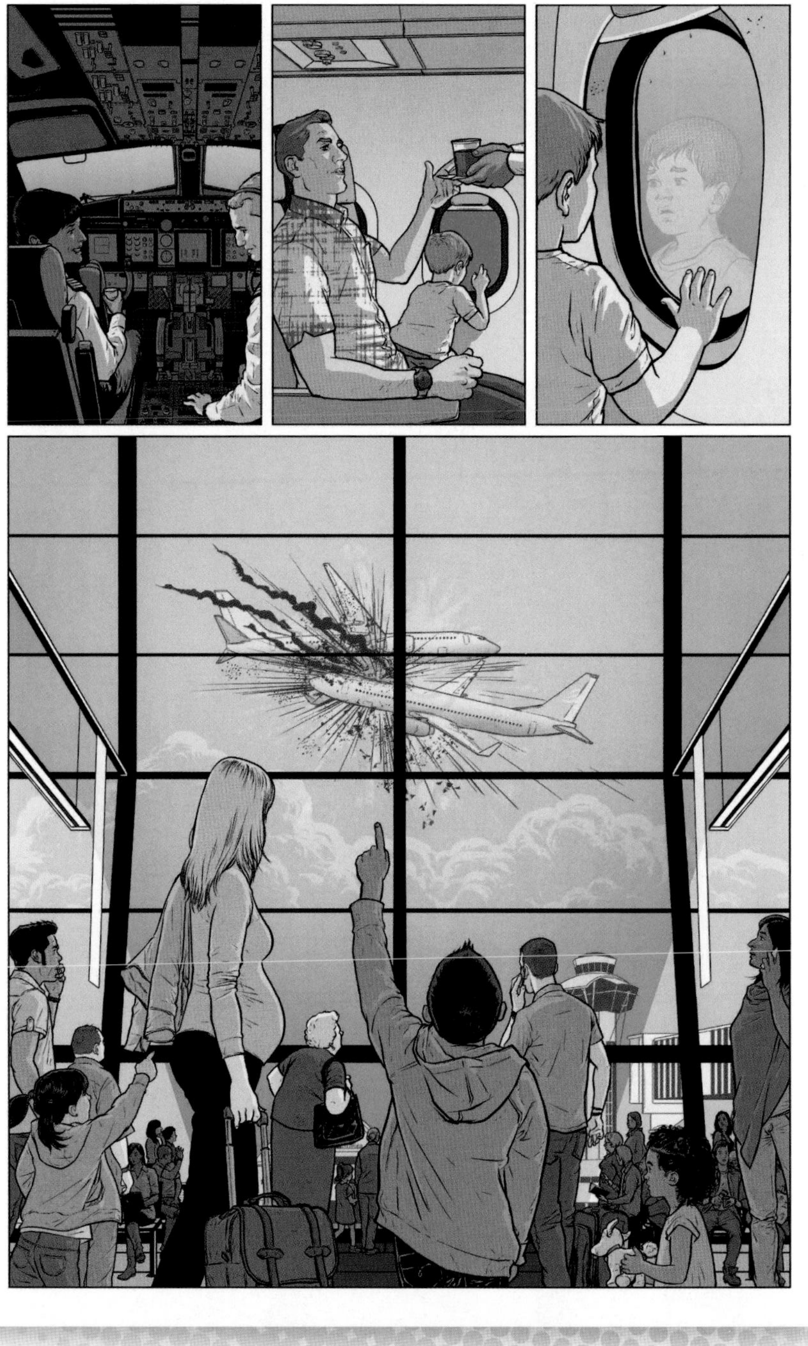

ART BY RAÚL ALLÉN AND PATRICIA MARTÍN

Originally presented in LIVEWIRE #1 PRE-ORDER EDITION.

When I was developing Pan de Santos, I was thinking about fear - causing it in others - and the draining of energy and courage. Amanda is so powerful that, to me, the worst enemy/obstacle that can stand against her is herself.

My mind immediately went to the story of when the Olympian gods were fighting their father, Cronus, and the Titans, and to the mythological character Pan, who claimed that it was he that scared the Titans so badly that they retreated. Before I had the specifics of the antagonist's power set, I knew then that they had to be some sort of mirror - because in order to redeem Amanda, we first have to show her where she has failed.

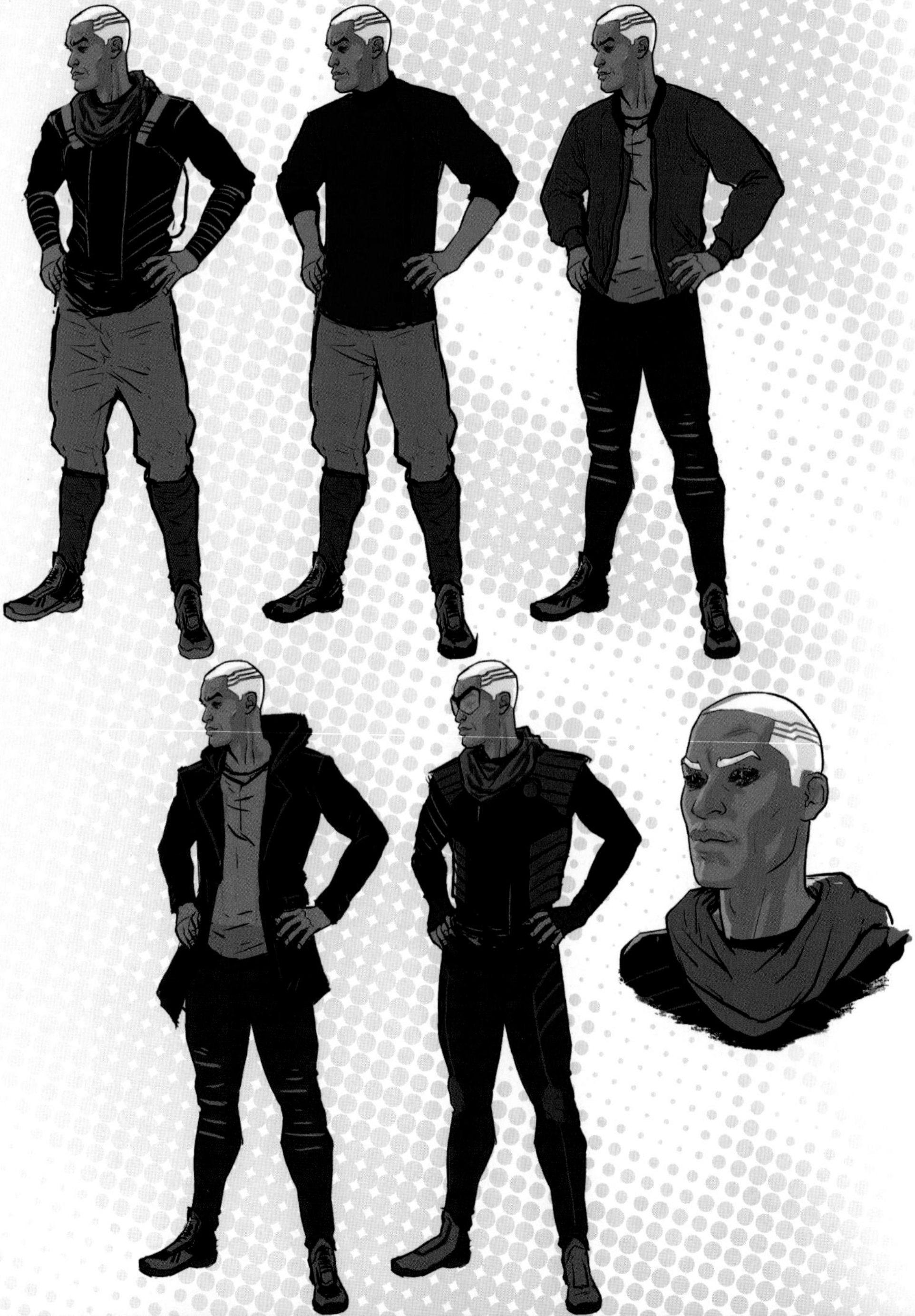

EARLY CONCEPT SKETCHES BY **RAÚL ALLÉN**

Pan is of Latinx descent. They are a psiot mercenary. They have the ability to absorb the electrical energy from people, and as a byproduct absorb their memories temporarily. I was thinking maybe they could almost be like a vampire this way - they live off the energy.

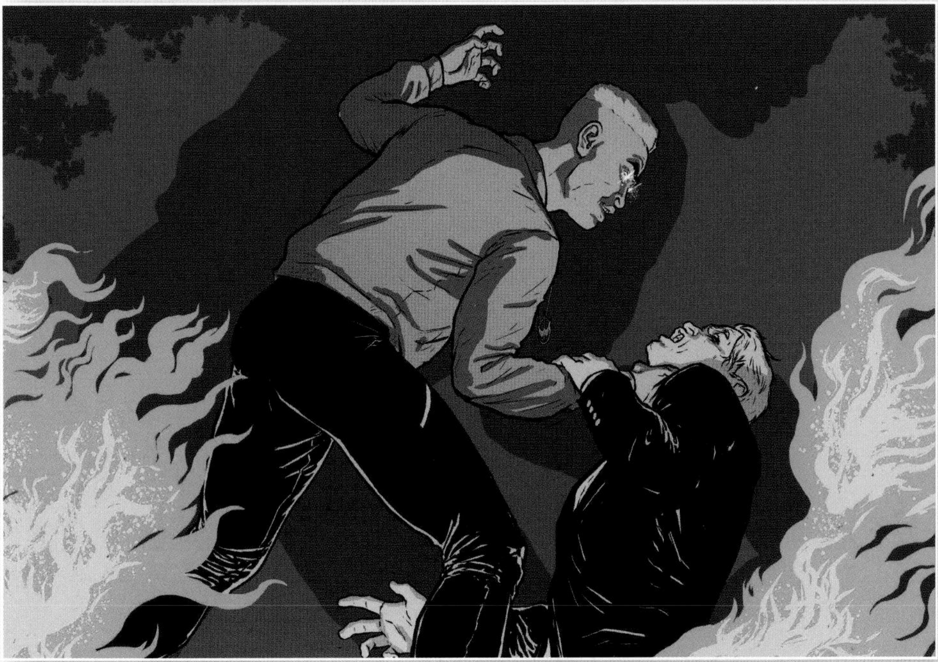

Design-wise, I was not sure if they should be intimidating or look innocent/non-threatening. They would have to be strong enough to be able to physically battle with Amanda, but their real power comes from draining their victims, so they didn't have to be a brute. Going back to Pan, satyrs are not big, but they are strong and crafty.

Pan is a Harada truther, so I wanted to have a slightly altered version of the Harbinger symbol on their clothing somewhere. Clearly recognizable and related, but altered somehow. The necklace that Raúl and Patricia brought to the design was perfect.

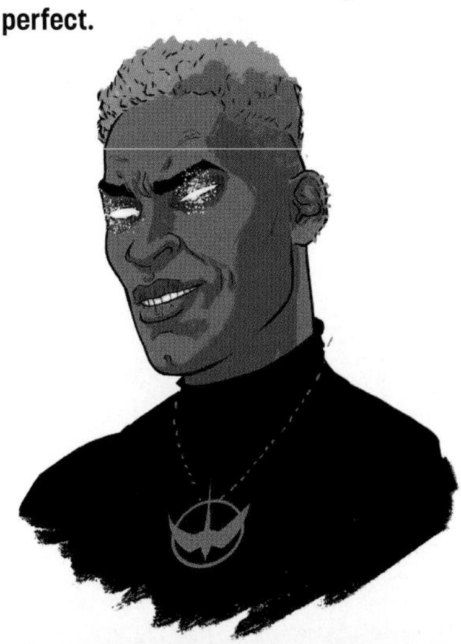

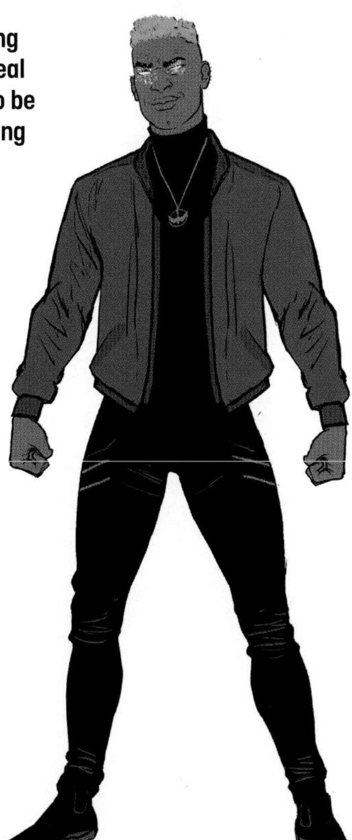

ART BY **RAÚL ALLÉN** AND **PATRICIA MARTÍN**

Originally presented in LIVEWIRE #2 PRE-ORDER EDITION

SPARK FROM THE PAST WITH SERIES WRITER VITA AYALA

In issue three, we make Livewire doubt the very foundation of her conviction. It is the final piece of breaking Amanda down, so that she is able to really work towards healing and rebuilding herself.

There is a story that I heard once. Someone claimed it was an African proverb, but I am not sure that it is true. The story goes that a mother monkey had two babies – twins – one clung to her back, and the other (her favorite), she cradled in her arms. The favorite grew plump and healthy, and the other grew thin and weathered. One day a leopard came, and the mother was forced to release her favorite child in order to get away. The little fat baby fell and was devoured by the leopard, because it was unused to holding on for itself, but the other baby was strong and managed to hold fast.

Amanda is no pampered darling, by far, but Pan has had to endure things – DO things – that are almost unfathomable to survive, as they were cast off by Harada even as Livewire was exalted.

Pan is a True Believer in Toyo's vision. What Amanda did is a monstrous betrayal in their eyes completely unforgivable. I imagi them almost like a religious zeal but not the kind that prays – the kind that burns witches for their god. They are going to draw out their "sister's" death, make her understand how wicked she was in her actions before killing her.

They are two sides to the same coin, the two paths that diverge in the wood, and they have come back together now to face off.

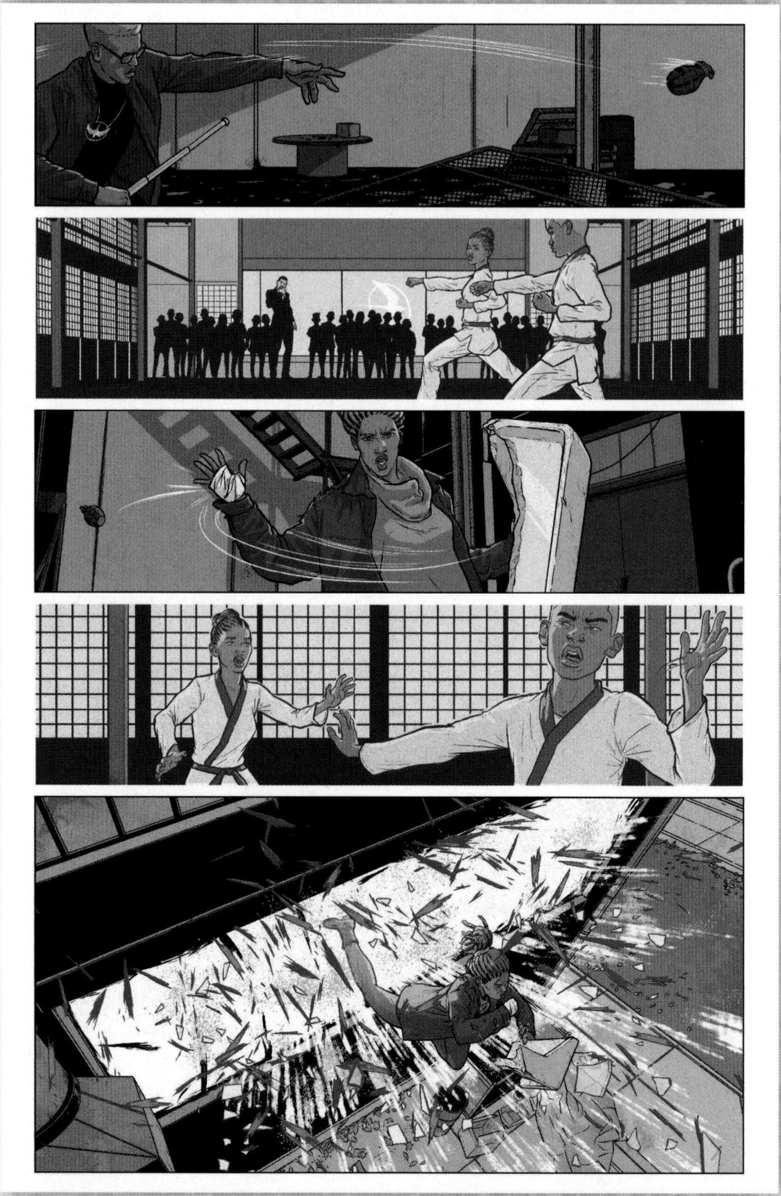

ART BY RAÚL ALLÈN AND PATRICIA MARTÍN

ee this page as a kind of verted version of HARBINGER Page 4 (our first introduction Peter).

of the visual noise that we ve come to associate with Amanda being around is gone. Things seem muted somehow, just a TINY BIT out of focus. Things seem much more still somehow than in the last two issues. I wanted to find a way to visually incorporate the LACK of her hearing/feeling technology.

The bruises from Amanda's fight with Kyle are fading, but still on her.

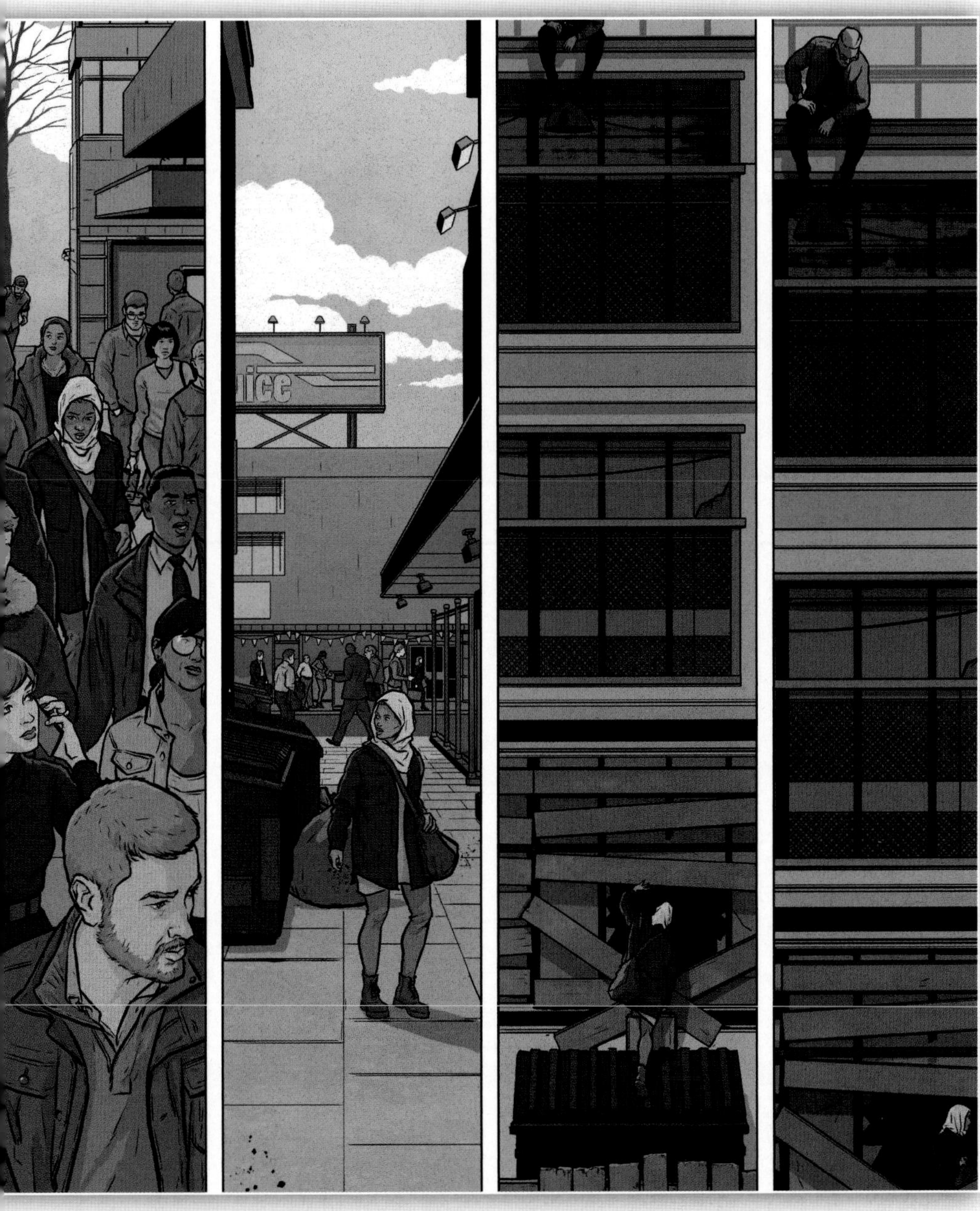

Coming into this issue, Amanda has finally realized/acknowledged her responsibility for the people who got hurt during Harbinger Wars 2.

Though she was protecting her kids, and fighting a government who was hunting and killing her kind (psiots) wholesale (many of them innocent), her actions in opposing them caused a lot of bad things to happen. Though it wasn't her goal to sow bad things to innocent people, Amanda is responsible for all the pain and suffering caused by turning off the power to the country.

In this issue, she will have to (emotionally) decide what she wants to do and be. Will she let Pan kill her, or will she fight back? SHOULD she let Pan kill her, for what she has done, or is living with the guilt and letting it guide her decisions from now on better?

She will come to understand that there is no action she can take that will atone for the pain she caused, but she will also decide that she will spend the rest of her life doing good/helping people/saving people. She will do this because she believes, at her core, that helping people is the greatest good, and her responsibility towards those that she hurt demands it. She will reemerge from her fight with Pan a fugitive hero.

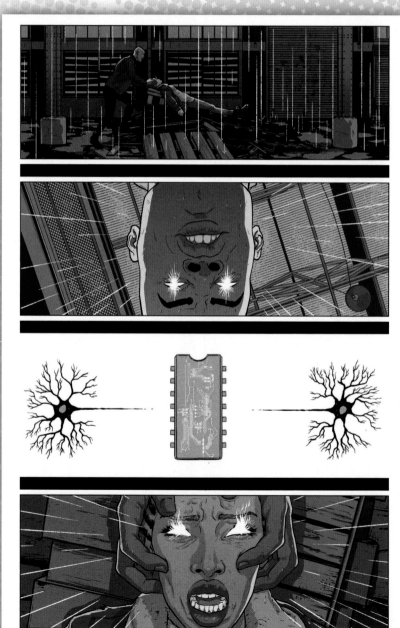

is the emotional wrap up of the arc. We already erstand where Amanda stands, with herself, and now we get to see where she stands with the kids. It will be difficult, but hopeful.

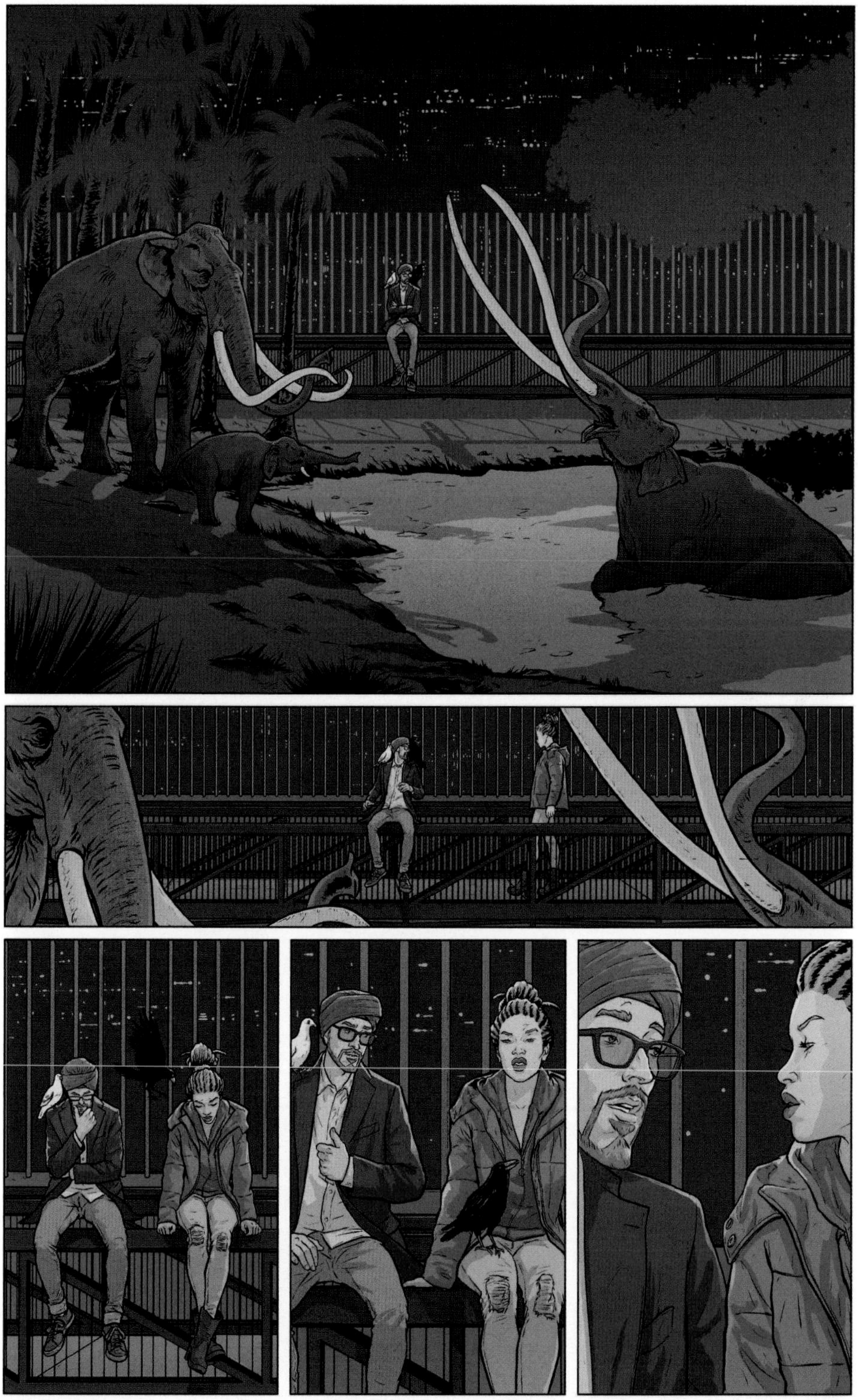

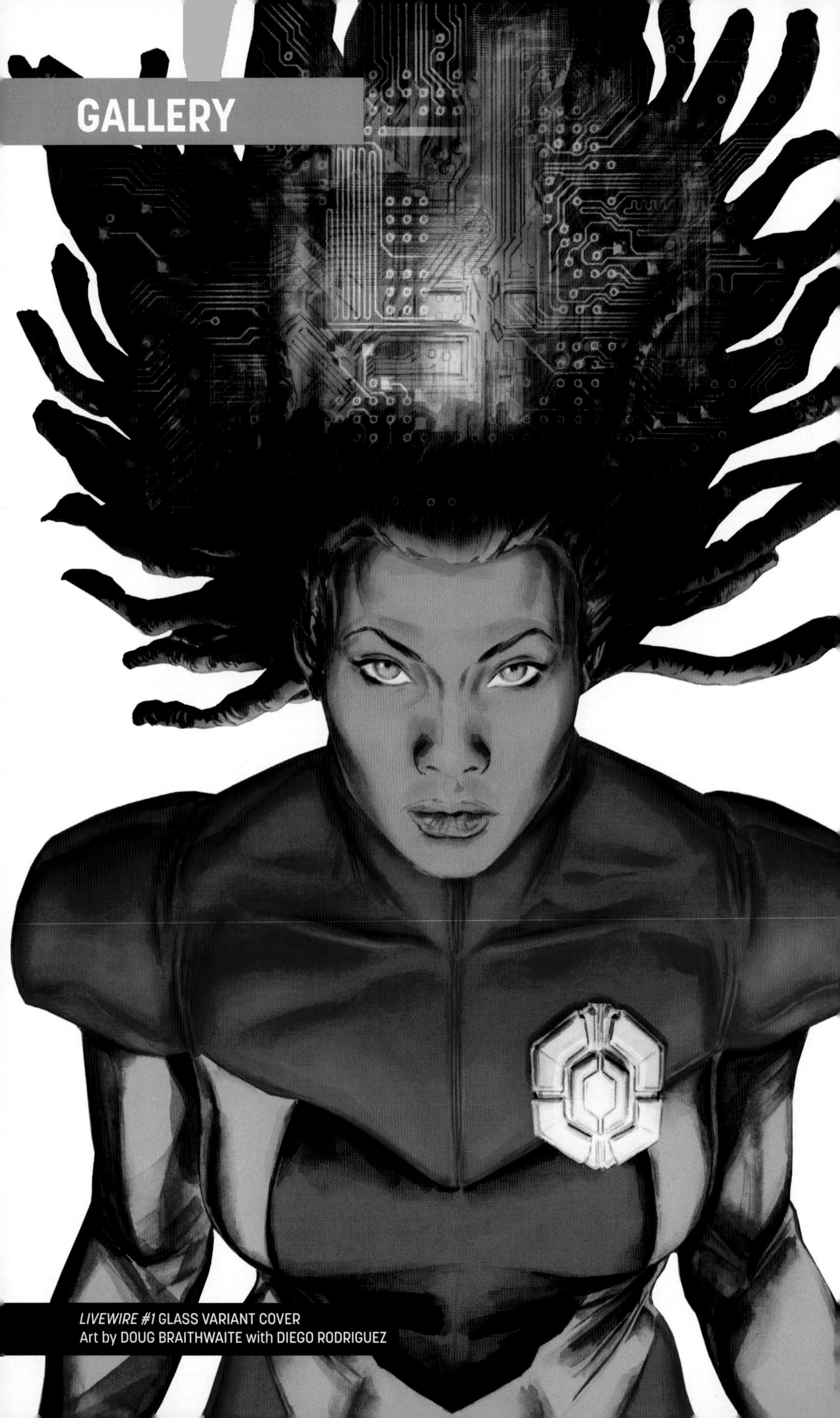

LIVEWIRE #1 GLASS VARIANT COVER
Art by DOUG BRAITHWAITE with DIEGO RODRIGUEZ

LIVEWIRE #1 COVER B
Art by HARVEY TOLIBAO with DIEGO RODRIGUEZ

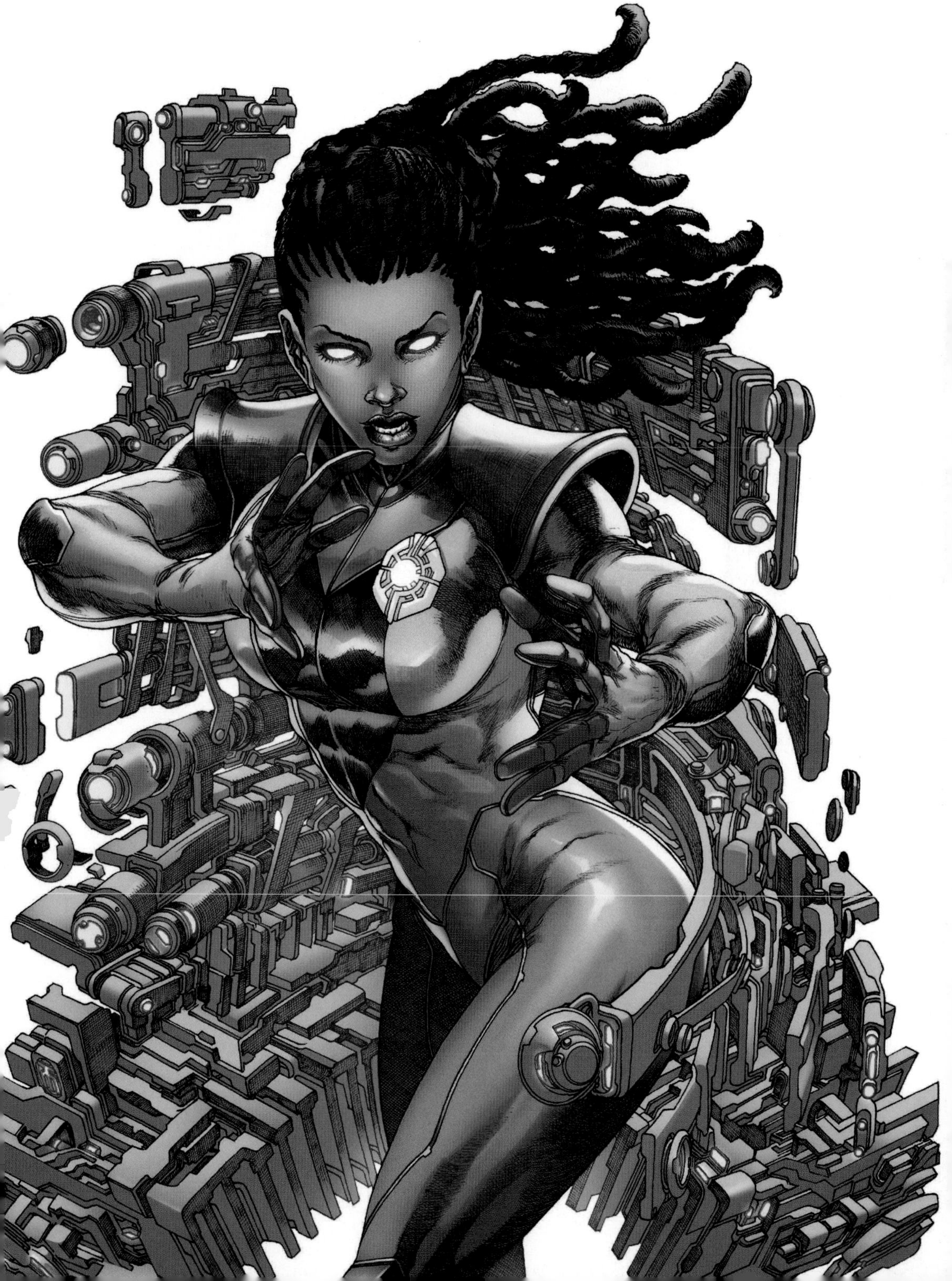

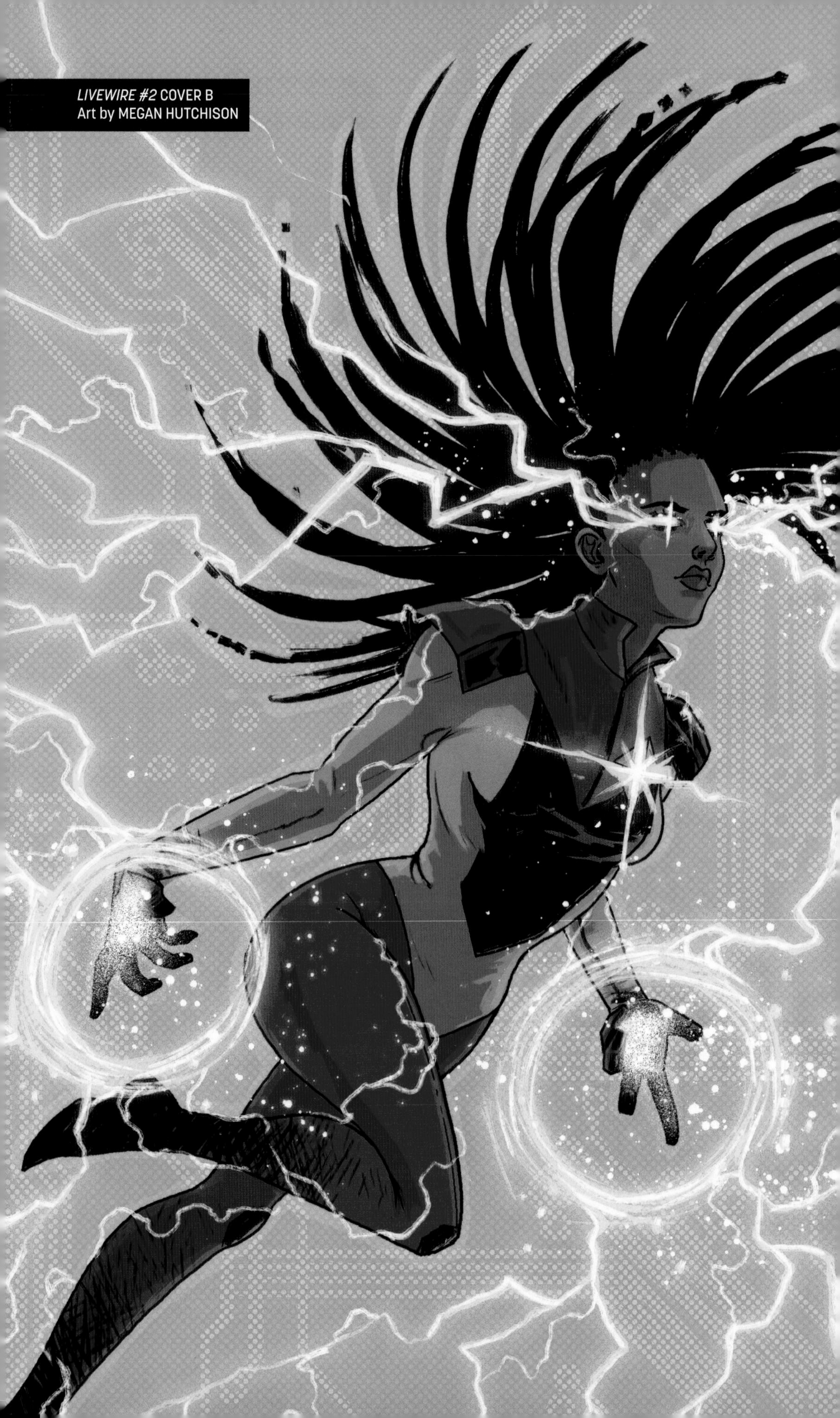

LIVEWIRE #2 COVER B
Art by MEGAN HUTCHISON

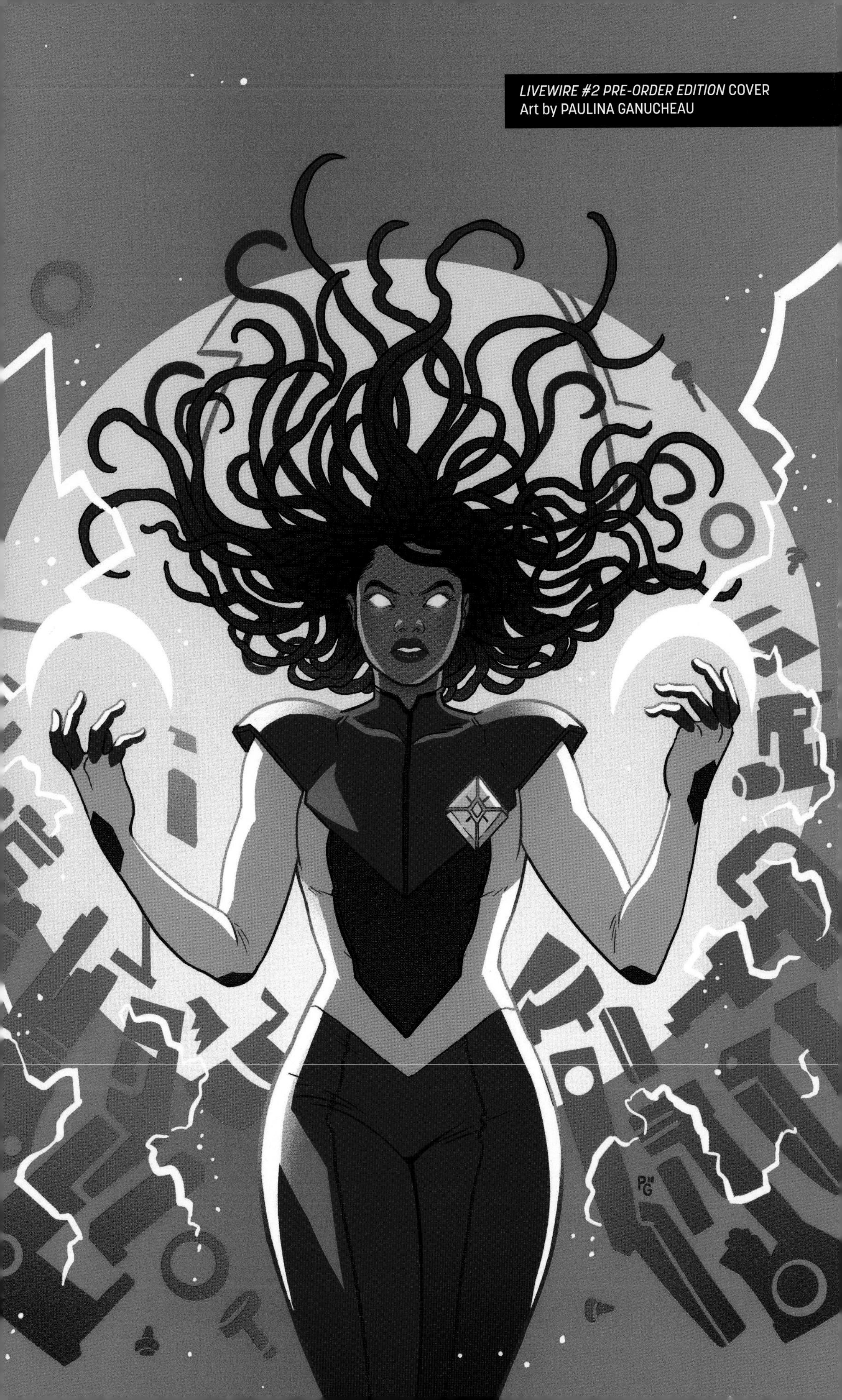

LIVEWIRE #2 PRE-ORDER EDITION COVER
Art by PAULINA GANUCHEAU

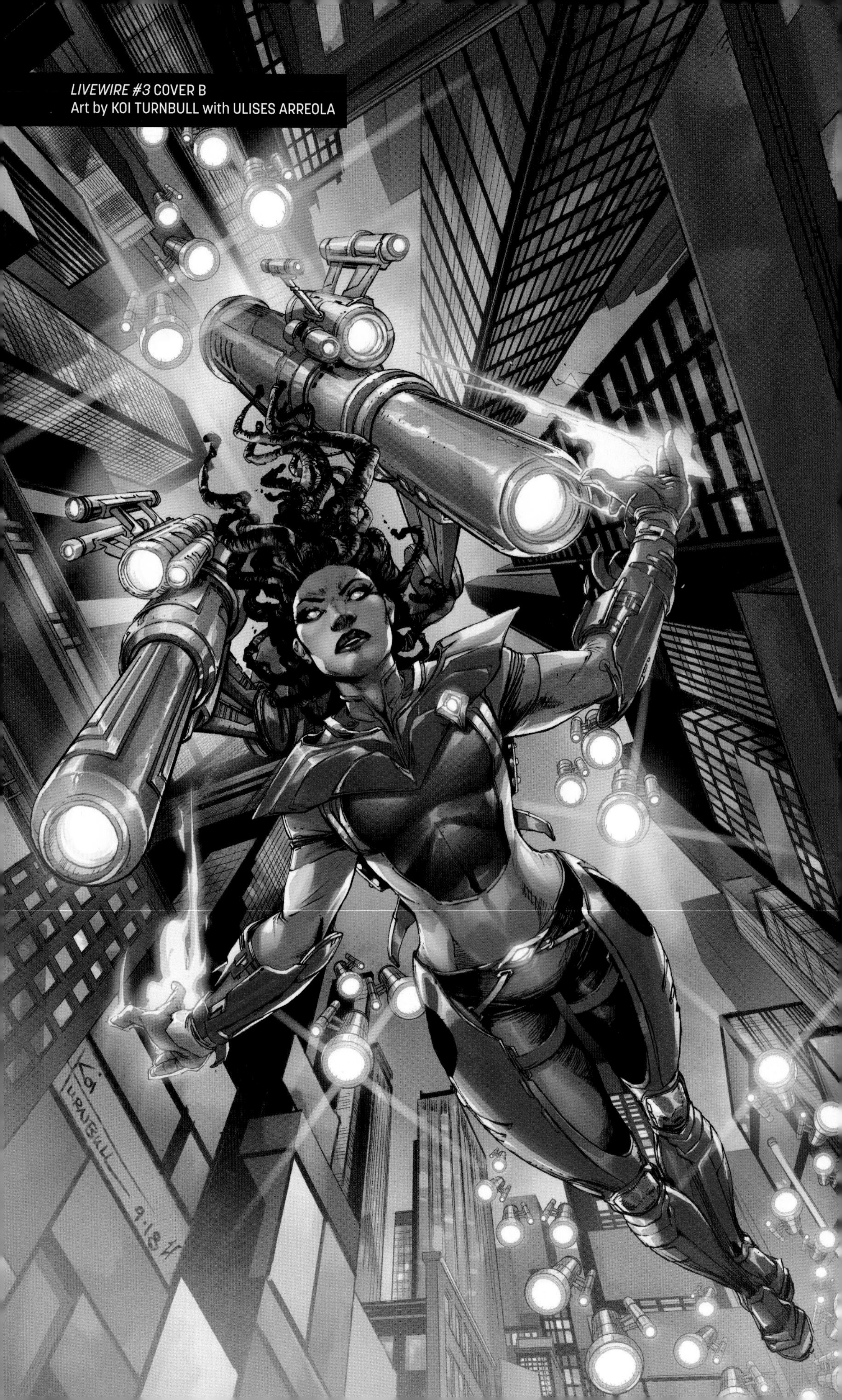

LIVEWIRE #3 COVER B
Art by KOI TURNBULL with ULISES ARREOLA

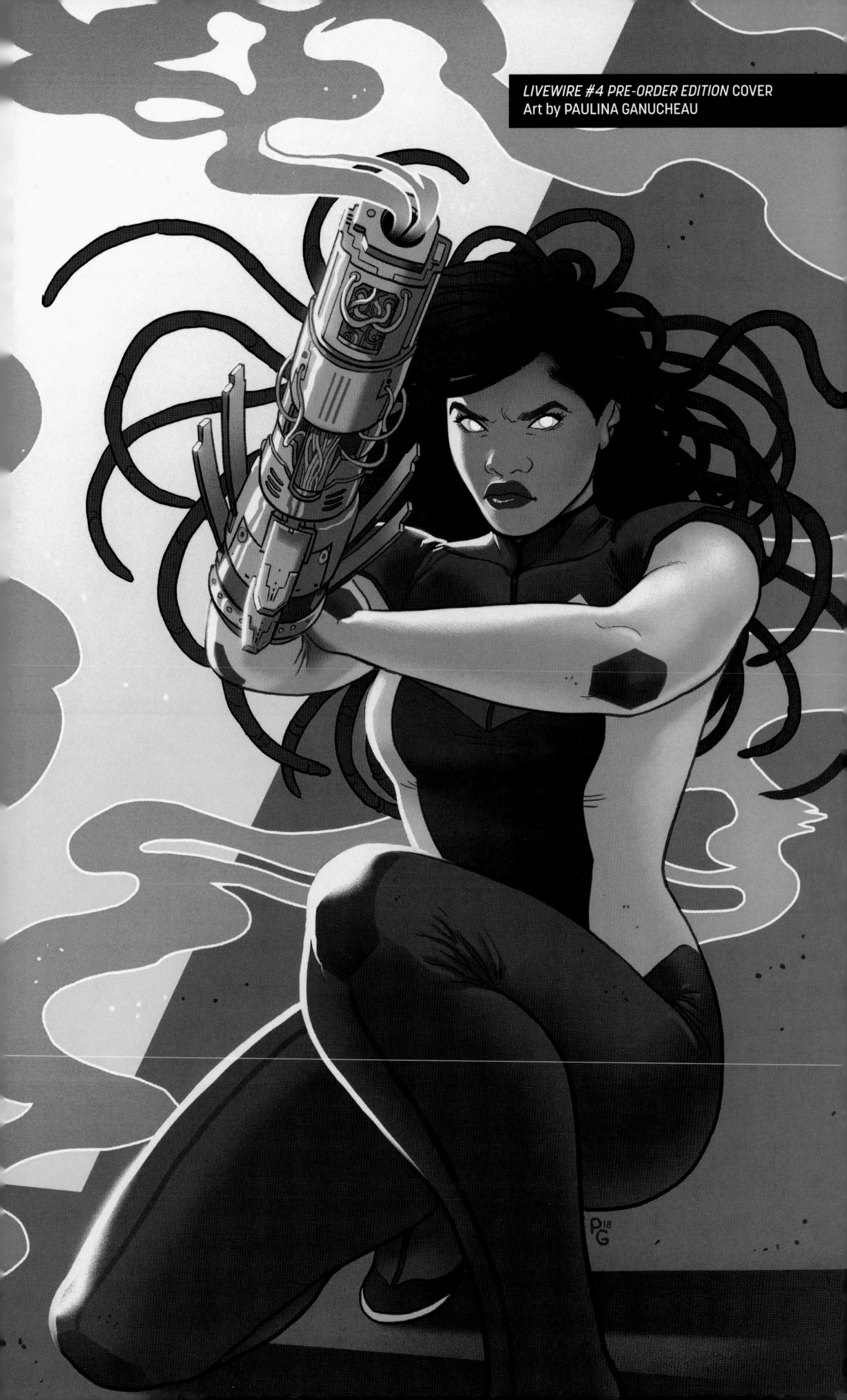
PG 18

LIVEWIRE #4 PRE-ORDER EDITION COVER
Art by PAULINA GANUCHEAU

LIVEWIRE #2, p. 6
Process and line art by RAÚL ALLÉN and PATRICIA MARTÍN

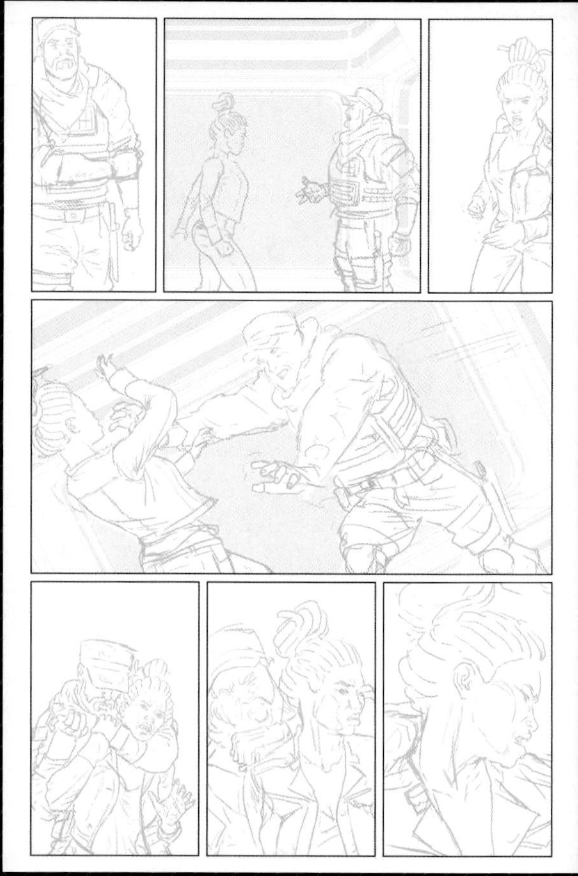

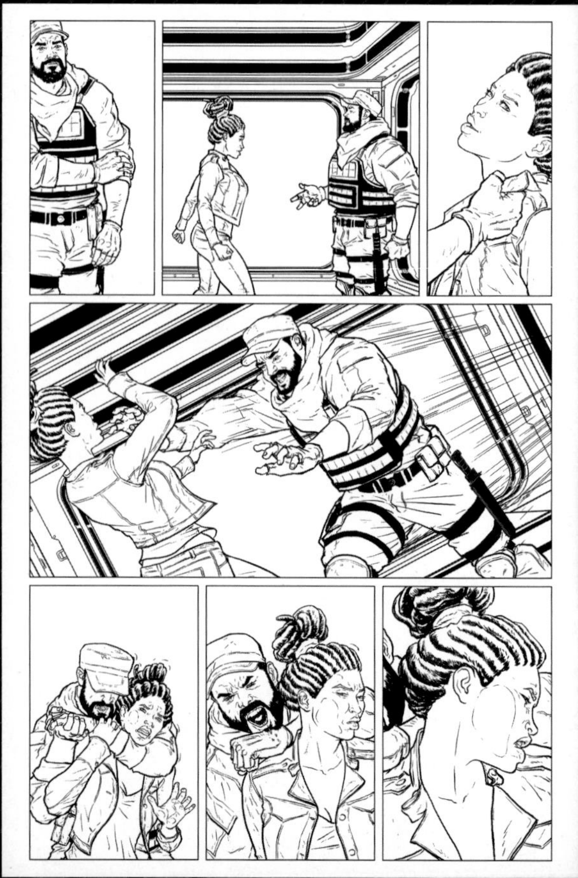

LIVEWIRE #2, p. 14
Process and line art by RAÚL and PATRICIA MARTÍN

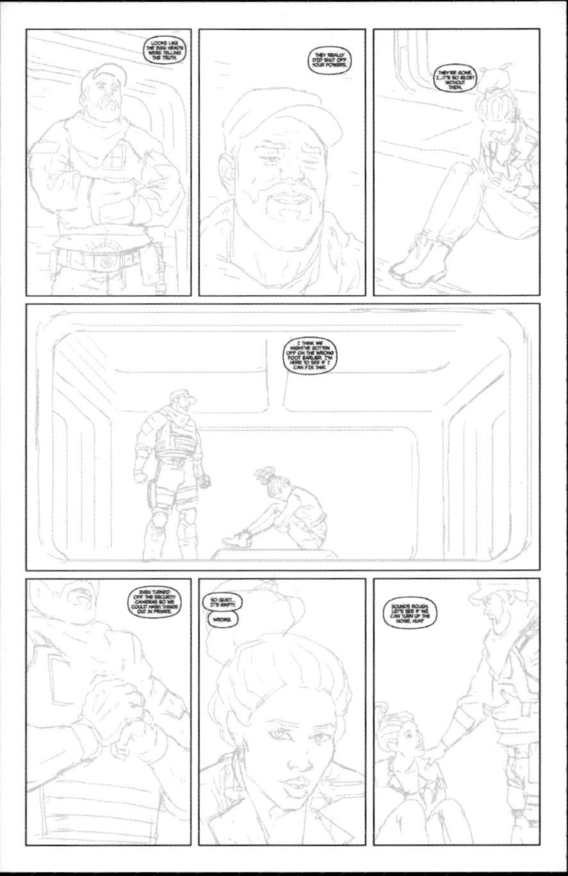
LOOKS LIKE THE BIG HEADS WERE TELLING THE TRUTH.
THEY REALLY DID SHUT OFF YOUR POWERS.
THEY'RE GONE. I...IT'S SO QUIET WITHOUT THEM.
I THINK WE MIGHT'VE GOTTEN OFF ON THE WRONG FOOT EARLIER. I'M HERE TO SEE IF I CAN FIX THAT.
EVEN TURNED OFF THE SECURITY CAMERAS SO WE COULD HASH THINGS OUT IN PRIVATE.
SO QUIET... IT'S EMPTY.
WRONG.
SOUNDS ROUGH. LET'S SEE IF WE CAN TURN UP THE NOISE, HUH?

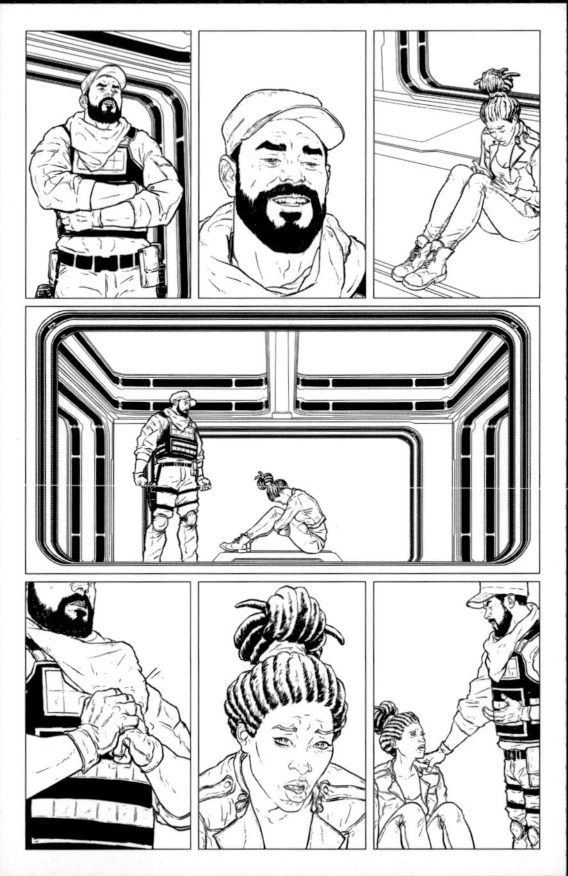

LIVEWIRE #3, p. 8
Process and line art by RAÚL ALLÉN
and PATRICIA MARTÍN

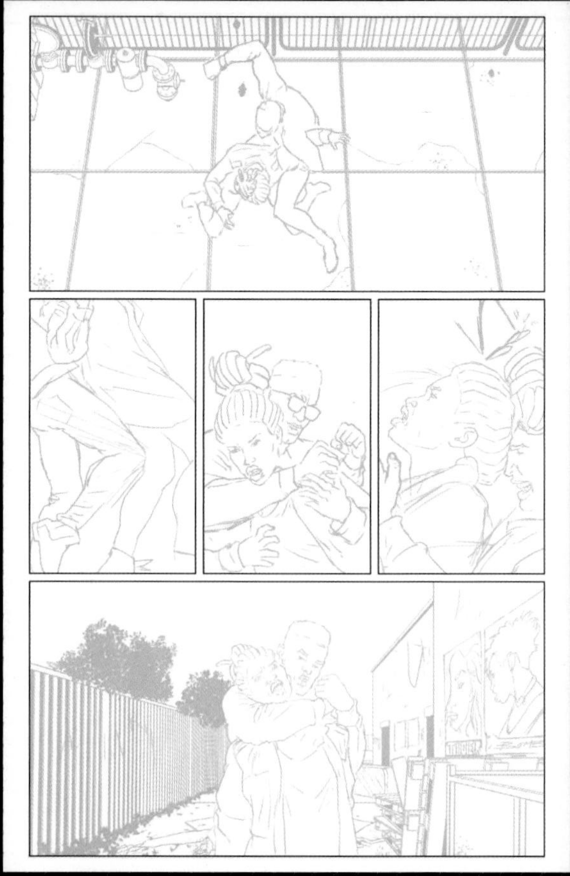

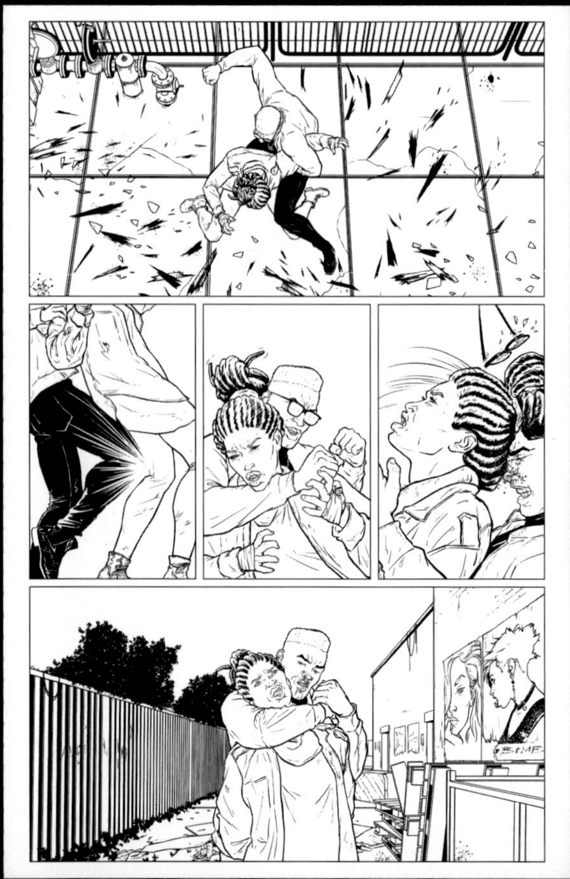

LIVEWIRE #3, p. 11
Process and line art by R
and PATRICIA MARTÍN

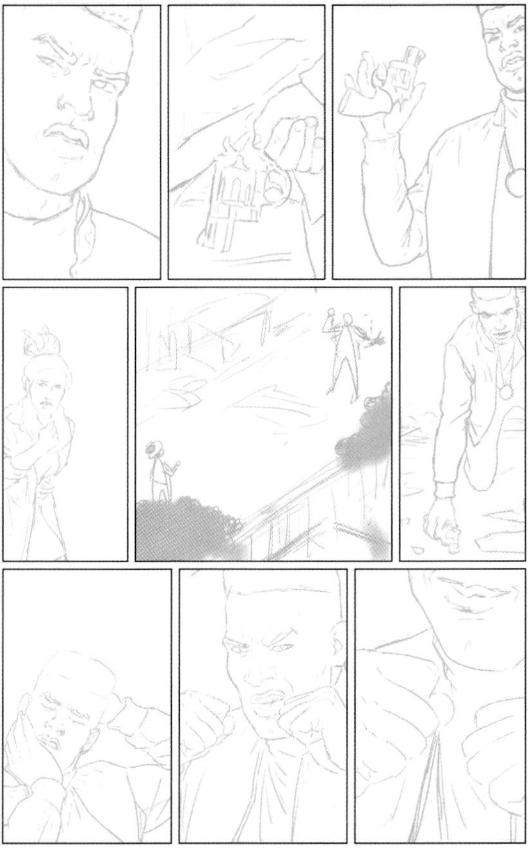

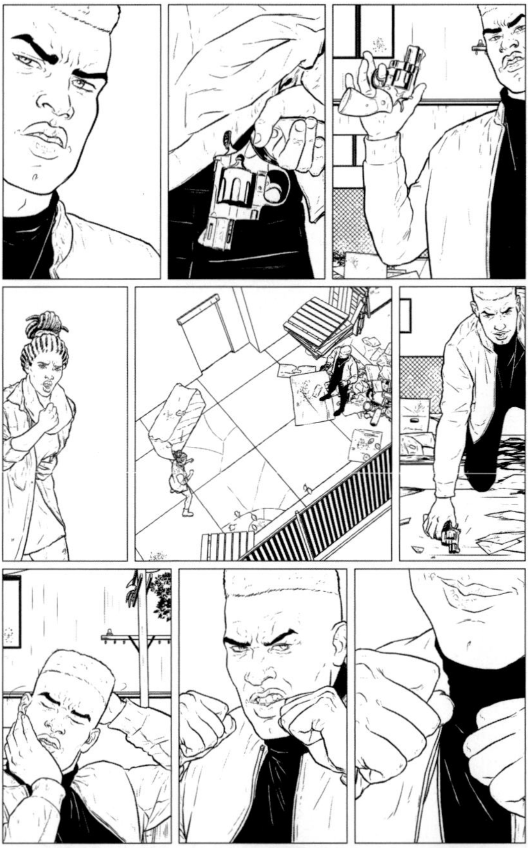

EXPLORE THE VALIANT

ACTION & ADVENTURE

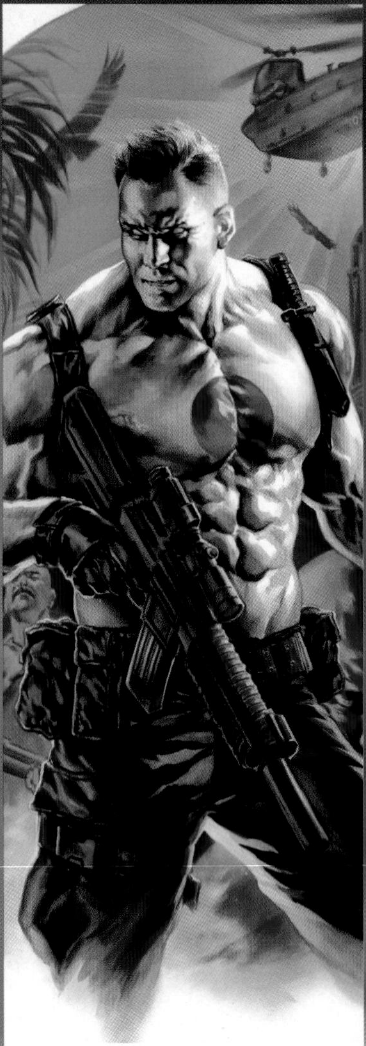

BLOODSHOT SALVATION VOL. 1: THE BOOK OF REVENGE
ISBN: 978-1-68215-255-3
NINJA-K VOL. 1: THE NINJA FILES
ISBN: 978-1-68215-259-1
SAVAGE
ISBN: 978-1-68215-189-1
WRATH OF THE ETERNAL WARRIOR VOL. 1: RISEN
ISBN: 978-1-68215-123-5
X-O MANOWAR (2017) VOL. 1: SOLDIER
ISBN: 978-1-68215-205-8

BLOCKBUSTER ADVENTURE

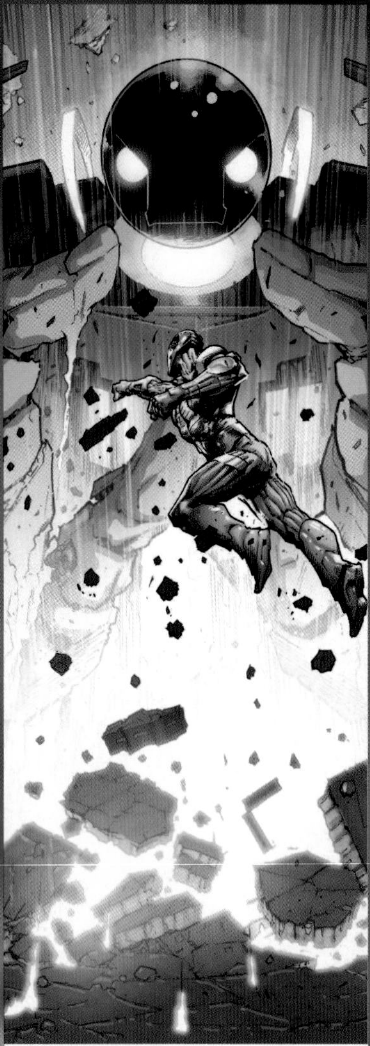

4001 A.D.
ISBN: 978-1-68215-143-3
ARMOR HUNTERS
ISBN: 978-1-939346-45-2
BOOK OF DEATH
ISBN: 978-1-939346-97-1
HARBINGER WARS
ISBN: 978-1-939346-09-4
THE VALIANT
ISBN: 978-1-939346-60-5

COMEDY

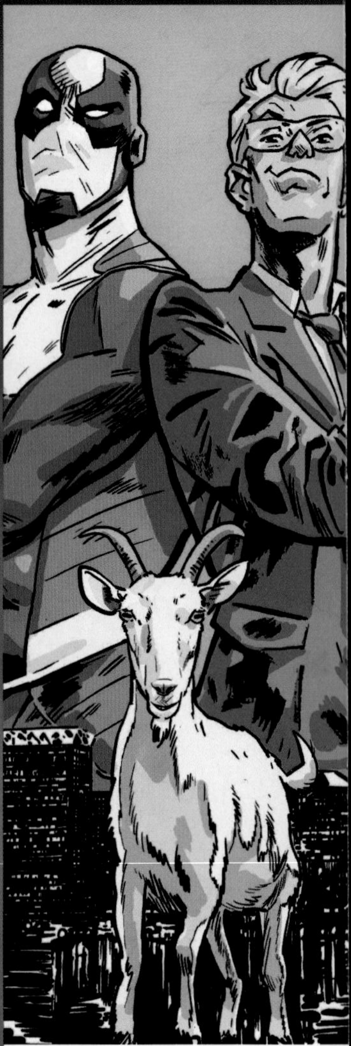

A&A: THE ADVENTURES OF ARCHER & ARMSTRONG VOL. 1: IN THE BAG
ISBN: 978-1-68215-149-5
THE DELINQUENTS
ISBN: 978-1-939346-51-3
QUANTUM AND WOODY! (2017) VOL. 1: KISS KISS, KLANG KLANG
ISBN: 978-1-68215-269-0

NIVERSE FOR ONLY $9.99

HORROR & MYSTERY

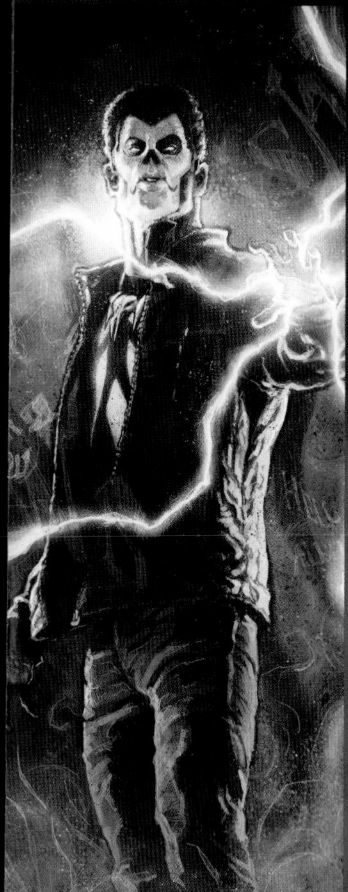

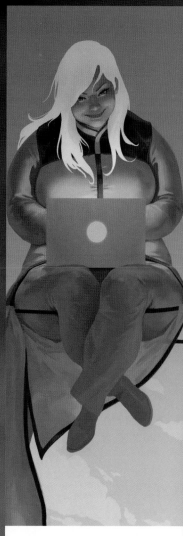

BRITANNIA
ISBN: 978-1-68215-185-3
THE DEATH-DEFYING DOCTOR MIRAGE
ISBN: 978-1-939346-49-0
RAPTURE
ISBN: 978-1-68215-225-6
SHADOWMAN (2018) VOL. 1: FEAR OF THE DARK
ISBN: 978-1-68215-239-3

SCIENCE FICTION & FANTASY

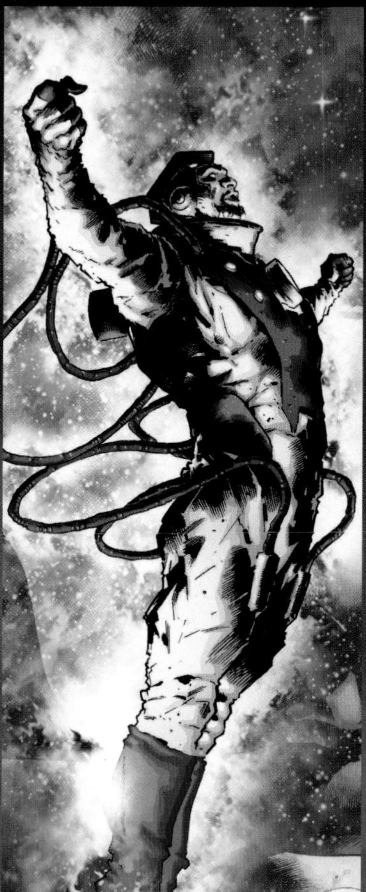

DIVINITY
ISBN: 978-1-939346-76-6
IMPERIUM VOL. 1: COLLECTING MONSTERS
ISBN: 978-1-939346-75-9
IVAR, TIMEWALKER VOL. 1: MAKING HISTORY
ISBN: 978-1-939346-63-6
RAI VOL. 1: WELCOME TO NEW JAPAN
ISBN: 978-1-939346-41-4
WAR MOTHER
ISBN: 978-1-68215-237-9

TEEN ADVENTURE

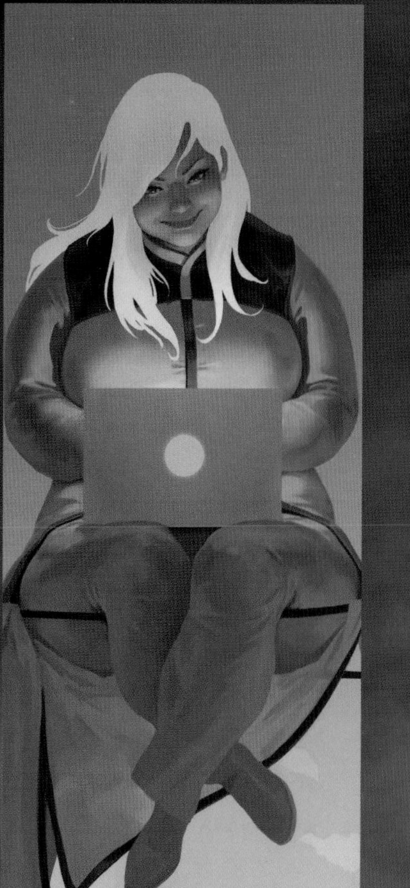

FAITH VOL. 1: HOLLYWOOD AND VINE
ISBN: 978-1-68215-121-1
GENERATION ZERO VOL. 1: WE ARE THE FUTURE
ISBN: 978-1-68215-175-4
HARBINGER RENEGADE VOL. 1: THE JUDGMENT OF SOLOMON
ISBN: 978-1-68215-169-3
LIVEWIRE VOL. 1: FUGITIVE
ISBN: 978-1-68215-301-7
SECRET WEAPONS
ISBN: 978-1-68215-229-4

Discover the entire Valiant Universe of titles at VALIANTENTERTAINMENT.COM/ALL-SERIES/

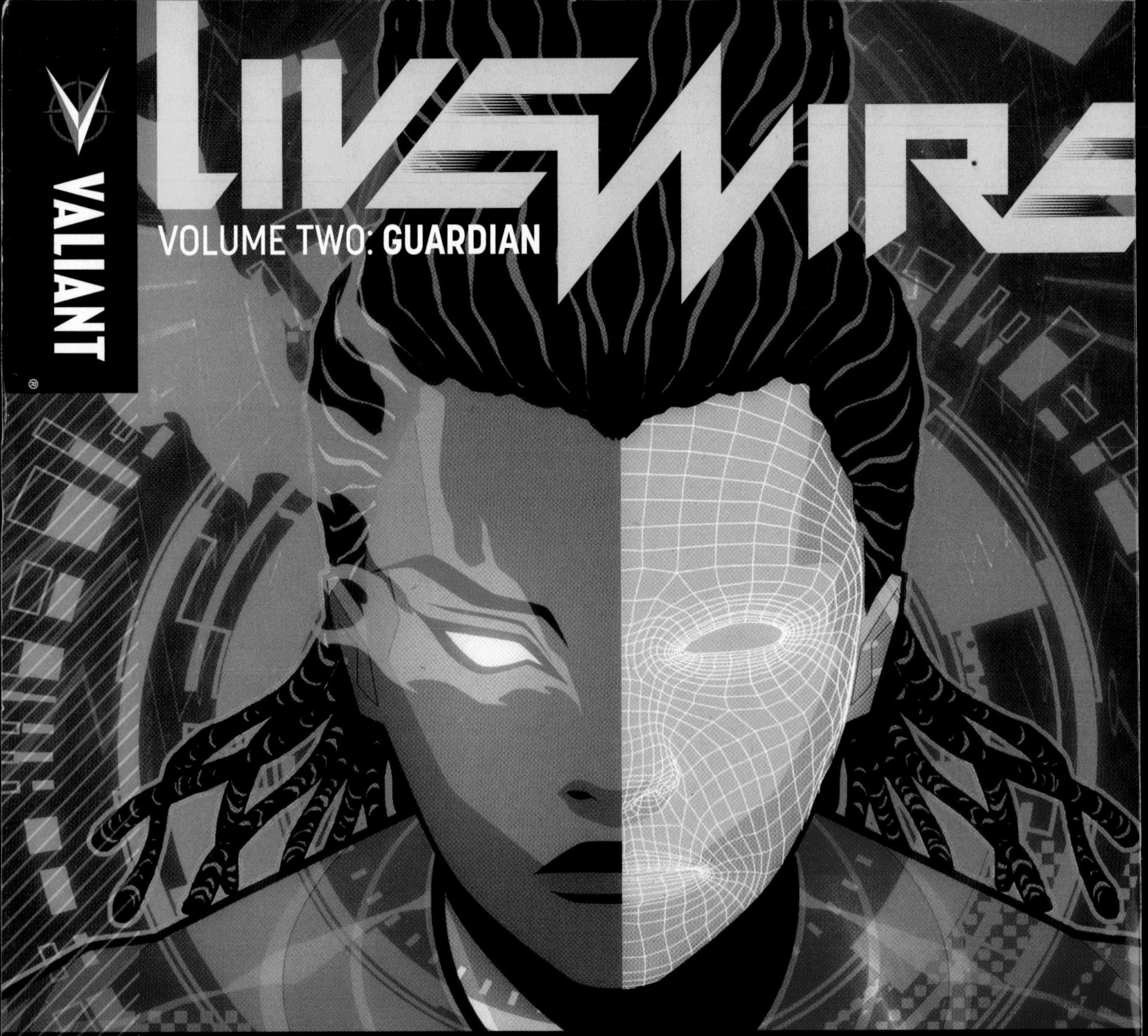
VALIANT
LIVEWIRE
VOLUME TWO: GUARDIAN

LIVEWIRE FINDS HERSELF FACE-TO-FACE WITH A BRAND-NEW FOE!

Investigating the disappearance of a young psiot girl, Livewire stumbles upon OMEN's answer to the psiot "problem," a facility where young psiots are taken and taught to control their powers. Is this facility the safe haven Livewire's dreamed of or is there something more sinister to this sanctuary?

One of the Valiant Universe's most powerful heroes continues down the road to redemption right here with rising star writer Vita Ayala (*Supergirl*) and artist Kano (*Gotham Central*)!

Collecting LIVEWIRE #5-8.

TRADE PAPERBACK
ISBN: 978-1-68215-326-0

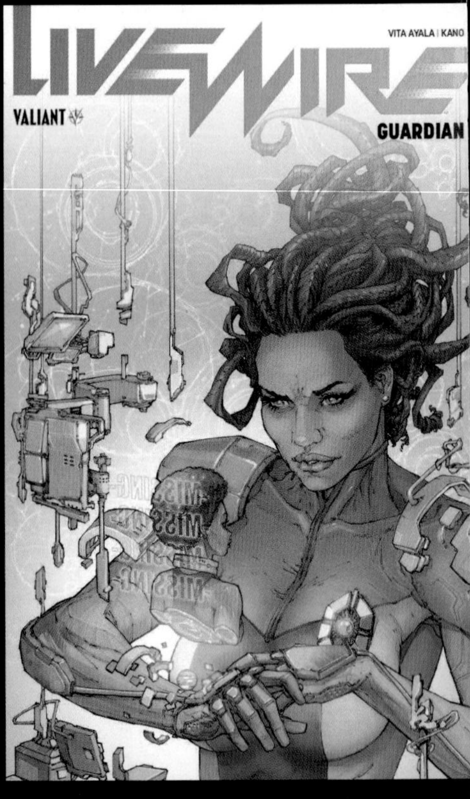
LIVEWIRE
VITA AYALA | KANO
VALIANT
GUARDIAN